D1713459

THE CONCEPT OF MORALS

THE CONCEPT OF MORALS

BY

W. T. STACE

*Emeritus Stuart Professor of Philosophy
in Princeton University*

NEW YORK
THE MACMILLAN COMPANY
1962

Copyright, 1937, by The Macmillan Company

All rights reserved — no part of this book may be repro-
duced in any form without permission in writing from the
publisher, except by a reviewer who wishes to quote brief
passages in connection with a review written for inclusion
in magazine or newspaper.

Macmillan Paperbacks Edition 1962

The Macmillan Company, New York
Brett-Macmillan Ltd., Galt, Ontario

Printed in the United States of America

PREFACE

THIS book is quite independent of my previous writings. Yet it constitutes, in a sense, the completion of a plan, or at least of a development of the various philosophical disciplines foreseen by me vaguely, though not in any detail, about ten years ago. Between *The Meaning of Beauty*, which I published in 1929, *The Theory of Knowledge and Existence*, published in 1932, and the present book there appears to be, on the surface, little connection. They treat of utterly different subjects, the first of esthetics, the second of epistemology and metaphysics, the third of morals. Systematic thinkers in the past have often developed some single grand philosophical conception—usually in the field of metaphysics—and then applied it rigorously in all branches of philosophy, sometimes forcing and twisting their material to suit the preconceived plan. Their ethic and esthetic have appeared as direct deductions from their metaphysic. I neither claim nor desire for my philosophy any such unity as this. In the three books referred to I have attempted to explore in each case a different terrain, and to describe disinterestedly just what I found in each, without deciding beforehand what I expected to find. Certainly I had no thought of insisting that the same type of scenery must keep on repeating itself in them all.

Nevertheless the three books have, in a sense, a common theme. They are connected together by a single idea, however loosely upon the thread of it their details are strung. To make clear what this idea is I must explain what I conceived to be the central problem with which philosophy, in view of the special and peculiar temper of our age, is faced. Philosophy, I believe, is organic to human culture, and has a task to perform in helping that culture to attain higher levels. It is a serious matter, and not a mere playing with ideas which are of no importance to humanity at large. It is not a set of intellectual Chinese puzzles cultivated idly and for their own sakes by academic minds out of touch with life. Or at any rate I never had any sympathy with philosophy so conceived—though I admit it is good policy to allow the specialist sometimes to live in his own world, to imagine it cut off from the sphere of mundane things, and to play with problems of which the human import may seem negligible. Every age has its special problems and it is the business of philosophy to help in solving them. Only thus can it be of service to humanity.

The present age is obsessed with the notion of relativity. I do not refer to the well known theory of physics which goes by that name. Relativity in that sense does not concern us. I refer to the growing belief that the things which are most valuable to human beings—beauty, knowledge, and moral goodness—are *relative* to the circumstances, the time, and the place of their appearance, as well as to the natures of men. On this view, since different men have different natures, and since their circumstances are always changing, there will be no constant truth or beauty or goodness; but these values will be in a perpetual state of variation. This is what I mean by the doctrine of relativity.

Formerly we used to hear of "absolute values." Knowledge was supposed to consist in a passive subjugation of the mind to a ready-made external world; so that what

was true once was true always. Beauty and moral goodness too were somehow rooted in the objective world, and
what we had to do was to discern and conform to them.
But against all this there has been a widespread revolt.
These values, we are told, are wholly subjective and relative to the human mind. They are man-made, and they
are different for different men and for different times and
places.

With this modern tendency I am in sympathy. Our
own natures surely enter at least as participants into the
creation of truth and beauty and goodness. But it has
appeared to me that the modern idea is running to dangerous excess. It is the way of the human animal to os-
cillate between extremes. Philosophy advances on a zig-
zag path. But in this matter of values it seemed to me
that philosophers were riding their hobby-horse of relativity towards the abyss.

If truth is *wholly* subjective and relative, then any one
assertion is as good as any other. This would be to destroy
the distinction between truth and falsehood altogether.
To say that the pragmatist teaches that the truth is whatever anyone chooses to think would no doubt be to caricature his doctrine. Yet the art of the caricaturist too
is a way of telling the truth about a man. And for this
particular caricature there is at least as much ground as
there is for any other. It may be correct that human
purposes have a share in the creation of truth. But this
ought not to be taken to mean that a man is entitled to
embrace as "truth" whatever religious belief happens to
make him personally feel comfortable; nor that if men,
some centuries ago, found that belief in a flat world
worked well enough for them, it was really a truth in
those days that the world was flat.

Likewise it is the modern tendency to deny any sort of objectivity to esthetic taste. That too is completely subjective and relative. But if there is no kind of standard by which the music of Beethoven can be judged superior to any barbarian's beating of the tom-tom, then what is the sense of esthetic education? Why trouble to teach our children to reverence what we believe to be great art and to contemn what we believe to be inferior? As pragmatism tends—at least when it runs to extremes—to destroy the distinction between truth and error, so does this way of thinking obliterate the difference between superior and inferior art.

In morals finally we have the doctrine of "ethical relativity." It is the same story over again. Morality is doubtless human. It has not descended upon us out of the sky. It has grown out of human nature, and is relative to that nature. Nor could it have, apart from that nature, any meaning whatever. This we must accept. But if this is interpreted to mean that whatever any social group thinks good *is* good (for that group), that there is no common standard, and that consequently any one moral code is as good as any other, then this relativism in effect denies the difference between good and evil altogether, and makes meaningless the idea of progress in moral conceptions.

Against the fundamental notions of humanism and relativism I make no complaint. Absolutism is dead. (If it is urged against this statement that there are still many who believe in absolutism, and that therefore it is incorrect to say that it is dead, I shall retort that in every age there are multitudes of minds which feed upon dead ideas. Let the dead live upon the dead.) But any tendency, however good in itself, can destroy us if we allow it to run away with us. And this, I think, is our present danger in philosophy. Relativism has run riot, become insane. When it goes the length of destroying the distinctions between the true and the false, between the fair and the foul, between the moral and the immoral, then it is on the way to making chaos of our spiritual and cultural lives.

Would there not be room then for a philosophy which should attempt a sane appraisal of the issue? Which should study one by one the departments of man's spiritual life and attempt in each to apportion their proper shares to relativism and universalism, to subjectivity and objectivity? This at least is the idea which has guided all my writings. To take up first the realm of beauty, then the realm of knowledge, and finally the realm of the morally good; to show that in spite of the principle of relativity—and admitting to it its proper place—there is yet in each case something of *real* value (not merely something which men, through some strange delusion, *think* valuable), something worth fighting for, something genuinely good and right to be distinguished from what is bad and wrong; to show that in each case there is a real lower and a real higher, so that progress is possible; that in none of these matters is it true that any one man's opinion and taste is as good as any other's; and that in consequence man's cultural life is not that futile beating of the air which an excessive and extravagant relativism would make it out to be—these have been my aims. And this plan—if a venture which was not undertaken in the spirit of a rigid and preconceived notion ought to be called a plan—I bring now to completion with this book on ethics.

There are indeed many contemporary writers who have

wished to secure the values of science, philosophy, art, and morals. But unfortunately most of them seem to have minds more fitted to convince our forebears of fifty years ago than to address the modern world. They have no tincture of modernism. The remedy which they suggest for our evils is to put the clock back. They mouth ancient formulas, unaware that all meaning has gone out of them. They preach an idealism or an absolutism which might have impressed—which did impress—our grandfathers, but which sounds to us like the echo of an almost forgotten world.

This is useless. The modern mind is empirical, positivistic, realistic, relativistic. It is merely stupid to rail against it, to demand that it revive within itself a temper which it scarcely any longer even understands. The age must solve its problems *in its own terms*. Every age has to do this—ours no less. Therefore the remedy for extreme relativism is not to go back to an out of date absolutism. The remedy is to discover a *sane* relativism—in metaphysic, in esthetic, in ethic. This is what I have attempted in my philosophizing to do.

Mr. J. A. Irving and Mr. David Bowers, both of Princeton University, read through the whole book in manuscript, and made important criticisms and suggestions. This has enabled me to improve many passages in the text. I am most grateful for their help. Neither, of course, is in any way responsible for what I say.

W. T. S.

PRINCETON, NEW JERSEY
June, 1937

CONTENTS

THE CONCEPT OF MORALS

CHAPTER I

ETHICAL RELATIVITY (I)

THERE is an opinion widely current nowadays in philosophical circles which passes under the name of "ethical relativity." Exactly what this phrase means or implies is certainly far from clear. But unquestionably it stands as a label for the opinions of a group of ethical philosophers whose position is roughly on the extreme left wing among the moral theorizers of the day. And perhaps one may best understand it by placing it in contrast with the opposite kind of extreme view against which, undoubtedly, it has arisen as a protest. For among moral philosophers one may clearly distinguish a left and a right wing. Those of the left wing are the ethical relativists. They are the revolutionaries, the clever young men, the up to date. Those of the right wing we may call the ethical absolutists. They are the conservatives and the old-fashioned.

According to the absolutists there is but one eternally true and valid moral code. This moral code applies with rigid impartiality to all men. What is a duty for me must likewise be a duty for you. And this will be true whether you are an Englishman, a Chinaman, or a Hottentot. If cannibalism is an abomination in England or America, it is an abomination in central Africa, notwithstanding that the African may think otherwise. The fact that he sees nothing wrong in his cannibal practices does not make them for him morally right. They are as much contrary to morality for him as they are for us. The only difference is that he is an ignorant savage who does not know this. There is not one law for one man or race of men, another for another. There is not one moral standard for Europeans, another for Indians, another for Chinese. There is but one law, one standard, one morality, for all men. And this standard, this law, is absolute and unvarying.

Moreover, as the one moral law extends its dominion over all the corners of the earth, so too it is not limited in its application by any considerations of time or period. That which is right now was right in the centuries of Greece and Rome, nay, in the very ages of the cave man. That which is evil now was evil then. If slavery is morally wicked today, it was morally wicked among the ancient Athenians, notwithstanding that their greatest men accepted it as a necessary condition of human society. Their opinion did not make slavery a moral good for them. It only showed that they were, in spite of their otherwise noble conceptions, ignorant of what is truly right and good in this matter.

The ethical absolutist recognizes as a fact that moral customs and moral ideas differ from country to country and from age to age. This indeed seems manifest and not to be disputed. We think slavery morally wrong, the Greeks thought it morally unobjectionable. The inhabitants of New Guinea certainly have very different moral ideas from ours. But the fact that the Greeks or the inhabitants of New Guinea think something right does not make it right, even for them. Nor does the fact that we think the same things wrong make them wrong. They are *in themselves* either right or wrong. What we have to do is to discover which they are. What anyone thinks makes no difference. It is here just as it is in matters of physical science. We believe the earth to be a globe. Our ancestors may have thought it flat. This does not show that it *was* flat, and is *now* a globe. What it shows is that men having in other ages been ignorant about the shape of the earth have now learned the truth. So if the Greeks thought slavery morally legitimate, this does not indicate that it was for them and in that age morally legitimate, but rather that they were ignorant of the truth of the matter.

The ethical absolutist is not indeed committed to the opinion that his own, or our own, moral code is the true one. Theoretically at least he might hold that slavery is ethically justifiable, that the Greeks knew better than we do about this, that ignorance of the true morality lies with us and not with them. All that he is actually committed to is the opinion that, whatever the true moral code may be, it is always the same for all men in all ages. His view is not at all inconsistent with the belief that humanity has still much to learn in moral matters. If anyone were to assert that in five hundred years the moral conceptions of the present day will appear as barbarous to the people of that age as the moral conceptions of the middle ages appear to us now, he need not deny it. If anyone were to assert that the ethics of Christianity are by no means final, and will be superseded in future ages by vastly nobler moral ideals, he need not deny this either. For it is of the essence of his creed to believe that morality is in some sense objective, not man-made, not produced by human opinion; that its principles are real truths about which men have to learn—just as they have to learn about the shape of the world—about which they may have been ignorant in the past, and about which therefore they may well be ignorant now.

Thus although absolutism is conservative in the sense that it is regarded by the more daring spirits as an out of date opinion, it is not necessarily conservative in the sense of being committed to the blind support of existing moral ideas and institutions. If ethical absolutists are sometimes conservative in this sense too, that is their personal affair. Such conservativism is accidental, not essential to the absolutist's creed. There is no logical reason, in the nature of the case, why an absolutist should not be a communist, an anarchist, a surrealist, or an upholder of free love. The fact that he is usually none of these things may be accounted for in various ways. But it has nothing to do with the sheer logic of his ethical position. The sole opinion to which he is committed is that whatever is morally right (or wrong)—be it free love or monogamy or slavery or cannibalism or vegetarianism—is morally right (or wrong) for all men at all times.

Usually the absolutist goes further than this. He often maintains, not merely that the moral law is the same for all the men on this planet—which is, after all, a tiny speck in space—but that in some way or in some sense it has application everywhere in the universe. He may express himself by saying that it applies to all "rational beings"— which would apparently include angels and the men on Mars (if they are rational). He is apt to think that the moral law is a part of the fundamental structure of the universe. But with this aspect of absolutism we need not, at the moment, concern ourselves. At present we may think of it as being simply the opinion that there is a single moral standard for all human beings.

This brief and rough sketch of ethical absolutism is intended merely to form a background against which we may the more clearly indicate, by way of contrast, the theory of ethical relativity. Up to the present, therefore, I have not given any of the reasons which the absolutist can urge in favour of his case. It is sufficient for my purpose at the moment to state *what* he believes, without going into the question of *why* he believes it. But before proceeding to our next step—the explanation of ethical relativity—I think it will be helpful to indicate some of the historical causes (as distinguished from logical reasons) which have helped in the past to render absolutism a plausible interpretation of morality as understood by European peoples.

Our civilization is a Christian civilization. It has grown up, during nearly two thousand years, upon the soil of Christian monotheism. In this soil our whole outlook upon life, and consequently all our moral ideas, have their roots. They have been moulded by this influence. The wave of religious scepticism which, during the last half century, has swept over us, has altered this fact scarcely at all. The moral ideas even of those who most violently reject the dogmas of Christianity with their intellects are still Christian ideas. This will probably remain true for many centuries even if Christian theology, as a set of intellectual beliefs, comes to be wholly rejected by every educated person. It will probably remain true so long as our civilization lasts. A child cannot, by changing in later life his intellectual creed, strip himself of the early formative moral influences of his childhood, though he can no doubt modify their results in various minor ways. With the outlook on life which was instilled into him in his early days he, in large measure, lives and dies. So it is with a civilization. And our civilization, whatever religious or irreligious views it may come to hold or reject, can hardly escape within its lifetime the moulding influences of its Christian origin. Now ethical absolutism was, in its central ideas, the product of Christian theology.

The connection is not difficult to detect. For morality has been conceived, during the Christian dispensation, as issuing from the will of God. That indeed was its single and all-sufficient source. There would be no point, for the naïve believer in the faith, in the philosopher's questions regarding the foundations of morality and the basis of moral obligation. Even to ask such questions is a mark of incipient religious scepticism. For the true believer the author of the moral law is God. What pleases God, what God commands—that is the definition of right. What displeases God, what he forbids—that is the definition of wrong. Now there is, for the Christian monotheist, only one God ruling over the entire universe. And this God is rational, self-consistent. He does not act upon whims. Consequently his will and his commands must be the same everywhere. They will be unvarying for all peoples and in all ages. If the heathen have other moral ideas than ours—inferior ideas—that can only be because they live in ignorance of the true God. If they knew God and his commands, their ethical precepts would be the same as ours.

Polytheistic creeds may well tolerate a number of diverse moral codes. For the God of the western hemisphere might have different views from those entertained by the God of the eastern hemisphere. And the God of the north might issue to his worshippers commands at variance with the commands issued to other peoples by the God of the south. But a monotheistic religion implies a single universal and absolute morality.

This explains why ethical absolutism, until very recently, was not only believed by philosophers but *taken for granted without any argument*. The ideas of philosophers, like the ideas of everyone else, are largely moulded by the civilizations in which they live. Their philosophies are largely attempts to state in abstract terms and in self-consistent language the stock of ideas which they have breathed in from the atmosphere of their social environment. This accounts for the large number of so-called "unrecognized presuppositions" with which systems of philosophy always abound. These presuppositions are simply the ideas which the authors of the systems have breathed in with the intellectual atmospheres by which they happen to be surrounded—which they have taken over therefore as a matter of course, without argument, without criticism, without even a suspicion that they might be false.

It is not therefore at all surprising to find that Immanuel Kant, writing in the latter half of the eighteenth century, not only took the tenets of ethical absolutism for granted, but evidently considered that no instructed person would dispute them. It is a noticeable feature of his ethical philosophy that he gives no reasons whatever to support his belief in the existence of a universally valid moral law. He assumes as a matter of course that his readers will accept this view. And he proceeds at once to enquire what is the metaphysical foundation of the universal moral law. That alone is what interests him. *Assuming* that there does exist such a law, how, he asks, can this be the case, and what, in the way of transcendental truth, does it imply? It never occurs to him to reflect that any philosopher who should choose to question his fundamental assumption could outflank his whole ethical position; and that if this assumption should prove false his entire moral philosophy would fall to the ground like a pack of cards.

We can now turn to the consideration of ethical relativity which is the proper subject of this chapter. The revolt of the relativists against absolutism is, I believe, part and parcel of the general revolutionary tendency of our times. In particular it is a result of the decay of belief in the dogmas of orthodox religion. Belief in absolutism was supported, as we have seen, by belief in Christian monotheism. And now that, in an age of widespread religious scepticism, that support is withdrawn, absolutism tends to collapse. Revolutionary movements are as a rule, at any rate in their first onset, purely negative. They attack and destroy. And ethical relativity is, in its essence, a purely negative creed. It is simply a denial of ethical absolutism. That is why the best way of explaining it is to begin by explaining ethical absolutism. If we understand that what the latter asserts the former denies, then we understand ethical relativity.

Any ethical position which denies that there is a single moral standard which is equally applicable to all men at all times may fairly be called a species of ethical relativity. There is not, the relativist asserts, merely one moral law, one code, one standard. There are many moral laws, codes, standards. What morality ordains in one place or age may be quite different from what morality ordains in another place or age. The moral code of Chinamen is quite different from that of Europeans, that of African savages quite different from both. Any morality, therefore, is relative to the age, the place, and the circumstances in which it is found. It is in no sense absolute.

This does not mean merely—as one might at first sight

be inclined to suppose—that the very same kind of action which is *thought* right in one country and period may be *thought* wrong in another. This would be a mere platitude, the truth of which everyone would have to admit. Even the absolutist would admit this—would even wish to emphasize it—since he is well aware that different peoples have different sets of moral ideas, and his whole point is that some of these sets of ideas are false. What the relativist means to assert is, not this platitude, but that the very same kind of action which *is* right in one country and period may *be* wrong in another. And this, far from being a platitude, is a very startling assertion.

It is very important to grasp thoroughly the difference between the two ideas. For there is reason to think that many minds tend to find ethical relativity attractive because they fail to keep them clearly apart. It is so very obvious that moral ideas differ from country to country and from age to age. And it is so very easy, if you are mentally lazy, to suppose that to say this means the same as to say that no universal moral standard exists,—or in other words that it implies ethical relativity. We fail to see that the word "standard" is used in two different senses. It is perfectly true that, in one sense, there are many variable moral standards. We speak of judging a man by the standard of his time. And this implies that different times have different standards. And this, of course, is quite true. But when the word "standard" is used in this sense it means simply the set of moral ideas current during the period in question. It means what people *think* right, whether as a matter of fact it *is* right or not. On the other hand when the absolutist asserts that there exists a single universal moral "standard," he is not using the word in this sense at all. He means by "standard" what *is* right as distinct from what people merely think right. His point is that although what people think right varies in different countries and periods, yet what actually is right is everywhere and always the same. And it follows that when the ethical relativist disputes the position of the absolutist and denies that any universal moral standard exists he too means by "standard" what actually is right. But it is exceedingly easy, if we are not careful, to slip loosely from using the word in the first sense to using it in the second sense; and to suppose that the variability of moral beliefs is the same thing as the variability of what really is moral. And unless we keep the two senses of the word "standard" distinct, we are likely to think the creed of ethical relativity much more plausible than it actually is.

The genuine relativist, then, does not merely mean that Chinamen may think right what Frenchmen think wrong. He means that what *is* wrong for the Frenchman may *be* right for the Chinaman. And if one enquires how, in those circumstances, one is to know what actually is right in China or in France, the answer comes quite glibly. What is right in China is the same as what people think right in China; and what is right in France is the same as what people think right in France. So that, if you want to know what is moral in any particular country or age all you have to do is to ascertain what are the moral ideas current in that age or country. Those ideas are, *for that age or country*, right. Thus what is morally right is identified with what is thought to be morally right, and the distinction which we made above between these two is simply denied. To put the same thing in another way, it is denied that there can be or ought to be any distinction between the two senses of the word "standard." There is only one kind of standard of right and wrong, namely, the moral ideas current in any particular age or country.

Moral right *means* what people think morally right. It has no other meaning. What Frenchmen think right is, therefore, right *for Frenchmen*. And evidently one must conclude—though I am not aware that relativists are anxious to draw one's attention to such unsavoury but yet absolutely necessary conclusions from their creed— that cannibalism is right for people who believe in it, that human sacrifice is right for those races which practice it, and that burning widows alive was right for Hindus un- til the British stepped in and compelled the Hindus to behave immorally by allowing their widows to remain alive.

When it is said that, according to the ethical relativist, what is thought right in any social group is right for that group, one must be careful not to misinterpret this. The relativist does not, of course, mean that there actually is an objective moral standard in France and a different objec- tive standard in England, and that French and British opinions respectively give us correct information about these different standards. His point is rather that there are no objectively true moral standards at all. There is no single universal objective standard. Nor are there a variety of local objective standards. All standards are subjective. People's subjective feelings about morality are the only standards which exist.

To sum up. The ethical relativist consistently denies, it would seem, whatever the ethical absolutist asserts. For the absolutist there is a single universal moral standard. For the relativist there is no such standard. There are only local, ephemeral, and variable standards. For the absolutist there are two senses of the word "standard."

Standards in the sense of sets of current moral ideas are relative and changeable. But the standard in the sense of what is actually morally right is absolute and unchanging. For the relativist no such distinction can be made. There is only one meaning of the word standard, namely, that which refers to local and variable sets of moral ideas. Or if it is insisted that the word must be allowed two meanings, then the relativist will say that there is at any rate no actual example of a standard in the absolute sense, and that the word as thus used is an empty name to which nothing in reality corresponds; so that the distinction between the two meanings becomes empty and useless. Finally—though this is merely saying the same thing in another way—the absolutist makes a distinction between what actually is right and what is thought right. The relativist rejects this distinction and identifies what is moral with what is thought moral by certain human beings or groups of human beings.

It is true that the relativist may object to my statement of his case on the ground that it does not specify precisely *who* the human beings are whose thinking makes what is right right and what is wrong wrong; and that he himself would not think of defining right as "that which people think right"—using the vague word "people" as if morality were determined by what any chance persons, anyone or everyone, happen to think moral. We shall see later that there is a real and incurable ambiguity in the relativist's position here (and not merely in my statement of it), and that he himself has difficulty in saying who are the "people" whose ideas are to constitute moral standards. But he cannot deny, at any rate, that his creed does identify morality with the subjective thinking of human beings. And that is the only point which I am at present trying to make clear. To *what* human beings he means to refer will be a matter for our future discussion.

In the preceding pages I have attempted to place absolutism and relativism over against one another in sharp contrast. In order not to blur the contrast I shall refrain, throughout the discussion in Chapters 1 and 2, from mentioning or discussing other possible and intermediate views on the matters in dispute. In the end neither absolutism nor relativism will be upheld in this book as being the truth. They are both, in my opinion, unreasonable extremes of opinion. Between black and white there are many shades of grey. For the present, however, I shall continue, for the sake of simplicity, to talk as if there were only the two views, absolutism and relativism, in existence. I trust the reader will not be misled by this procedure into supposing that, if I reject ethical relativity, this must be because I wish to embrace absolutism and to argue in favour of it. This would be a complete misapprehension of my position.

I shall now proceed to consider, first, the main arguments which can be urged in favour of ethical relativity; and secondly, the arguments which can be urged against it. In both cases I shall have to be very brief, nor is it pretended that the summary of arguments here to be given can constitute at all an adequate or complete discussion. My purpose in this book is to develop in detail a view of ethics very different from that of either the absolutist or the relativist; and for me the controversy between these two is no more than a necessary background for the presentation of my own view.

There are, I think, four main arguments in favour of ethical relativity. The first is that which relies upon the

actual varieties of moral "standards" found in the world.
It was easy enough to believe in a single absolute morality
in older times when there was no anthropology, when all
humanity was divided clearly into two groups, Christian
peoples and the "heathen." Christian peoples knew and
possessed the one true morality. The rest were savages
whose moral ideas could be ignored. But all this is
changed. Greater knowledge has brought greater toler-
ance. We can no longer exalt our own morality as alone
true, while dismissing all other moralities as false or inferior. The investigations of anthropologists have shown
that there exist side by side in the world a bewildering variety of moral codes. On this topic endless volumes have
been written, masses of evidence piled up. Anthropologists have ransacked the Melanesian Islands, the jungles of
New Guinea, the steppes of Siberia, the deserts of Aus-
tralia, the forests of central Africa, and have brought
back with them countless examples of weird, extravagant,
and fantastic "moral" customs with which to confound
us. We learn that all kinds of horrible practices are, in
this, that, or the other place, regarded as essential to
virtue. We find that there is nothing, or next to nothing,
which has always and everywhere been regarded as morally good by all men. Where then is our universal morality? Can we, in face of all this evidence, deny that it is
nothing but an empty dream?

This argument, taken by itself, is a very weak one. It
relies upon a single set of facts—the variable moral customs of the world. But this variability of moral ideas is
admitted by both parties to the dispute, and is capable of
ready explanation upon the hypothesis of either party.
The relativist says that the facts are to be explained by
the non-existence of any absolute moral standard. The

absolutist says that they are to be explained by human ignorance of what the absolute moral standard is. And he can truly point out that men have differed widely in their opinions about all manner of topics including the subject-matters of the physical sciences—just as much as they differ about morals. And if the various different opinions which men have held about the shape of the earth do not prove that it has no one real shape, neither do the various opinions which they have held about morality prove that there is no one true morality.

Thus the facts can be explained equally plausibly on either hypothesis. There is nothing in the facts themselves which compels us to prefer the relativistic hypothesis to that of the absolutist. And therefore the argument fails to prove the relativist conclusion. If that conclusion is to be established, it must be by means of other considerations.

This is the essential point. But I will add some supplementary remarks. The work of the anthropologists, upon which ethical relativists seem to rely so heavily, has as a matter of fact added absolutely nothing *in principle* to what has always been known about the variability of moral ideas. Educated people have known all along that the Greeks tolerated sodomy, which in modern times has been regarded in some countries as an abominable crime; that the Hindus thought it a sacred duty to burn their widows; that trickery, now thought despicable, was once believed to be a virtue; that terrible torture was thought by our own ancestors only a few centuries ago to be a justifiable weapon of justice; that it was only yesterday that western peoples came to believe that slavery is immoral. Even the ancients knew very well that moral customs and ideas vary—witness the writings of Herodotus. Thus the principle of the variability of moral ideas was well understood long before modern anthropology was ever heard of. Anthropology has added nothing to the knowledge of this principle except a mass of new and extreme examples of it drawn from very remote sources. But to multiply examples of a principle already well known and universally admitted adds nothing to the argument which is built upon that principle. The discoveries of the anthropologists have no doubt been of the highest importance in their own sphere. But in my considered opinion they have thrown no new light upon the special problems of the moral philosopher.

Although the multiplication of examples has no logical bearing on the argument, it does have an immense *psychological* effect upon people's minds. These masses of anthropological learning are impressive. They are propounded in the sacred name of "science." If they are quoted in support of ethical relativity—as they often are—people *think* that they must prove something important. They bewilder and over-awe the simple-minded, batter down their resistance, make them ready to receive humbly the doctrine of ethical relativity from those who have acquired a reputation by their immense learning and their claims to be "scientific." Perhaps this is why so much ado is made by ethical relativists regarding the anthropological evidence. But we must refuse to be impressed. We must discount all this mass of evidence about the extraordinary moral customs of remote peoples. Once we have admitted—as everyone who is instructed must have admitted these last two thousand years without any anthropology at all—the principle that moral ideas vary, all this new evidence adds nothing to the argument. And the argument itself proves nothing for the reasons already given.

A second argument for relativism is that which asserts that all moral ideas are based upon "emotions." That which men regard with such emotions as resentment and disgust they disapprove and call immoral. That which they view with admiration they approve and call good. But emotions are notoriously variable. What disgusts some people pleases others. What angers one person does not anger another. Hence moral standards will vary with the emotions upon which they are based.

This argument is not approved by all relativists. By Westermarck it is made the mainstay of his position.[1] By Dewey, on the other hand it is belittled as being based upon an out of date dualistic psychology.[2] I do not propose to comment upon it in this chapter. We shall have to advance a great deal further in our enquiries before we are in a position to appraise it. I list it here for the sake of completeness, and pass on.

The third argument in favour of ethical relativity is, I think, an exceedingly powerful and important one. But it depends wholly upon the acceptance of the general philosophical attitude known as "radical empiricism." The present writer accepts that attitude, and this book is an attempt to give a satisfactory radical empiricist account of morals. It is written wholly from that standpoint. But there are many people to whom radical empiricism is antipathetic, and to them perhaps this third argument will not appear as powerful as it does to me. It is, however, quite impossible to undertake here the defence of a doctrine which is not specially concerned with ethics but covers the whole field of philosophy. And I shall therefore do no more than state the argument in its baldest terms.

[1] Edward Westermarck, *Ethical Relativity*.
[2] John Dewey, *Human Nature and Conduct*, Chap. V.

Radical empiricism is a philosophical attitude of which it may be said, perhaps, that its first great prophet was David Hume. It does indeed appear sporadically in the work of some of Hume's predecessors, though with them it is not an explicitly stated principle. Berkeley's writings, for example, are full of arguments which are really based upon it. In modern times it has been powerfully advocated by William James, and the recent school of "logical positivism" is a product of it. Modern "realism" and the teachings of the "Cambridge analysts" in large measure reflect its spirit. It is, however, a mistake to identify it with the teachings of any special school, such as that of the logical positivists. Logical positivism is, many of us think, a peculiarly narrow and contorted version of it, and I am anxious not to be understood as endorsing the special dogmas of that, or indeed of any of the other above-mentioned "schools." Radical empiricism is rather the pervading spirit of most of the vital thinking of our day than the peculiar possession of any particular sect.

Radical empiricists hold that no word has cognitive meaning unless what it refers to, or purports to refer to, is something of a kind whose elements are at least theoretically capable of being directly experienced. Concepts are derived from experience, and therefore must at least refer to the experience from which they have been derived. Or even if we believe, as Kant did, that some concepts are *a priori* and not derived from experience, yet even these concepts apply to experience (or in other words refer to it), and could have no meaning unless we could find in experience something to which they apply. This was implicitly recognized by Kant himself when he wrote the words "concepts without percepts are empty."

The concept "red" has meaning because it refers to the red things which we find in experience. The concept "centaur" has meaning because, although we do not experience centaurs, we do experience men and horses, and the concept "centaur" has no content which is not referable to one or other of these things. But a concept which purported to stand for something the elements of which never have been, and in principle never could be, experienced, would be meaningless. It would not really *be* a concept at all. It would be a mere word. Thus though the word "potentiality" may, if properly used, have good meaning, it is sometimes used in a way which has none. Suppose I say "Oaks are potentially present in acorns." If all I intend to assert is that, given certain conditions, oaks grow out of acorns, my statement is meaningful, since the growth of acorns into oaks is an experiencible fact. If what I intend is that a sufficiently powerful microscope would detect a minute oak wrapped up inside the acorn, this is also meaningful (though probably false). For the tiny oak asserted to exist would be *visible*, at least theoretically, and therefore experiencible. But if what is intended is that there is now present in the acorn, not an actually existing oak tree however small, but a "potentially existing" one, then this is meaningless. For what does not actually exist could not conceivably be experienced. The essence of the theory of meaning which radical empiricists hold is that any word which purports to stand for an entity which could not possibly be experienced by any conceivable mind in any conceivable circumstances is entirely meaningless; and that any sentence which affirms the reality or existence of any such entity is also entirely meaningless. Now an entity whose being is not actual but potential could not possibly be experienced by any mind—even by the mind of God. For if it were experienced that very fact would show it to be an *actual* existence. Hence "potential existence" is a very good example of a phrase which, on radical empiricist principles, is quite meaningless.[1]

We have now to apply this theory of meaning to the ethical problem before us. When we do so we find that absolutism involves the use of conceptions which have no meaning, while, on the other hand, the relativist account of morals is wholly meaningful.

The key word of morals is the word "ought." Morality means simply that which men ought to do. But in the light of the empirical criterion of meaning just explained has the word "ought" any meaning? This question presents a real difficulty. For it is obvious that only what *is* is capable of being experienced, and that no being could ever conceivably experience what only ought to be but is not. The difficulty is really identical with that which Hume discovered in the notion of natural, as distinguished from logical, necessity. It is possible to experience something which actually is the case—for example, the fact that the sun rises. But how can one ever experience the fact that anything must *necessarily* be the case—for example that the sun *must* rise? In the same way, no being can ever experience the fact that something *ought* to be the case. But if this is true, it would seem that the word "ought," since its objective referent is not to be found in

---

[1] There are, of course, many difficulties in the theory of meaning suggested above which I have here simply ignored. What, for example, is the exact definition of the vague word "experience"? Again, *by whom* have the elements of a meaningful concept to be experiencible? I cannot discuss these difficulties here and have to content myself with the very rude sketch of radical empiricism given in the text. Some of the difficult problems referred to are discussed in my article "Metaphysics and Meaning," in *Mind*, XLIV, N.S. No. 176.

experience, is meaningless. And in that case morality collapses.

Fortunately there is more to be said. I am going to call all sentences which state that something ought (or ought not) to be the case, or that something ought (or ought not) to be done, by the name "ought sentences." And I am going to call all sentences which merely state that something is (or is not) the case by the name "is sentences." According to what has been said it will then be clear that all "ought" sentences are meaningless, but that "is" sentences are meaningful. If then an "ought" sentence can be wholly translated, without loss of intended content, into an "is" sentence—if the word "ought" can be got rid of from it—it may in that way be shown to have meaning. It may be the case that what is *verbally* an "ought" sentence is in reality, according to its true meaning, an "is" sentence. We may have said that something ought to be the case when what we really mean is only that something is the case. And in that case our sentence will have meaning even though by mistake, or for some convenience of speech, we have used the meaningless word "ought" in it.

This is often the real state of affairs. I say, for example, "You ought not to over-eat." It seems quite clear here that I have left part of my meaning to be understood. What I really mean is "You ought not to over-eat, *if* you wish to retain your health." And this can be translated into "Abstention from over-eating *is* one of the means to health." This is an "is" sentence, and the "ought" sentence "You ought not to over-eat" has been translated into it, thus showing that it possesses meaning. What has really been stated as to the way to retain one's health is a matter of *fact* which is *empirically verifiable*,

namely, the fact that over-eating leads to ill-health.
Further examination will show that *hypothetical* "ought"
sentences—sentences of the form "*if* you want so and so,
then you ought to do so and so"—are all thus translatable into "is" sentences, since they all merely state that
the best way of attaining some desired end *is* to adopt
such and such means. All such sentences are therefore
meaningful. But *categorical* "ought" sentences—which
have the form "You absolutely ought to do so and so
without any conditions whatsoever"—are not so translatable. There is no way, in them, of getting rid of the
word "ought" and replacing it by the word "is." They do
not state that something is the case, for example that the
best means to some end is to adopt certain measures. They
purport to state unconditionally that something absolutely
ought to be the case, and the "ought" in them is therefore
totally intractable.

Now absolutism implies that moral judgments are categorical. It therefore involves the use of a meaningless
conception, that of the absolute and unconditional
"ought," and it thereby stands condemned. Relativism,
on the other hand, implies that moral judgments are
hypothetical, and therefore its account of morals is intelligible.

According to relativism a moral imperative is always
relative to the time, the place, and the circumstances.
And this means that its obligation is not absolute and
unconditional but dependent and conditional. Polygamy,
for example, is not absolutely immoral. But it may be
immoral in America where the social conditions favour
monogamy, where women have achieved a status such
that they cannot be kept in the state of relative inferiority
to men which is implied in the keeping of a harem. "You

ought not to have several wives" means therefore that,
if you live in a country like America, and *if* you wish to
avoid the social maladjustments which polygamy would
there entail, then you should be monogamous. Again,
the moral judgment which might have been passed in
Canaan "You ought to sacrifice your child to Moloch"
means that such a sacrifice is the best way to appease
the anger of that god, to stand well with your tribe, to
make the fruits of the soil prosper. Such a judgment may
perhaps be superstitious and untrue. But that is not to
the point. It is perfectly meaningful, because it is an "is"
sentence, a statement of alleged fact which can be empirically checked.

On the other hand absolutism implies categorical imperatives. For these imperatives are said to be binding
upon all men in *all* circumstances, that is, without any
conditions whatever. You are not to be honest merely *if*
it is good policy, or *if* you want to prosper in your trade.
To be honest is an absolute and unconditional "ought."
And since absolutism depends upon the meaningless idea
of the absolute "ought," it must itself be rejected as
meaningless.

This is the argument. Upon one point in it a little further elucidation seems necessary before we proceed to
our comments. When it is said that the word "ought,"
taken absolutely, is meaningless, it is not of course meant
that it conveys no idea whatever to the mind. This
would certainly be nonsense, since it would then be
impossible to explain how human beings ever came to
suppose that it had a meaning. And obviously when a
despot issues an absolute command to a subject, the latter
does receive some mental impression, usually a very
strong one. What is intended by saying that it is meaning-

less is that it has no *cognitive* meaning, that is, it does not convey any information about the world, it does not make any statement of alleged fact which could be either true or false. In order for a sentence to be either true or false it must at least purport to convey some information. There are many perfectly good sentences in language which do not do this. For example, if I say "May the sun shine on my wedding tomorrow," I am not even pretending to state any kind of fact about the actual state of the weather or about anything else in the world. I am giving expression to a feeling or a hope. And if I say "Go and get my umbrella," here too I am not giving any information about anything, but I am issuing a command. The purpose of such sentences is not to give information but to express emotions or to influence people's actions. Such sentences cannot be said to be strictly true or false, for they do not assert anything to be, or not to be, a fact. Of course it is no doubt a fact that I have the emotion or that I issue the command, but this is not what these sentences specifically say. And these sentences are, therefore, "meaningless" in the technical sense of that term which is employed in the argument which we are discussing. But of course they are not meaningless in the ordinary sense of conveying nothing at all to the minds of their hearers.

So too it is with categorical "ought" sentences. It is not denied that they may have a very powerful effect upon people's minds, call up in them various ideas, feelings, images, hopes, fears, and cause them to act in the way the speaker of the sentences desires. But they are meaningless in the technical sense that they do not make any statements of alleged fact, and that therefore they cannot be either true or false. Now it is essential for absolutism that the categorical "ought" should be meaningful in the technical sense of being either true or false. For the whole philosophy of absolutism is summed up in the view that some moral judgments, that is, some categorical "ought" sentences, are true, namely those which accord with the one true moral standard; and that some are false, namely those which do not accord with it. Thus the contention of the radical empiricist does destroy the absolutist's position without implying the absurdity that the word "ought" conveys no idea to one's mind.

I said, in introducing this argument, that it is an exceedingly powerful one. Nevertheless it fails, in my opinion, to establish the kind of conclusion which the ethical relativist usually wishes to establish, namely, that there exists a variety of moral standards all equally binding upon the races or groups who accept them. All that it does actually prove is that *a moral judgment can only be true (or false) if it is hypothetical*. It shows that all moral duties are relative to human needs, desires, and ends. For it is only *if* a man desires to achieve some end that it can be true to say that he *ought* to do this or that. And this establishes that moral obligations cannot be severed from the human ends which they subserve, and that they would cease to be obligations if they did not subserve these ends. And this conclusion does, to a large extent, undermine the position of the absolutist. But it does not show that there must be many variable moral standards all equally valid for those who accept them. For suppose that there exists some end or set of ends, some need or set of needs, which is common to all human beings. There might be founded upon these needs and ends a set of universal hypothetical "ought" judgments. A proposition of the form "If you want x, then you ought to do y" might give expression to an obligation applicable to *all* men. This would be true if, as a matter of fact, all men wanted x. A set of such obligations would be perfectly meaningful, because hypothetical, and might constitute a universal code of morality.

Such a possibility cannot be neglected. Suppose for the moment that we turn our attention from strictly moral maxims to maxims of physical health. "You ought not to over-eat" might well be claimed to be universally applicable to all men, since all men presumably desire health. It is true that some lunatics and would-be suicides might have to be excepted. But it would still be true that such a maxim would be applicable to all normal men in all ages and in all countries. It would not be the case that this maxim would be valid for Frenchmen but not for Italians, or that it would be a good rule in one century but not in the next. It would have a degree of uniformity remote from the quite chaotic kind of variability postulated in morals by the ethical relativists. It would be, for all practical purposes, universal in its application. And if this is true in the sphere of physical culture, why should not something similar be true in the higher sphere of morality? If, for example, there is any sense in which it is true that all men desire happiness, could there not be founded upon this fact a set of universal moral obligations? I am not for the moment saying that anything like this *is* true. That will be a matter for our future investigation. But the mere fact that it *might* be true is sufficient to show that this third argument does not prove the impossibility of a universal moral standard.

But at absolutism in the older sense, at absolutism in its more extreme forms, the argument from radical empiricism does strike a mortal blow. Since it shows that morality must at least be relative to human needs, it seems no longer possible to talk of a morality applicable to angels and the men on Mars, of a morality which is part of the structure of the universe, so that it would still be real and objective if no race of men existed at all. We can no longer expect to find a moral code binding upon "all rational beings," since there may be rational beings with needs quite other than ours.

While therefore I do not accept the position of ethical relativity, I shall accept the results which, in my opinion, follow from the argument of radical empiricism. The account of morality to be given in this book must exhibit it as human, as an outgrowth of human needs, and as contingent upon them. I shall have to find a meaning for the moral "ought" such that it can always be translated into an "is"; such that any moral judgment can always be shown to assert or deny some supposed matter of fact which may be true or false. I am committed to an empirical ethic.

The fourth argument in favour of ethical relativity is also a very strong one. And it does not suffer from the disadvantage that it is dependent upon the acceptance of any particular philosophy such as radical empiricism. It makes its appeal to considerations of a quite general character. It consists in alleging that no one has ever been able to discover upon what foundation an absolute morality could rest, or from what source a universally binding moral code could derive its authority.

If, for example, it is an absolute and unalterable moral rule that all men ought to be unselfish, from whence does this *command* issue? For a command it certainly is, phrase it how you please. There is no difference in meaning between the sentence "You ought to be unselfish" and the sentence "Be unselfish." Now a command implies a commander. An obligation implies some authority which obliges. Who is this commander, what this authority? Thus the vastly difficult question is raised of *the basis of moral obligation*. Now the argument of the relativist would be that it is impossible to find any basis for a universally binding moral law; but that it is quite easy to discover a basis for morality if moral codes are admitted to be variable, ephemeral, and relative to time, place, and circumstance.

In this book I am assuming that it is no longer possible to solve this difficulty by saying naïvely that the universal moral law is based upon the uniform commands of God to all men. There will be many, no doubt, who will dispute this. But I am not writing for them. I am writing for those who feel the necessity of finding for morality a basis independent of particular religious dogmas. And I shall therefore make no attempt to argue the matter.

The problem which the absolutist has to face, then, is this. The religious basis of the one absolute morality having disappeared, can there be found for it any other, any secular, basis? If not, then it would seem that we cannot any longer believe in absolutism. We shall have to fall back upon belief in a variety of perhaps mutually inconsistent moral codes operating over restricted areas and limited periods. No one of these will be better, or more true, than any other. Each will be good and true for those living in those areas and periods. We shall have to fall back, in a word, on ethical relativity.

For there is no great difficulty in discovering the foundations of morality, or rather of moralities, if we adopt the relativistic hypothesis. Even if we cannot be quite certain *precisely* what these foundations are—and relativists themselves are not entirely agreed about them—we can at least see in a general way the *sort* of foundations they must have. We can see that the question on this basis is not in principle impossible of answer—although the details may be obscure; while, if we adopt the absolutist hypothesis—so the argument runs—no kind of answer is conceivable at all.

Relativists, speaking generally, offer two different solutions of the problem, either of which, or perhaps some compromise between the two, might be correct. According to some the basis of morality is in "emotion." According to others it is in "customs." I do not intend to examine these rival suggestions in detail. An understanding of the general principles involved in them will be quite sufficient for our purpose.

According to the first view emotions such as that of resentment give rise to the idea that the things or actions resented are immoral and bad. Westermarck, who is the chief exponent of this type of opinion, makes further distinctions. Not any resentment, but only impartial or "disinterested" resentment, is the source of moral disapproval. But with these refinements we need not concern ourselves. We can see, easily enough, that if in one community a particular type of act, say sodomy, comes for any reason—biological, historical, or merely accidental—to be resented by the majority of the members of the group, it will come to be regarded as "wrong" by that group. If in another community no such feeling of resentment or dislike arises, it will be thought to be morally unobjectionable. The sense of moral obligation and the commands of morality, then, have their source in *feelings*. And since the feelings of men, and of different groups of men, are variable, the moral codes which are based upon them will be variable too.

Moreover an emotion is not—at any rate according to the psychology implied by Westermarck's conceptions—anything rational. An emotion, as such, cannot be true or false, right or wrong. It simply *is*. If therefore one group of people feels resentment at murder, while another does not, it cannot be said that the moral ideas of the former are any better or more true or more right than those of the latter. They are simply different. What is right *means* simply what arouses certain kinds of feelings, say those of approval. What is wrong *means* simply what arouses resentment or disapproval. There is consequently no sense in asking whether a race of men is right in approving this or that kind of action. Their approving it is what makes it right. For them, therefore, it *is* right. And if another race disapproves it, then, for that race, it *is* wrong.

According to the other view it is custom which is the source of moral standards and ideas. That is "wrong" in any community which is contrary to the customs of that community. That is "right" which is in accordance with them. A moral standard, in fact, is simply identifiable with the set of customs which are in force in any particular region at any particular time. And as customs are variable, so are moral standards. Here too there can be no question of declaring that one set of customs is morally better than another. For the fact that something is the custom is what makes it morally good. And according to this view the sense of moral obligation is simply the force of social custom making itself felt in the individual consciousness.

These two views are not really incompatible. For customs surely have their roots in men's feelings. And to say that morality is based on customs is in the end the same as to say that it is based on feelings. One view emphasizes the outward behaviour which exhibits itself in customs; the other view emphasizes the inward feelings which give rise to this behaviour. The dispute is a professional one between rival schools of psychology. It does not affect the larger issues with which we are concerned.

No such easy solution of the problem of the basis of moral obligation is open to the absolutist. He believes in moral commands obedience to which is obligatory on all men, whether they know it or not, whatever they feel, and whatever their customs may be. Such uniform obligation cannot be founded upon feelings, because feelings are—or are said to be—variable. And there is no set of customs which is more than local in its operation. The will of God as the source of a universal law is no longer a feasible suggestion. And there is obviously no mundane authority, king, or Pope, or super-state, to which all men admit allegiance, and which could have the recognized right to issue universally binding decrees. Where then is the absolutist to turn for an answer to the question? And if he cannot find one, he will have to admit the claims of the ethical relativist; or at least he will have to give up his own claims.

Nevertheless attempts have been made by absolutists to discover a secular basis for an absolute morality, a philosophical foundation which will replace the lost religious foundation upon which absolutism was originally built. And we cannot, without examining them, dismiss the possibility that one or other of these suggested foundations might prove satisfactory. And if a satisfactory secular basis for an absolute morality could be discovered, this fourth argument in favour of ethical relativity would fall to the ground. It will be better, however, to consider the attempts of the absolutists to find such a basis in a new chapter.

CHAPTER 2

ETHICAL RELATIVITY (II)

IN this chapter I shall, firstly, mention four attempts to find for absolutism a secular philosophical basis. My discussion of these will have to be exceedingly brief. I am, it must be remembered, still engaged in outlining the case for ethical relativity, and it is no part of my purpose to discuss other ethical doctrines at length here. When I have finished such discussion of these attempts as is here possible I shall, in the latter part of the chapter, turn to consider the arguments which can be urged *against* ethical relativity.

The first attempt to found absolutism philosophically which I shall consider is one which proceeds from the type of philosophy technically known as "rationalism." The clearest exponent of this kind of thinking in ethics was Immanuel Kant. Difficult as is his moral philosophy in its details, its fundamental idea is profoundly simple. According to Kant, morality is founded, not on "emotions," but on "reason." Emotions are supposed to vary from person to person, from race to race, and from age to age. But reason is said to be "universal," to be the same for all men. As far as mere feelings are concerned, one man may resent what another man welcomes. But the laws of logic, which are the laws of reason, are absolute, and do not vary. If a piece of reasoning is valid for one man, it is valid for every other. Thus it would be absurd to suggest that a piece of mathematical reasoning might be valid in France, but not in China. Hence, if the source

of morality is in emotion, morality will be variable. There
will be many different moralities. But if its source is in
reason, then there will be only one morality which will be
absolutely true, not only for all men, but for all rational
beings.

Kant accordingly attempted to show that the law of
contradiction, as being the highest law of "reason," is the
source of the moral law. It could be shown, he thought,
that to act immorally is always to involve oneself in some
way in a logical contradiction. For example, to make a
promise intending to break it is wrong because this implies acting upon two principles which contradict one another. For if it is right for me to do this, it must be right
for everyone. And if everyone did it, all faith in promises
would be destroyed and no one would ever believe any
promises. Therefore my act implies the principle that *it is
right that no one should ever believe a promise*. But at the
same time my act is based upon the principle that *people
ought to believe my promises*. And these two principles
contradict one another. Hence the duty of keeping one's
promises follows directly from the logical law that one
ought not to contradict oneself.

The usual criticism of this is that a formal logical
principle, such as the law of contradiction, can yield no
positive content in the way of moral duties any more
than it can give material truth in the sciences. All it can
do is to guarantee consistency—in action, as in science.
Since logical consistency in action is by Kant equated
with moral goodness, a consistently wicked man would
have to be considered, on Kant's hypothesis, to be morally
good. We need not discuss the particular example of the
duty of keeping promises given above. It is sufficient to
say, regarding this, that Kant, while pretending to con-

sider only pure logical consistency, illicitly introduces the question of the evil *consequences* which would follow from a universal breaking of promises—a proceeding which is not in keeping with his principles. It is clear that a formal logical law cannot give rise to a material body of moral truths, or to any kind of moral code either absolute or relative. And Kant cannot escape from this conclusion.

Professor Broad has remarked that Kant might defend himself against this criticism by pointing out that "it is no more the business of ethics to provide rules of conduct than it is the business of logic to provide arguments. The business of ethics is to provide a test for rules of conduct, just as it is the business of logic to provide a test for argument." [1] This will mean that just as logic can never tell you *what* the truth is, but only that *if* one proposition is true then another (which follows from it) must also be true; so the ethics of Kant, though it can never tell you *what* is your duty, can tell you that *if* you have a certain duty then you must never do anything which by implication contradicts it. Such a defence may be, within narrow limits, satisfactory. But it is quite useless if Kant's ethical system is to provide a bulwark against ethical relativity. For it admits by implication that the actual source of any particular moral obligation is extra-logical. When once ethical obligations have been obtained from some source other than reason, say from emotion, then logic can come in and admonish us as to their implications, convict us of inconsistency in regard to them, and so forth. Logic can coördinate and systematize the various obligations derived from some other source, just as it can coördinate and systematize the material truths derived from sense-experience. But if reason is to replace

[1] *Five Types of Ethical Theory*, page 123.

the will of God as a basis for a universally valid moral code, then reason must be the actual source of our obligations, not the mere coördinator of obligations derived from elsewhere. If the source of particular obligations lies in emotions or customs, and not in reason, then the obligations themselves will of course vary with the emotions or customs, and we shall be at the mercy of moral relativity once more. A worshipper of Moloch might with complete justification argue that, human sacrifice being in his country a moral institution, all that Kant's ethics would require of him would be that he should never do anything inconsistent with the principles of human sacrifice.

We must therefore conclude that Kant's attempt to found an absolute moral law upon reason was a failure.

What may be considered a second attempt is that of H. Sidgwick among the utilitarians. Mill had proclaimed that the supreme end of human actions ought to be to achieve "the greatest happiness of the greatest number." Those actions are morally right which tend to increase as much as possible the general happiness; those wrong which tend to decrease it. Now even if we admit that this is true as far as it goes—and of course it is not admitted by all ethical philosophers, perhaps not now by many—it fails to give any account of the *basis* of moral obligation. It tells us at best *what* we are obliged to do, namely to increase the happiness of humanity, but it does not tell us *why* we are obliged to do this. It may be an admirable *description* of our duties, but it fails even to suggest by what authority these duties are imposed upon us. That is to say, it does nothing towards solving the problem as to the source, or foundation, of moral obligations.

If one sticks to the view of philosophical egoism—that all morality is based upon "intelligent self-interest"—this problem should present no difficulties. For in that case the reason why I ought to do all I can to increase the happiness of others is that I believe this is, in the end, the best way to secure my own. The basis of my obligation will be my own interest. But the utilitarians did not take this view. Their morality was to be, not egoistic, but high-mindedly altruistic. And in that case the problem of the basis of obligation becomes for them acute. Why I should advance my own happiness is not difficult to understand. But why should I advance yours? To work for the greatest happiness of the greatest number may sometimes be disastrous for my own interests. To do so may be my duty. But why should I do my duty? To this vital question Mill had given no intelligible reply.

Sidgwick undertook to do so. Obligation was based, he supposed, upon what he called the "axiom" of rational benevolence. The axiom is that "each one is morally bound to regard the good of any other individual as much as his own, except in so far as he judges it to be less, when impartially viewed, or less certainly knowable as attainable by him." [1] Or—as another statement of the axiom—"I ought not to prefer my own lesser good to the greater good of another." [2] This amounts to saying that the basis of morality is a self-evident moral axiom just as the basis of geometry is (or was formerly believed to be) a set of self-evident geometrical axioms. If this were true, we should have to believe in an absolute morality. For a necessary truth, a self-evident axiom, must necessarily be true for all men, indeed for all rational beings.

[1] H. Sidgwick, *The Methods of Ethics*, page 382.
[2] *Op. cit.*, page 383.

On this it must be remarked, in the first place, that our faith in self-evident axioms of any kind has been gravely shaken since the time of Sidgwick's book. The axioms of geometry, it is now believed, are all either disguised definitions or pure assumptions. They are no longer claimed to be self-evidently true. And the general tendency of the day is to disbelieve altogether in axioms, to take the view (in technical phrase) that all *a priori* propositions are analytic. This view, though characteristically modern, is by no means universally accepted, and may quite possibly be mistaken. It is, however, fair to say that the possibility of the very existence of any self-evident axioms, whether ethical or otherwise, has been placed in grave doubt by modern enquiries, that this is therefore not an opportune moment for founding ethics upon one, and that neither Sidgwick nor anyone else could succeed in doing so without first undertaking a most elaborate defence of the notion of axioms designed to dispel modern doubts.

I do not wish to stand, however, upon this disputable ground. Let us assume, therefore, for the sake of argument, that there are or might be self-evident truths. Can it be said that Sidgwick's proposition has any claim to stand among them? The question is posed why I ought to work for the happiness of anyone other than myself. Sidgwick replies simply, in effect, that the fact that I ought to do so is self-evident. Now I can understand what is meant, or what was once meant, when it was said that the so-called axiom "two straight lines cannot enclose a space" is self-evident. Place two straight lines on a piece of paper, or call them up in imagination. Put them in any position you please, turn them around how you will, you cannot even imagine that they could enclose a space.

That they should do so seems inconceivable. To enclose a space, the two ends of the two lines must coincide each with each. But if the ends coincide then the entire lines will coincide, will become one line, and no space will be enclosed. As soon therefore as one understands what is meant by the axiom one seems to see, not only that it is true as a matter of fact, but that it is necessarily true, that it could not conceivably be otherwise. (I am not, of course, disputing the validity of non-Euclidean geometries or attempting to resurrect outmoded views of the foundations of geometry. I am merely pointing out what was meant by these views.) But no consideration of this sort will apply, surely, to Sidgwick's axiom. To hold the view that I am under no obligation to trouble myself about the happiness of other people may appear to be very shocking. But it can hardly be said that there is an actual logical impossibility in holding such a view. And this is what is necessary if we are to argue successfully that Sidgwick's axiom is in any strict sense "self-evident." The fact is that it seems quite obvious to most of us, with centuries of altruistic ethical tradition behind us, that we ought to be unselfish. We take it for granted in theory, though our actions so often belie it. No one ordinarily would think of denying it. But this kind of "obviousness" must not be mistaken for logical self-evidence. This is the mistake, I think, which is made by those who would have us believe that altruism is a self-evident duty. We do often use the expression "self-evident" in this loose way, as if it imported nothing but what is in ordinary conversation called "obvious." We say it is self-evident that Caesar was a great man, that the earth goes round the sun, that knowledge is a good thing, that there exist other minds besides our own. None of these things is, in the logical sense, self-evident. We are doubtless quite justified in calling them self-evident for the purposes of everyday conversation. But to introduce this kind of loose talk into philosophical discussion is unpardonable.

The ethics of Kant and of Sidgwick, so unlike each other in most respects, are alike in this, that they both attempt to found morality upon logically necessary truths or axioms. Kant appeals to the logical law of contradiction, Sidgwick to a supposed ethical axiom. They fail, however, for opposing reasons. Kant's axiom may really be a necessary truth because it is merely formal and empty. But for that very reason we cannot believe that material moral truths can be extracted from it. Sidgwick's axiom does contain material (ethical) content, and for that very reason we cannot believe that it is really an axiom.

A third and very different attempt to find for absolute morality a secular basis takes its rise in connection with the view that moral value is a kind of *quality*.[1] There is more than one possible variant of this theory. It may be held, for example, that certain things, situations, or states of affairs, which exist objectively in the world, possess the quality of goodness in much the same way as a flower possesses the quality of yellowness. Such things as pleasure, knowledge, beautiful art, might possess this quality.

[1] Perhaps I ought to ward off a possible misconception. I refer in the text to this, and the other three ethical philosophies discussed in this chapter, as attempts to find a secular basis for an absolute morality. I do not, however, mean that the authors of these philosophies themselves necessarily had that aim, or that they specifically had in mind the controversy between absolutism and relativism. They might well disclaim any such idea. I only mean that, in whatever connection or with whatever purpose they developed their views, these views might be thought of (perhaps by other people) as possible bases for a defence of absolutism.

A moral action is then defined as one which tends to increase as much as possible the number of things or states of affairs which have this quality. An immoral action is defined in the opposite way. Morality then becomes a means to the achievement of these good ends. Another possible variant of the same kind of view would hold that the quality of goodness attaches to our moral actions themselves, and not to their consequences. In that case morality is not a means, but an end in itself.

It is usually held that the quality of goodness is something unanalysable and ultimate in the same sense as the quality of yellowness is ultimate and unanalysable. Yellow may be caused by certain ether vibrations, but it cannot itself be analysed into these vibrations. It cannot be defined. It can only be pointed out. A man either knows yellow by direct acquaintance, or he does not know it at all. It is just the same, so it is alleged, with value-quality. It is not, indeed, seen by the eyes, as yellow is, nor perceived by any of the physical senses. It is presumably immediately apprehended by the mind. But, like yellow, it cannot be analysed or defined. A man either perceives the goodness of a thing or action, or he does not. If he does not, he is then in the same sort of position as a blind man who cannot see colour.

If this view were true, it might be possible to defend belief in an absolute morality on the basis of it. For in that case it would be as much a question of hard *fact* whether a thing or action had the quality of being good as it is a question of hard fact whether a flower is yellow. Value-quality would be objective in the same sense as colour is objective. It is true that there are some philosophers who think that colour is subjective. But that is not as a rule the opinion of those who preach the ethical doctrine which we are discussing. And in any case, the question of the colour is certainly, in some sense, a question of fact, regarding which there may be right and wrong views. It is not a mere question of personal taste or whim what colour we find a thing to be. And in the same way, if goodness is a quality, then a thing or action either has that quality or does not have it. Whether an act is moral or immoral cannot in that case be a mere matter of personal opinion, tradition, customary belief, or taste. If it is moral, then anyone who thinks it immoral is mistaken. And if it is immoral, then anyone who thinks it moral is mistaken. Hence if the same action is thought moral by Chinamen and immoral by Frenchmen, one or other of them must be wrong. There can only be one true opinion about what is moral or immoral. And this is the same as saying that there exists only one single universal true moral standard.

The view that goodness is a quality is beset by many difficulties. An attempt to discuss these would take us too far afield, and is not necessary here. For one can point out at once that, even if it is true that goodness is a quality, this fact is quite insufficient to afford a basis for moral obligation. The fact that something has a quality does impose upon me the purely intellectual, or theoretical, obligation to admit that it has that quality. But how can it impose upon me any obligation to *act?* Why should I *do* anything about it? If it is pointed out to me that a certain flower is yellow, and if I see this with my own eyes, then I can understand that I am obliged to admit the truth of the proposition "This flower is yellow." I cannot indeed do otherwise. I may, of course, for some peculiar reason of my own, still refuse to admit it *to you*. But in my own mind, intellectually,

I *have* to accept it. But this cannot possibly oblige me
to any kind of action. It cannot oblige me, for example,
to pick the flower. I shall only do this if I like yellow
flowers, or have some other inclination which prompts
me to pick it. So too, if it is pointed out to me that a
thing or an action has the quality of being good, and if I
myself perceive this, I can see that this will compel me to
admit the truth of the proposition "This is good." But
it cannot impose on me any *practical* obligation whatsoever. I shall still not do anything, unless it happens that
I like good things. And in that case it is my inclination
which obliges me, not the theoretical truth which has
been pointed out to me. And I may very likely say "I
recognize clearly the quality of goodness which you point
out to me. But I do not happen to be interested in this
quality of things. In fact in this case I dislike it because
it conflicts with my interests and pleasures." In that
case the question "*why* should I pursue goodness"? remains
unanswered. The basis of moral obligation has not been
disclosed. This means that goodness as a quality cannot
be the source of a moral *law*, whether relative or absolute.

The fourth and last attempt to find a basis for absolutism which I shall mention here consists in the suggestion that value—we are only interested in moral value,
but the suggestion is usually applied to all kinds of
value—is a "subsistent" entity, timeless, spaceless, and
eternal. It is—so this theory states—like logical and
mathematical entities. It is a Platonic universal. Values,
therefore, are not variable as the ethical relativists would
have us believe. They are eternally immutable. And
therefore the obligations founded upon them must be
universal and unchangeable.

It is exceedingly doubtful whether the word "subsistence," as employed in this theory, is not entirely meaningless when judged by the empirical test of meaning described in the last chapter. In that case the whole theory of subsistent entities, whether it is applied to values, to mathematical conceptions, or to any other kind of universal, is a mere empty game of words. But to establish this position would require a prolonged analysis which would be out of place in a book on ethics. I shall therefore content myself with pointing out that, even if we assume for the purpose of argument that there are subsistent entities and that values are among them, this theory—like the theory of value as a quality, and for the same reason—cannot provide a basis for moral obligation.

Here, as in the previous case, only a theoretical or intellectual obligation could arise, never a practical one. If goodness is an eternal subsistent reality, and if this can be pointed out to me in experience, then I shall be compelled to admit intellectually the truth of the proposition "Goodness is a subsistent reality." But why should I *do* anything, or refrain from doing anything, because of this? The mere fact that there exists, or subsists, in the universe, some quality, thing, entity, value, universal, cannot of itself alone put me under an obligation to do anything except to admit the existence or subsistence of this quality, entity, thing, value, or universal. I can take off my hat to this eternally subsistent goodness, thereby politely recognizing its reality, and thereafter take no further notice of it.

We can now gather together the threads of this rather long and complicated discussion. The fourth argument in favour of ethical relativity, which I began to describe at the end of the last chapter,[1] pointed out that, if there is a single absolute morality, whose commands are obligatory on all rational beings, or even on all men, there must be some authority which is the source of this universal obligation. If no such authority can be indicated, then there can be no such universal obligation. The religious basis of absolutism has decayed, and all attempts to find a secular basis for it have failed. We have examined four of the most famous such attempts and have found them all unsatisfactory. We can hardly expect to have better luck with others less well known. And in any case the onus is upon the absolutist to produce a theory of the foundation of his absolute obligation, and to produce evidence that his theory is true. He has not done this; he cannot do it. And therefore his absolutism falls to the ground. The only alternative with which we are left is ethical relativity.

This argument is undoubtedly very strong. It *is* absolutely essential to solve the problem of the basis of moral obligation if we are to believe in any kind of moral standards other than those provided by mere custom or by irrational emotions. It is idle to talk about a universal morality unless we can point to the source of its authority—or at least to do so is to indulge in a faith which is without rational ground. To cherish a blind faith in morality may be, for the average man whose business is primarily to live aright and not to theorize, sufficient. Perhaps it is his wisest course. But it will not do for the philosopher. His function, or at least one of his functions, is precisely to discover the rational grounds of our everyday beliefs— if they have any. Philosophically and intellectually,

[1] Page 27.

then, we cannot accept belief in a universally binding morality unless we can discover upon what foundation its obligatory character rests.

But in spite of the strength of the argument thus posed in favour of ethical relativity, it is not impregnable. For it leaves open one loop-hole. It is always possible that some theory, not yet examined, may provide a basis for a universal moral obligation. The argument rests upon the negative proposition that *there is no theory which can provide a basis for a universal morality*. But it is notoriously difficult to prove a negative. How can you prove that there are no green swans? All you can show is that none have been found so far. And then it is always possible that one will be found tomorrow. So it is here. The relativist shows that no theory of the basis of moral obligation has yet been discovered which could validate a universal morality. Perhaps. But it is just conceivable that one might be discovered in the course of this book.

It is time that we turned our attention from the case in favour of ethical relativity to the case against it. Now the case against it consists, to a very large extent, in urging that, if taken seriously and pressed to its logical conclusion, ethical relativity can only end in destroying the conception of morality altogether, in undermining its practical efficacy, in rendering meaningless many almost universally accepted truths about human affairs, in robbing human beings of any incentive to strive for a better world, in taking the life-blood out of every ideal and every aspiration which has ever ennobled the life of man. In short, the charge against it is that it revolts and outrages man's moral *feelings*.

To all such arguments it is always possible to reply

that they are merely pragmatic, mere appeals to feeling which have no logical cogency and no scientific value. I will not for the moment argue the question whether feelings have any value at all in the search for truth, or whether they ought to be utterly disregarded. That matter may be left for a later page. For the moment let us rather see what these arguments of the anti-relativist are. We will frankly recognise from the outset their quasi-emotional character. If we do this, we shall perhaps be saved from disappointment and misunderstanding. The reader should not be either disappointed or surprised if in what follows I seem to him to be merely appealing to feelings and not to facts or logic. This in fact is what I shall be doing. And I shall be doing it because it is the only way in which the case of the anti-relativist can be communicated to the reader. We can judge of all this afterwards. Perhaps we shall find that the purely logical and scientific procedure, which would rule out all feeling as irrelevant, is not wholly applicable to the subject-matter of morals; that it rests upon a too rigorous dichotomy between feeling and cognition. But however that may be, let us hear what the anti-relativist has to say. It cannot be wrong, it cannot be irrelevant for us, and for the relativist himself, to see what his doctrine actually implies in the way of practical consequences; to see how it tallies with the demands of the "moral consciousness." Other arguments, of a more definitely empirical and scientific character, can be left for discussion in later chapters.

First of all, then, ethical relativity, in asserting that the moral standards of particular social groups are the only standards which exist, renders meaningless all propositions which attempt to compare these standards with one another in respect of their moral worth. And this is a very serious matter indeed. We are accustomed to think that the moral ideas of one nation or social group may be "higher" or "lower" than those of another. We believe, for example, that Christian ethical ideals are nobler than those of the savage races of central Africa. Probably most of us would think that the Chinese moral standards are higher than those of the inhabitants of New Guinea. In short we habitually compare one civilization with another and judge the sets of ethical ideas to be found in them to be some better, some worse. The fact that such judgments are very difficult to make with any justice, and that they are frequently made on very superficial and prejudiced grounds, has no bearing on the question now at issue. The question is whether such judgments have any *meaning*. We habitually assume that they have.

But on the basis of ethical relativity they can have none whatever. For the relativist must hold that there is no *common* standard which can be applied to the various civilizations judged. Any such comparison of moral standards implies the existence of some superior standard which is applicable to both. And the existence of any such standard is precisely what the relativist denies. According to him the Christian standard is applicable only to Christians, the Chinese standard only to Chinese, the New Guinea standard only to the inhabitants of New Guinea.

What is true of comparisons between the moral standards of different races will also be true of comparisons between those of different ages. It is not unusual to ask such questions as whether the standard of our own day is superior to that which existed among our ancestors five hundred years ago. And when we remember that our ancestors employed slaves, practiced barbaric physical tortures, and burnt people alive, we may be inclined to think that it is. At any rate we assume that the question is one which has meaning and is capable of rational discussion. But if the ethical relativist is right, whatever we assert on this subject must be totally meaningless. For here again there is no common standard which could form the basis of any such judgments.

This in its turn implies that the whole notion of moral *progress* is a sheer delusion. Progress means an advance from lower to higher, from worse to better. But on the basis of ethical relativity it has no meaning to say that the standards of this age are better (or worse) than those of a previous age. For there is no common standard by which both can be measured. Thus it is nonsense to say that the morality of the New Testament is higher than that of the Old. And Jesus Christ, if he imagined that he was introducing into the world a higher ethical standard than existed before his time, was merely deluded.

There is indeed one way in which the ethical relativist can give some sort of meaning to judgments of higher or lower as applied to the moral ideas of different races or ages. What he will have to say is that we assume *our* standards to be the best simply because they are ours. And we judge other standards by our own. If we say that Chinese moral codes are better than those of African cannibals, what we *mean* by this is that they are better *according to our standards*. We mean, that is to say, that Chinese standards are *more like our own* than African standards are. "Better" accordingly *means* "more like us." "Worse" means "less like us." It thus becomes clear that judgments of better and worse in such cases do not express anything that is really true at all. They merely give expression to our perfectly groundless satisfaction

with our own ideas. In short, they give expression to
nothing but our egotism and self-conceit. Our moral
ideals are not really better than those of the savage. We
are simply deluded by our egotism into thinking they are.
The African savage has just as good a right to think his
morality the best as we have to think ours the best. His
opinion is just as well grounded as ours, or rather both
opinions are equally groundless. And on this view Jesus
Christ can only have been led to the quite absurd belief
that his ethical precepts were better than those of Moses
by his personal vanity. If only he had read Westermarck
and Dewey he would have understood that, so long as
people continued to believe in the doctrine of an eye for
an eye and a tooth for a tooth, that doctrine was morally
right; and that there could not be any point whatever in
trying to make them believe in his new-fangled theory of
loving one's enemies. True, the new morality would
become right as soon as people came to believe in it, for it
would then be the accepted standard. And what people
think right is right. But then, if only Jesus Christ and
persons with similar ideas had kept these ideas to themselves, people might have gone on believing that the old
morality was right. And in that case it would have *been*
right, and would have remained so till this day. And that
would have saved a lot of useless trouble. For the change
which Jesus Christ actually brought about was merely a
change from one set of moral ideas to another. And as
the new set of ideas was in no way better than the set it
displaced—to say that it was better would be meaningless
for the reasons already given—the change was really a
sheer waste of time. And of course it likewise follows that
anyone who in the future tries to improve the moral ideas
of humanity will also be wasting his time.

Thus the ethical relativist must treat all judgments comparing different moralities as either entirely meaningless; or, if this course appears too drastic, he has the alternative of declaring that they have for their meaning-content nothing except the vanity and egotism of those who pass them. We are asked to believe that the highest moral ideals of humanity are not really any better than those of an Australian bushman. But if this is so, why strive for higher ideals? Thus the heart is taken out of all effort, and the meaning out of all human ideals and aspirations.

The ethical relativist may perhaps say that he is being misjudged. It is not true that, on the basis of his doctrine, all effort for moral improvement is vain. For if we take such a civilization as our own, and if we assume that the standard of morals theoretically accepted by it is that of Christian ethics, then there is surely plenty of room for improvement and "progress" in the way of making our practice accord with our theory. Effort may legitimately be directed towards getting people to live up to whatever standards they profess to honour. Such effort will be, on the relativistic basis, perfectly meaningful; for it does not imply a comparison of standards by reference to a common standard, but only a comparison of actual achievements with an admitted and accepted standard within a social group.

Now I do not believe that even this plea can be accepted. For as soon as it comes to be effectively realized that our moral standard is no better than that of barbarians, why should anyone trouble to live up to it? It would be much easier to adopt some lower standard, to preach it assiduously until everyone believes it, when it would automatically become right. But even if we waive this point, and admit that the exhortation to practice what we preach may be meaningful, this does not touch the issue which was raised above. It will still be true that efforts to improve moral *beliefs*, as distinguished from moral *practice*, will be futile. It will still be true that Jesus Christ would have done better had he tried only to persuade humanity to live up to the old barbaric standards than he did in trying to propagate among them a new and more enlightened moral code. It will still be true that any reformer in the future who attempts to make men see even more noble ideals than those which we have inherited from the reformers of the past will be wasting his time.

I come now to a second point. Up to the present I have allowed it to be taken tacitly for granted that, though judgments comparing different races and ages in respect of the worth of their moral codes are impossible for the ethical relativist, yet judgments of comparison between individuals living within the same social group would be quite possible. For individuals living within the same social group would presumably be subject to the same moral code, that of their group, and this would therefore constitute, as between these individuals, a common standard by which they could both be measured. We have not here, as we had in the other case, the difficulty of the absence of any common standard of comparison. It should therefore be possible for the ethical relativist to say quite meaningfully that President Lincoln was a better man than some criminal or moral imbecile of his own time and country, or that Jesus was a better man than Judas Iscariot.

But is even this minimum of moral judgment really possible on relativist grounds? It seems to me that it is not. For when once the whole of humanity is abandoned as the area covered by a single moral standard, what smaller areas are to be adopted as the *loci* of different standards? Where are we to draw the lines of demarcation? We can split up humanity, perhaps,—though the procedure will be very arbitrary—into races, races into nations, nations into tribes, tribes into families, families into individuals. Where are we going to draw the *moral* boundaries? Does the *locus* of a particular moral standard reside in a race, a nation, a tribe, a family, or an individual? Perhaps the blessed phrase "social group" will be dragged in to save the situation. Each such group, we shall be told, has its own moral code which is, for it, right. But what *is* a "group"? Can anyone define it or give its boundaries? This is the seat of that ambiguity in the theory of ethical relativity to which reference was made on an earlier page.[1]

The difficulty is not, as might be thought, merely an academic difficulty of logical definition. If that were all, I should not press the point. But the ambiguity has practical consequences which are disastrous for morality. No one is likely to say that moral codes are confined within the arbitrary limits of the geographical divisions of countries. Nor are the notions of race, nation, or political state likely to help us. To bring out the essentially practical character of the difficulty let us put it in the form of concrete questions. Does the American nation constitute a "group" having a single moral standard? Or does the standard of what I ought to do change continuously as I cross the continent in a railway train? Do different States of the Union have different moral codes? Perhaps every town and village has its own peculiar standard. This may at first sight seem reasonable enough. "In Rome do as

[1] Page 12.

Rome does" may seem as good a rule in morals as it is in etiquette. But can we stop there? Within the village are numerous cliques each having its own set of ideas. Why should not each of these claim to be bound only by its own special and peculiar moral standards? And if it comes to that, why should not the gangsters of Chicago claim to constitute a group having its own morality, so that its murders and debaucheries must be viewed as "right" by the only standard which can legitimately be applied to it? And if it be answered that the nation will not tolerate this, that may be so. But this is to put the foundation of right simply in the superior force of the majority. In that case whoever is stronger will be right, however monstrous his ideas and actions. And if we cannot deny to any set of people the right to have its own morality, is it not clear that, in the end, we cannot even deny this right to the individual? Every individual man and woman can put up, on this view, an irrefutable claim to be judged by no standard except his or her own.

If these arguments are valid, the ethical relativist cannot really maintain that there is anywhere to be found a moral standard binding upon anybody against his will. And he cannot maintain that, even within the social group, there is a common standard as between individuals. And if that is so, then even judgments to the effect that one man is morally better than another become meaningless. All moral valuation thus vanishes. There is nothing to prevent each man from being a rule unto himself. The result will be moral chaos and the collapse of all effective standards.

Perhaps, in regard to the difficulty of defining the social group, the relativist may make the following suggestion. If we admit, he may say, that it is impossible or very difficult to define a group territorially or nationally or geographically, it is still possible to define it logically. We will simply define an ethical group as any set of persons (whether they live together in one place or are scattered about in many places over the earth) who recognize one and the same moral standard. As a matter of fact such groups will as a rule be found occupying each something like a single locality. The people in one country, or at least in one village, tend to think much alike. But theoretically at least the members of an ethical group so defined might be scattered all over the face of the globe. However that may be, it will now be possible to make meaningful statements to the effect that one individual is morally better or worse than another, so long as we keep within the ethical group so defined. For the individuals of the ethical group will have as their common standard the ethical belief or beliefs the acknowledgment of which constitutes the defining characteristic of the group. By this common standard they can be judged and compared with one another. Therefore it is not true that ethical relativity necessarily makes all such judgments of moral comparison between individuals meaningless.

I admit the logic of this. Theoretically judgments of comparison can be given meaning in this way. Nevertheless there are fatal objections to the suggestion. In the first place, this is certainly not what the relativist ordinarily understands his doctrine to mean. He never talks in terms of ethical groups defined in this purely logical way. He talks in terms of actual social groups, nations, tribes, or historically existing communities of some kind. We are told that the moral customs of the Athenians of the fifth century B.C. were the only effective standards for the Athenians of the fifth century B.C.; that the moral customs of present day Hottentots are the only effective standards for present day Hottentots; and so on. The suggestion which we are now considering gives to the usual doctrine of relativism a twist which renders it unrecognizable. And if it be said that the logical ethical group is *in fact* usually at least roughly identical with some actual territorial or social group—since people living together tend to share the same moral ideas—I can only reply by denying the truth of this. In the same social group all sorts of different moral ideas may thrive. This is the point of the second objection to the relativist's present suggestion.

The second objection is that the suggested criterion will be useless in practice. For how can I ever know whether two persons whom I wish to compare belong to the same ethical group or not? I wish to say that Jesus was a morally nobler man than Judas Iscariot. If the relativist cannot admit this, then surely his creed revolts our moral sense. But I cannot make this statement unless I have first made certain that Jesus and Judas had the same moral ideals. But had they? Personally I should think it almost certain that they had not. Judas may have paid homage, in some sort, to the moral teachings of his master. He may even have been quite sincere. But it seems to me incredible that he could ever really have made them parts of his mental and moral outlook, or even that he could have effectively understood them. Consequently the judgment that Jesus was better than Judas is meaningless after all. It is almost certain that the Chicago gangsters do not hold the same moral views (if it has any meaning to attribute moral views to them at all) as President Roosevelt. Therefore a judgment of moral comparison between the president and the gangster will be meaningless. I think it would be in general true to say that wherever there is between people a very wide discrepancy of moral practice, there is almost sure to be also a wide discrepancy of moral belief. And in no such case could we, on the relativistic basis suggested, make meaningful moral comparisons. It can hardly be said, therefore, that this suggestion at all helps the case of the ethical relativist.

But even if we assume that the difficulty about defining moral groups has been surmounted, a further difficulty presents itself. Suppose that we have now definitely decided what are the exact boundaries of the social group within which a moral standard is to be operative. And we will assume—as is invariably done by relativists themselves—that this group is to be some actually existing social community such as a tribe or nation. How are we to know, even then, what actually *is* the moral standard within that group? How is anyone to know? How is even a member of the group to know? For there are certain to be within the group—at least this will be true among advanced peoples—wide differences of opinion as to what is right, what wrong. Whose opinion, then, is to be taken as representing *the* moral standard of the group? Either we must take the opinion of the majority within the group, or the opinion of some minority. If we rely upon the ideas of the majority, the results will be disastrous. Wherever there is found among a people a small band of select spirits, or perhaps one man, working for the establishment of higher and nobler ideals than those commonly accepted by the group, we shall be compelled to hold that, for that people at that time, the majority are right, and that the reformers are wrong and are preaching what is immoral. We shall have to maintain, for example, that

Jesus was preaching immoral doctrines to the Jews. Moral goodness will have to be equated always with the mediocre and sometimes with the definitely base and ignoble. If on the other hand we say that the moral standard of the group is to be identified with the moral opinions of some minority, then what minority is this to be? We cannot answer that it is to be the minority composed of the best and most enlightened individuals of the group. This would involve us in a palpably vicious circle. For by what standard are these individuals to be judged the best and the most enlightened? There is no principle by which we could select the right minority. And therefore we should have to consider every minority as good as every other. And this means that we should have no logical right whatever to resist the claim of the gangsters of Chicago—if such a claim were made—that their practices represent the highest standards of American morality. It means in the end that every individual is to be bound by no standard save his own.

The ethical relativists are great empiricists. *What* is the actual moral standard of any group can only be discovered, they tell us, by an examination on the ground of the moral opinions and customs of that group. But will they tell us how they propose to decide, when they get to the ground, which of the many moral opinions they are sure to find there is *the* right one in that group? To some extent they will be able to do this for the Melanesian Islanders— from whom apparently all lessons in the nature of morality are in future to be taken. But it is certain that they cannot do it for advanced peoples whose members have learnt to think for themselves and to entertain among themselves a wide variety of opinions. They cannot do it unless they accept the calamitous view that the ethical opinion of the majority is always right. We are left therefore once more with the conclusion that, even within a particular social group, anybody's moral opinion is as good as anybody else's, and that every man is entitled to be judged by his own standards.

Finally, not only is ethical relativity disastrous in its consequences for moral theory. It cannot be doubted that it must tend to be equally disastrous in its impact upon practical conduct. If men come really to believe that one moral standard is as good as another, they will conclude that their own moral standard has nothing special to recommend it. They might as well then slip down to some lower and easier standard. It is true that, for a time, it may be possible to hold one view in theory and to act practically upon another. But ideas, even philosophical ideas, are not so ineffectual that they can remain for ever idle in the upper chambers of the intellect. In the end they seep down to the level of practice. They get themselves acted on.

Speaking of the supposedly dangerous character of ethical relativity Westermarck says "Ethical subjectivism instead of being a danger is more likely to be an advantage to morality. Could it be brought home to people that there is no absolute standard in morality, they would perhaps be on the one hand more tolerant, and on the other hand more critical in their judgments." [1] Certainly, if we believe that any one moral standard is as good as any other, we *are* likely to be more tolerant. We shall tolerate widow-burning, human sacrifice, cannibalism, slavery, the infliction of physical torture, or any other of the thousand and one abominations which are, or have been, from time to time approved by one moral code or another. But this is not the kind of toleration that we want, and I do not

[1] *Ethical Relativity*, page 59.

think its cultivation will prove "an advantage to morality."

These, then, are the main arguments which the anti-relativist will urge against ethical relativity. And perhaps finally he will attempt a diagnosis of the social, intellectual, and psychological conditions of our time to which the emergence of ethical relativism is to be attributed. His diagnosis will be somewhat as follows.

We have abandoned, perhaps with good reason, the oracles of the past. Every age, of course, does this. But in our case it seems that none of us knows any more whither to turn. We do not know what to put in the place of that which has gone. What ought we, supposedly civilized peoples, to aim at? What are to be our ideals? What is right? What is wrong? What is beautiful? What is ugly? No man knows. We drift helplessly in this direction and that. We know not where we stand nor whither we are going.

There are, of course, thousands of voices frantically shouting directions. But they shout one another down, they contradict one another, and the upshot is mere uproar. And because of this confusion there creeps upon us an insidious scepticism and despair. Since no one knows what the truth is, we will deny that there is any truth. Since no one knows what right is, we will deny that there is any right. Since no one knows what the beautiful is, we will deny that there is any beauty. Or at least we will say—what comes to the same thing—that what people (the people of any particular age, region, society)—think to be true is true *for them;* that what people think morally right is morally right *for them;* that what people think beautiful is beautiful *for them.* There is no common and objective standard in any of these matters. Since all the voices contradict one another, they must be all equally right (or equally wrong, for it makes no difference which we say). It is from the practical confusion of our time that these doctrines issue. When all the despair and defeatism of our distracted age are expressed in abstract concepts, are erected into a philosophy, it is then called relativism—ethical relativism, esthetic relativism, relativity of truth. Ethical relativity is simply defeatism in morals.

And the diagnosis will proceed. Perhaps, it will say, the current pessimism as to our future is unjustified. But there is undoubtedly a wide spread feeling that our civilization is rushing downwards to the abyss. If this should be true, and if nothing should check the headlong descent, then perhaps some historian of the future will seek to disentangle the causes. The causes will, of course, be found to be multitudinous and enormously complicated. And one must not exaggerate the relative importance of any of them. But it can hardly be doubted that our future historian will include somewhere in his list the failure of the men of our generation to hold steadfastly before themselves the notion of an (even comparatively) unchanging moral idea. He will cite that feebleness of intellectual and moral grasp which has led them weakly to harbour the belief that no one moral aim is really any better than any other, that each is good and true for those who entertain it. This meant, he will surely say, that men had given up in despair the struggle to attain moral truth. Civilization lives in and through its upward struggle. Whoever despairs and gives up the struggle, whether it be an individual or a whole civilization, is already inwardly dead.

And the philosophers of our age, where have they stood? They too, as is notorious, speak with many voices. But those who preach the various relativisms have taken upon themselves a heavy load of responsibility. By formulating abstractly the defeatism of the age they have made themselves the aiders and abettors of death. They are injecting poison into the veins of civilization. Their influence upon practical affairs may indeed be small. But it counts for something. And they cannot avoid their share of the general responsibility. They have failed to do what little they could to stem the tide. They have failed to do what Plato did for the men of his own age—find a way out of at least the intellectual confusions of the time.

We may now sum up the criticisms which have been made of ethical relativity. According to the anti-relativist, the doctrine of the relativist logically implies:

(1) That all propositions which adjudge the moral standards of one civilization to be better or worse than the moral standards of another civilization are either meaningless or express nothing except the groundless self-satisfaction of the person making the judgment.

(2) That all propositions which adjudge the moral standards of one age to be better or worse than those of another age are either meaningless or express only self-satisfaction.

(3) That the notion of progress in moral ideals (as distinguished from moral practice) is meaningless.

(4) That it is consequently useless for people to strive for higher moral ideals than those they already possess.

(5) That it is usually meaningless to judge that any one human being is morally better or worse than any other, for example that Jesus was better than Judas. Such judgments are only meaningful if one can be certain that the two persons compared hold exactly the same

moral beliefs. In practice one can almost never be certain of this, and one can usually be fairly certain of the opposite.

I think the anti-relativist is right in arguing that ethical relativity does imply these conclusions. What then? Suppose that the relativist accepts these deductions from his creed, and asserts that he believes them to be true. (This is what he is likely to do if he is both bold and honest, though the feebler type of relativist is likely to draw back, to try to pick holes in the logic of the deductions, and to assert that he is being mis-represented.) How can the anti-relativist deal with an antagonist who is audacious enough to take this ground? Now the full answer to this question can only be given, I believe, after a long and difficult analysis. And to give that full answer is, in part, one of the main aims of this book. For the moment, however, the anti-relativist is likely to reply simply that he rejects these conclusions because they revolt his moral sense. These conclusions, he will say, undermine the whole idea of morality. They make moral effort meaningless. They destroy the very roots of human aspiration. They are therefore unacceptable to anyone possessed of the slightest moral *feeling*. That is why I said earlier that the arguments of the anti-relativist are really appeals to feeling, rather than to facts or logic. And, as before stated, the relativist can always reply—if he is sufficiently "tough-minded"—that mere appeals to feeling, whether moral or any other, have no logical cogency and no scientific value.

Now I think we shall have to admit that arguments based upon feelings can never be, either to the scientist or the philosopher, finally and completely satisfactory and sufficient. To be a philosopher is to live the life of reason. Philosophy is rational or it is nothing. It must in

the last analysis base its conclusions upon rational considerations. It must stand the test of logic and of facts. To
take any other view is to desert the standard of philosophy. And if ethical relativity is to be rejected, if an
attempt is to be made to establish any kind of universal
morality, other evidence than that afforded by our mere
moral feelings will have to be adduced. The position of
the anti-relativist, as it has appeared so far in the argument,
is therefore very far from being satisfactory.

But to admit all this is not at all to admit that human
feelings can be swept contemptuously aside as if they
possessed no value and no relevancy whatever in the
search for knowledge. This is far from being true. There
are men—and perhaps they are the majority of men—
who through insight, intuition, or feeling, attain a view
of moral truth which may be hidden from those who rely
exclusively upon what is called "scientific method." I
am not proposing to raise again the ancient and foolish
quarrel between "intuition" and "reason." Man does
not possess a kind of separate and supernatural "organ"
of intuition, a sort of super-eye which enables him to
contradict his reason. There are not two kinds of truth
standing in opposition to one another. But in the claims
of "intuition"—distorted, exaggerated, and fantastic as
they have often been—there is at least this element of
truth, that men frequently feel dimly, in the obscure
depths of their personality, a truth which, because it has
not yet risen to the surface of consciousness, is not for them
clothed in the forms of the understanding, is unexpressed
in words, and may even seem—for lack of successful ver-
balization—ineffable. In the end these ineffable insights,
these formless divinations of truth, must be capable of
receiving upon them the form and the stamp of rational

statement and expression. They must be capable of rational defence. Otherwise they would not *be* truths.

These instinctive "feelings" which men have for the truth, perhaps because they are biologically much older and more experienced than are the categories of logic and science—which were acquired by the human race only yesterday—are sometimes wiser than the latter. This is especially the case in those matters which more deeply concern human life, questions of value, moral questions, the conduct of affairs. In matters of pure physical fact, in chemistry, biology, astronomy, we may well trust the scientist. Indeed we should be foolish to trust anyone else. But in matters of human values humanity at large has sound instincts. These instincts or feelings are likely to be vague, inarticulate, and cloudy. But it is better to be vaguely right than to be precisely wrong. And the wise man will give ear to the feelings of humanity and endeavour to discover *what* is the truth which, deeply hidden within them, gives them their vitality. Or at least he will take it as a danger-sign if his theories seriously violate them. This is what is sound in the old appeals to "the facts of the moral consciousness" which a former generation of philosophers were wont to make. They knew that if an ethical theory violates and outrages the moral intuitions of mankind, this is probably a sign that something is wrong. And in this they were wiser than those who, in the interests of the latest scientific fad or fashion, are ready to deride or ignore the deepest convictions of humanity.

We have now very briefly reviewed arguments on both sides of this question. We are not yet in a position to reach any definite conclusions. But there are certain very modest and tentative results which seem to me to emerge from the discussion. And these may now be indicated.

Firstly, ethical absolutism will have to be rejected. The arguments of the ethical relativist do not conclusively demonstrate their favourite contention that there is no universal code of morals applicable to all human beings. But they do prove that morality is relative to human needs and has no meaning apart from human requirements.[1] They prove that there can be no such thing as an absolute categorical imperative. All imperatives must be hypothetical. It is only *if* human beings have need of attaining certain ends that they "ought" to do so and so. Apart from the need of attaining ends the word "ought" has no meaning. It is, therefore, impossible any longer to conceive morality as a law of the whole universe in the same way as mathematical propositions or the laws of logic are laws of the universe. There is not the slightest reason to suppose that the moral law is, like the proposition $2 + 2 = 4$, valid on Mars or that it binds all rational beings everywhere. The beings on Mars, or even the future supermen of our earth, may have a morality quite different from ours, since they may have different natures and different needs. Our (human) morality is relative to our (human) nature.

Secondly, the position as regards ethical relativity is still unclear. We may accept from it the view that morality is relative to human nature in general. But its characteristic concept is that morality is relative to the special natures of different social groups, and that there is, consequently, no morality which is applicable to all human

[1] What I am here stating is a summary of the conclusions reached on pages 25–27 to which the reader may turn back if what I am now saying is not clear to him.

beings. This, in fact, is what is commonly understood by the term ethical relativity. Now none of the arguments adduced so far by the anti-relativist demonstrate conclusively that this is false. For what they all amount to is that conclusions can be drawn from the view of the ethical relativist which contradict our subjective moral feelings. It has not been shown that they contradict any empirically verifiable objective *facts*. And this is what would be necessary if we were to have a conclusive demonstration that ethical relativity is false. The feelings which relativism outrages *may* be mere subjective and irrational emotions which have no bearing upon any objective truth and no scientific or philosophical cogency. If therefore the anti-relativist proposes to urge belief in any kind of universal morality, he will have to find for it some more solid and definitely factual basis than is afforded by "moral feelings." This is a challenge which believers in a universal morality must certainly accept.

The most that can at present be urged in favour of the contentions of the anti-relativist is that it is unwise wholly to ignore and over-ride natural human feelings. "Feeling" is a slippery word, and is used to cover many different things. Some "feelings" may be irrational. But others may not. What are vaguely called feelings may sometimes be instinctive and doubtless confused perceptions of truth. The radical empiricist is too apt to lump together such different experiences as anger and jealousy (which are genuine emotions) on the one hand, and men's vague intuitions of truth on the other; and to dismiss them both contemptuously as "mere emotions." The deep repugnance which moral minds feel to the conclusions of the ethical relativist may be based on a dim perception of genuine truth. That ethical relativity stands in flat con-

tradiction to moral feeling ought to be taken at least as a
danger signal.

I shall conclude this chapter by pointing to the general
direction in which I myself intend to move in this controversy. I shall reject ethical absolutism. But I shall also
reject ethical relativity. Morality, I shall try to show, is
relative in the sense that it is relative to the universal
needs of human nature. But it is not relative to the particular needs of particular nations, ages, or social groups.
Consequently it does not vary from place to place or from
time to time. Morality is universal, but it is not absolute.
So far I have used the two phrases "absolute morality"
and "universal morality" as practically synonymous.
But the time has come to make a distinction. By an absolute morality I shall mean in future one which is valid
independently of all conditions whatsoever, which resembles in this respect the laws of logic and mathematics,
which would be true (in some sense) even if the human
race were wiped out, which has application to all rational
beings. Such a morality, with all its transcendental and
non-empirical implications, I entirely reject. By a universal morality I mean one which applies, not merely to
this race or that during this age or that, but to all humanity in all ages. And I shall try to show that there is such a
morality. I shall try also to show that this does not involve the undesirable conclusions which ethical relativity
necessitates and does not do violence to men's moral
feelings, but satisfies them.

I shall accept the challenge of the empiricist to find for
this conception a factual and empirical basis. This means
that I shall have to discover evidence of its existence and
validity other than the feelings to which the anti-relativist
has so far made his appeal. Radical empiricism is sup-

posed, by some of its supporters, to imply ethical relativity.[1] My purpose, as a radical empiricist, is to show that this is not true, and that it is possible to be a good empiricist without destroying men's moral convictions.

The course of our enquiry will lead us to attempt an answer to the three following questions:

> What *is* the universal moral law? What is its actual content? What, in short, are its commands?
>
> In what *sense* is this law universal, and how can its universality be shown to be consistent with the actual plurality of moral codes in the world?
>
> What is the *basis and foundation* of this morality, and of the *obligation* which it imposes? and how can it be shown that the universal "ought" which it implies is empirically meaningful?

I shall take up these three questions in the order just given. The first is the most complicated, and will occupy us for many chapters. The reader should therefore suspend his judgment if he is inclined to exclaim "Yes, but this morality which you are expounding, and which may perhaps be *our* morality, is certainly not accepted by all men." He must expect to see both the problem of the universality of morals and the problem of the basis of moral obligation recede into the background for the present. We shall come to them in good time.

---

[1] See, for example, Professor J. A. Irving's contribution to the volume *American Philosophy Today and Tomorrow.*

CHAPTER 3

MORALS IN EXTENSION

IT will be relevant to our enterprise to enquire whether the sphere of morality is to be thought of as wide or narrow, whether in extension it covers the whole of life or only some limited portion of it. It has been common enough to distinguish the theoretical from the practical, and to think of morality as concerned either wholly, or at least primarily, with practical activities. But even if this distinction be taken as valid, is it enough? Should all practical activities, or only some, be regarded as the subjects of moral predicates?

In one sense, of course, the opinion that morality covers the whole of life is pretty obviously true. Practically every human action has, or may have, a moral aspect. Because the effects of what we do ramify indefinitely into the future, because of the vast network of causal relations between things and events, almost anything a man does may have consequences which bring it within the purview of moral judgment. To flicker the eyelid is not in itself, I should say, either moral or immoral. But it may be used as a signal to a confederate to commit a murder. To hammer nails in crookedly is not in itself a breach of the moral law. But it may be the sign of a slovenly and careless character, and so come rightfully under condemnation. And if a carpenter supplies a carelessly made box where a workmanlike article has been promised and is to be paid for, his conduct will be thought dishonest. The engineer who builds a bridge so badly that it collapses beneath the weight of traffic and kills innocent persons cannot escape an adverse moral judgment, as well as a censure on his technical skill.

No one will deny that, in this obvious sense, morality covers the whole of life. But there is another quite different and much less plausible doctrine which is likely to be confused with this. "Morals" writes Professor Dewey "has to do with all activity into which alternative possibilities enter. For wherever they enter a difference between better and worse arises. . . . Potentially therefore every and any act is within the scope of morals, being a candidate for possible judgment with respect to its better-or-worse quality." [1] This passage suggests that morality covers all the activities of life in the sense that every kind of "better" is, as such, a moral better, and every kind of "worse" a moral worse. It suggests that what we mean by morality is simply the carrying out of any and every human activity in the best way in which that particular activity can be carried out. Or, to put it in another way, that morality means in general doing things (things of any kind) well, while immorality means doing things badly.

I do not know, and I am not going to discuss, whether this is actually the meaning which Professor Dewey intends to express. He does often seem to me to write as if that were what he meant. But very likely it may not be. It is, in any case, a possible opinion, whether Professor Dewey or anyone else actually holds it or not. And I propose to discuss it as such.

We are accustomed to distinguish between different kinds of valuation, for example, between what is esthetically, and what is morally, good or bad. But on the view

[1] John Dewey, *Human Nature and Conduct*, Part 4, Section 1.

just suggested all such distinctions are implicitly denied. To be better in *any* way is to be morally better. And *any* choice is a moral choice. If I hammer a nail into a piece of wood I shall either do it in a moral or in an immoral way. For it is certainly "better" to hammer it in straight than to hammer it crooked. And if *every* kind of better and worse is a moral better or worse, then this is too. On this view again the skilful physician acts morally, the unskilful physician less morally.

This is an example of a concept of morals which is *too wide*. It ignores or obliterates vital distinctions such as exist between moral value, esthetic value, and economic value. Of course these different kinds of value are in actual life almost invariably intertwined with one another. A work of art has as a rule both esthetic and moral qualities. And one is therefore entitled to judge it both by esthetic and by moral standards. But the very fact that we use the word "both" indicates that the two are not the same. The beautiful is not thought to be the same as the morally good. It is a commonplace that a work of art may be morally indifferent or even objectionable and yet esthetically fine; and likewise that it may be morally impeccable or even edifying and yet artistically worthless. Economic standards, again, are not identical with either ethical or esthetic standards. A business deal may be carried out in the best possible way from a business point of view, and yet it may be neither moral nor beautiful. The moral quality of an activity cannot therefore be simply defined as its "better-or-worse" quality. There are different kinds of better and worse, and we have to discover what is the specific nature of the kind called moral.

The philosopher who identifies the moral quality of actions simply with their better or worse quality is inevitably led by his too wide concept to an exaggerated view of the variability of morals. He begins with a loose, vague concept of morality. He does not think it necessary, before he pronounces upon the question whether moral standards are variable or uniform or to what degree they are variable, that he should specify precisely what he is going to mean by the adjective "moral," what he will include under that heading and what he will exclude. He does not distinguish between the different kinds of approval and disapproval which men bestow upon things. Whatever is approved or liked in any place he will assume to be approved because it is in accordance with the moral standard of that place. Whatever is disapproved or disliked he will assume to be morally disapproved. Every custom becomes in his eyes a "moral custom." If any line of conduct is generally thought good in any community it becomes a custom. But it may be thought good on the basis of standards which have nothing to do with morality. And in that case it is not a moral custom at all. But if all customs are indiscriminately lumped together as "moral," one has only to point to the enormous variability of human customs to conclude that the moral ideas of humanity are an indescribable chaos of mutually contradictory conceptions in which can be found neither principle nor rationality nor order.

To proceed in this loose way is disastrous, for it heavily and quite unfairly weights the case in favour of ethical relativity. As a matter of fact men approve and disapprove, like and dislike, the activities of their fellows upon all sorts of different grounds. Some of these grounds are not moral at all. They may be perfectly good grounds, although not specifically moral. Or they may be mere irrational prejudices, taboos, superstitions, or even personal caprices. In that case they will, of course, be variable. And the customs founded upon these variable elements in the human make-up will, of course, be variable too. If then the philosopher adopts an unduly wide, general, and vague conception of morality, if he fails carefully to discriminate between different kinds of approval and disapproval, the theory of ethical relativity is likely to follow as a matter of course.

Regarding many, if not most, of the activities of our lives, the "best" way of carrying them out is largely a matter of personal taste, of fashion, of local custom, of individual caprice. Most people would think that hammering nails in straight is "better" than hammering them crooked. But there may be people who prefer their nails to be crooked. And if so, who is to say they are wrong? So long as the box, the table, the coffin, holds together, what matter though the nails are all askew? And if anyone thinks that crooked nails look better than straight ones, he has certainly the right to indulge his preference. Suppose then that there existed a tribe of people constituted in just that way. If we simply identify moral quality with any kind of "better-or-worse," as Professor Dewey appears to do, we shall have to describe the carpentering habits of these people as a "moral custom." And will it be any wonder, then, if we conclude to the relativity of morals? One tribe thinks straight nails "right." Another tribe thinks straight nails "wrong." What is right is therefore no more than a matter of local custom. And if no distinction is made between the kind of "better-or-worse" which exists in carpentry and the kind which exists in matters genuinely moral, we shall naturally conclude that *all* morality is, like people's preferences regarding straight or crooked nails, entirely relative.

The example here chosen is no doubt far-fetched and absurd. But it illustrates the principle none the less. It cannot be denied that in regard to all save a very few human activities there may be numerous equally "good" ways of doing the same thing, and that the way which is chosen is often a mere matter of local or individual preference. And if all the different ways of doing the same thing are to be regarded as implying different moral standards, we shall naturally fall into ethical relativity.

The nature of the fallacy involved should now be plain. On the specious pretext that morality should "cover the whole of life," it is first conceived in such wise that it includes the manner in which people get married, the customs they adopt at burials, their habits in regard to social gatherings, eating, drinking, and making love, and even perhaps the way in which they dress their hair. Since in most of these matters there are no definite rules of right and wrong, save such as are determined by tradition, custom, or personal preference, morality so defined is seen to be purely relative. From this wide and loose sense of the word "morals" we then slip over, unconsciously perhaps, to real morality—that is, to morality in a narrower, stricter, sense. We then find ourselves landed in the conclusions that human sacrifice is only evil in those countries where people happen to condemn it, that head hunting is morally good in Borneo, that the burning alive of widows was ethically admirable in the India of two centuries ago, that cannibalism is most praiseworthy in Africa, etc.

The mistake of confusing moral commands with commands based upon grounds which have nothing to do with morality is not confined to philosophers. It is common to most of humanity. It is indeed because philosophers have in this matter uncritically adopted the vague ideas of plain unthinking men that they have been misled. I will explain this by means of an example. Musulmans and Hebrews are forbidden by their respective religions to eat pork. Now this is commonly supposed to be a *moral* prohibition. According to my view it is not a moral rule at all, but simply a sanitary rule. The grounds upon which the disapproval of eating pork were based were simple considerations of health, not moral considerations. Pigs in the east are dirty feeders. To eat them was likely to spread disease. Hence the custom of forbidding their use for food. The rule has no more to do with morality than has the rule that one should dress warmly in the winter if one wishes to avoid colds. This view, of course, may be questioned, but I am not yet in a position adequately to defend it. For it is impossible to distinguish between moral and sanitary grounds of objection until we have before us a clear concept of the meaning of "moral"—in addition, no doubt, to a clear concept of the meaning of "sanitary." But the meaning of the concept "moral" is precisely what we are in search of and do not yet possess. I shall therefore ask the reader to allow me to assume without proof, for the present, that there *is* a distinction between moral rules and rules of conduct based upon sanitary or other grounds —though we do not yet know *what* the distinction is—and that the maxim "Do not eat pork" belongs to the latter of these two classes.

But now mark what happens. A primitive people are forbidden by their law-givers to eat pork. They are also forbidden to commit murders. The former prohibition is based upon sanitary, the latter upon moral, grounds. But the people themselves, being ignorant and unthinking, do not distinguish between the different kinds of reasons which lie behind different kinds of prohibition. All they know is that murder is something forbidden and that eating pork is also something forbidden. The two prohibitions are thus indiscriminately lumped together in the popular consciousness. Both come to be labelled "moral rules."

This confusion passes down the ages and clouds our minds today. It is taken for granted, not only by the masses, but by professional philosophers. These latter— or some of them—take over from the popular consciousness the vague confused ideas they find there and weave them into their systems without criticism and without sifting. It is assumed without question that the eating of pig-flesh is morally wrong among Musulmans and Hebrews but morally innocent among Christians. Therefore what is right in one country is wrong in another. Therefore we must believe in ethical relativity.

But the conclusion does not follow. What follows is simply that sanitary rules which are necessary in a tropical climate and in a country and age in which enlightened methods of pig farming have not been developed are quite unnecessary in other conditions. But this has nothing to do with any question of morality.

Numerous other examples could be given. Many of the rules of conduct connected with sex have, I believe, nothing to do with morality. Some are quite reasonable— though not based upon moral grounds. Others are based upon totally irrational prejudices and taboos. Yet in the popular consciousness every rule of sex is a moral rule. The result is that the different sexual customs of different peoples—all classed as "moral customs"—come to be widely quoted as evidences of ethical relativity. But before we could legitimately derive from them any such conclusion we ought to have carefully analysed the grounds upon which the different rules rest and distinguished those which are moral from those which are not.

Not only sanitary and sex rules, but all sorts of customs and habits based upon tradition, mere prejudice, local idiosyncrasy, irrational taboos, are in the same way commonly mixed up with morality. Those philosophers who insist that customs are the only moral standards are in this matter the chief sinners. They make as a rule no attempt to discriminate between customs which have a genuine ethical basis and customs which are without any specific moral character. Mere superstitions thus become classed as moral ideas. And since superstitions are irrational, unaccountable, variable, morality comes to be tarred with the same brush. No wonder that, in such circumstances, it is concluded that there is no common standard by which moral codes can be judged; that there is in morality no rhyme or reason, no order, no uniformity.

Had we not better attempt to discriminate? If we could come to some agreement as to what should be included under the heading "moral" and what should be excluded, perhaps morality might be seen to be less variable than is commonly supposed.

But to do this is a matter of extreme difficulty. We cannot appeal to popular usage. For this is precisely what has misled us in the past. We cannot even appeal to the way in which scholars and men of letters use the word "morality." For they are—as we have seen—infected with all the vagueness and confusion of popular thought. It would certainly be of no use to go to the inhabitants of New Guinea and say "What do *you* mean by the word moral?" (if there is such a word in their language) and to ask the same question of Frenchmen, Chinamen, Americans, and others, in the hope of arriving at some common concept. For in all countries people usually describe as immoral whatever they happen to regard with especially strong feelings of aversion. Whatever men feel very strongly about they think to be the centre of gravity of morality. The Moslem will insist that it is positively sinful, and not merely insanitary, to eat pork. And it is because sex arouses in men the most violent feelings that the words morality and immorality have come in many minds to be especially connected with it. If for some local or accidental reason violent feelings should happen to be aroused in any community against the use of parachutes or the wearing of silk hats, these matters would probably come to be regarded in that community as the especial concern of morality. People in general fail to distinguish between what they condemn on genuinely moral grounds and what they happen strongly to dislike for other reasons. That is to say, they make the strength of their feelings the test for distinguishing between what is morally objectionable and what is objectionable on other (non-moral) grounds. But this is a mistake. It is not the *strength* of our feelings, but their *kind* or quality, which puts the difference. Thus the difference between moral and esthetic feelings is not a difference of strength but of kind or quality. And my objection to an evil smell—which is simply a physical disgust—does not become moral simply because the disgust is so strong that I vomit.

For all these reasons, then, we cannot expect to discover the true concept of morality by appealing to the way in which any body of people, whether in one country or another, whether learned or unlearned, use the word. And if, on the other hand, we attempt to introduce some concept of our own—to say that such and such kinds of customs or maxims of conduct will be regarded by us as moral, while all other kinds of customs and maxims of conduct will be regarded as extra-moral—if we do this, we shall be liable to be accused of being simply arbitrary.

In these difficult circumstances I make the following suggestion. In the perplexed tangle of human relations, amid all the shifting customs, changing habits, variable rules, which now and in past time, here and elsewhere, govern and have governed human conduct, can we find anywhere any abiding element? Admitting that most rules of conduct are local and variable, can one find any which, without claiming to be "eternal" in any supernatural or transcendental sense, are yet sufficiently permanent and universal to be regarded as standards which could be used to measure and judge the more variable elements of human nature? If we could find such rules, could we not agree to call them moral and to exclude the rest from this title? If so we might reject ethical relativity and discover a universal—as distinguished from an absolute—morality.

As against any such suggestion there are two objections which will at once be made. In the first place the hope of finding any such abiding element in human rules of conduct will be thought chimerical. No such universal rules, it will be said, are discoverable. Not merely some, but all, rules of conduct ever proposed are relative to time, place, circumstance, and to the differing natures of different men. In this way our enterprise will be foredoomed to failure from the first. In the second place, even if there do exist any rules of conduct which happen to be, for some reason or other, relatively permanent and universal, in some sense or other, the proposal to limit the application of the word morality to just these particular rules and to exclude all others will be utterly arbitrary.

The first of these objections is one which I cannot hope to refute except by the sum-total of the investigations contained in the rest of this book. I cannot dispel the reader's antecedent scepticism, his disposition to disbelieve from the first in the possibility of discovering a universal element in the rules of human conduct, save by long and patient enquiry. But I shall endeavour at this stage to predispose the reader more favourably towards my enterprise by reminding him of certain facts of human nature. For it is on these facts that my own hope is founded.

Let us phrase a little more clearly the grounds upon which the reader's scepticism is likely to be founded. Morality (in any sense), he will perhaps say, arises through the interaction of human beings with their environment. It does not descend ready-made out of the sky. It is the outgrowth of human nature when faced with its surrounding world. Now human beings differ from one another, and they undergo change. Race differs from race, and one individual from another. The environment too is variable and undergoes constant change. Therefore morality, which is the product of these two variable factors, must itself be variable. Hence the hope of finding in it an unchanging element is foredoomed to failure.

Now as to the account here given of the nature and origin of morality I have no criticism to make. I am in entire agreement. Morals for an empiricist cannot be thought of as superhuman or as depending upon any transcendental mystery. They must have developed naturally out of human nature and its reactions to its environment. They are human or they are nothing. But I must point out that in all the variations of what is vaguely called human nature it is possible that there may be a relatively unchanging core. There may be a ground plan upon the basis of which men are built. Men of utterly different characters, men living in widely separated places and times, may all be variants upon a single theme—the human theme—just as the different varieties and individuals of an animal species are all variants of the theme common to the species. There may be common elements in the human psychological make-up as well as individual or racial differences, just as there are common elements in human anatomical structure. Upon these common psychological elements a uniform morality may well be founded.

Probably because we are ourselves human beings involved in the human imbroglio we tend very greatly to exaggerate the differences which exist among us. As one looks at an assemblage of ants in an ant-hill they seem to be, and indeed they are, as like one another as so many pins. The microscopical differences between them are trifling as compared with their fundamental similarity. Yet it may be that to them these differences seem enormous. Perhaps they distinguish, here and there among the crowd, a "great ant" as we distinguish a "great man." There may be famous ants, ants of immense reputation. There may be ants of genius and stupid ants. There may be saint y ants and wicked ants. There may even be different views as to what is the best way to lay eggs, to bring up one's young, and to go about the business of ant life generally. And I think that the actual differences between our great men and little men, and between the ways in which we think it best to conduct our lives (morality) may be as unimportant and trivial, in comparison with our fundamental human similarities, as are such differences among the ants. They would be microscopic, hardly to be at all detected, to a larger outside view. There is not a little truth in the suggestion that the greatest differences of human opinion, on what seem to us to be vastly important matters, are in truth but as the differences of those who quarrel as to whether a boiled egg should be opened at the big or the little end. A god, looking down upon the ant-hill of this planet, might well be unable to detect any differences whatever between human beings.

We exaggerate the differences because we are ourselves interested in them. They are important to us. And what is important to us seems large. How trifling and petty appear to us the matters at issue in a quarrel between our acquaintances in which we are not ourselves concerned. We cannot understand how sensible people can fight thus over nothing. Let but the same quarrel touch our own interests, and we take up arms immediately supposing that vast issues are at stake, and that profound moral principles are involved. Or to take a very different kind of example. Aristotle could see little except the differences between his own philosophy and that of Plato. We, looking at the controversy between the two men from a distance, perceive that the resemblance between them was in fact far greater than the difference. Ethical relativists, and indeed all of us, are perhaps involved in a similar illusion—the illusion which comes of seeing things too close to the eye. We exaggerate the differences which exist between men, between races, between the customs, habits, civilizations, of different countries and ages. To a large and impartial view the single theme upon which all men are variants, the ground plan and pattern of humanity, would stand out as vastly more real and more important.

It is not my purpose to argue that human nature never

changes. One has indeed listened *ad nauseam* to the idle dispute whether men are really much different now from what they were two, three, or five thousand years ago. As to this the reader may think what he likes. But whatever one thinks about the differences between ancient Babylonians and modern Americans, it cannot be denied that they are creatures of the same flesh and blood, of fundamentally the same passions, desires, needs, reasoning powers—that underneath all superficial differences there is visible the same fundamental human pattern. Then as now men faced the ancient problems of life and death. They faced, as we face, the battle against hunger, cold, famine, disease, loneliness, misery, death. Then as now men fought, strove, conquered, played, ate, drank, loved, hated, envied, were jealous, made friends and enemies, needed each other's help, pondered on the mystery of life. Fathers then felt for their sons much as we feel for ours. Their sorrows were like our sorrows, their joys like our joys. The scene has changed a little, the clothes of the actors, the weapons with which they fight. But the human drama is always really the same. This is why we can enter with sympathetic rapport into the art and the literature of peoples remote from us in time and space. This would be impossible if they were not, as we are, human, and made of the same humanity as ourselves. All this is evidence of the common elements in human nature, the ground plan which does not change from country to country or from age to age.

Admitting then that human conduct is governed by rules which grow out of human nature, and which have not been let down out of the sky, will it not be likely that the more fundamental of these rules will be everywhere and in all ages the same? Will there not tend to be some rules of life which correspond to, and arise out of, the common elements of human nature, and others which correspond to, and arise out of, special differences? And will not the former be permanent and universal and applicable to all men, the latter variable and relative?

After all there is nothing so very unlikely in this suggestion. Even in purely physical matters, in matters of diet for instance, there are universal rules. "Do not eat cyanide of potassium" is one of them. "You must eat some kind of organic matter" is another. These rules are universal because they are based upon common elements in the human physical make-up, upon universal structural similarities in the human anatomy. There are other rules which are not universal. "Do not eat any sugar" is a rule applicable only to diabetics. This is because it is based upon conditions of the body which are not common to all men but peculiar to diabetics. In our country it is customary to eat with knife and fork, in China with chopsticks. Neither custom is universal because neither is based on anything—either physical or mental—which is common to all men.

Now just as there are differences between human bodies, but underneath these differences a common structure, so it is, I suggest, with the human mind or spirit. Certainly different men have different likes and dislikes, different desires, different ideas. But underneath all this there may be a common psychological structure. And just as the common physical elements give rise to universal rules of health, so the common mental or spiritual characters of man will give rise to universal rules of conduct of the kind which I propose to call moral. Not only is there nothing surprising in this. It would be very surprising if it were otherwise.

But, it will be said, we have forgotten that morality is the product of *two* variable factors, human nature and its environment. And even if there is a permanent universal element in the first of these factors, yet if the second be variable the product will possess no uniformity. But man's environment is both physical and social. His physical environment is the seas, hills, and rivers amid which he lives. His social environment consists of the other men with whom he comes into contact. And I think it is Dewey who has pointed out somewhere that it is social environment which is the essentially determining factor in morality. It is the necessity of living with other human beings, it is the impact of their needs and their personalities upon us, which forces us to develop moral codes. Such a code is simply the set of rules which govern our relations with our fellow men. Hence the environment of human nature—so far as any question of ethics is concerned—is simply human nature itself, i.e., the natures of the other men with whom we associate. And this possesses, as we have seen, a relatively permanent and unchanging core. The social environment is permanent in precisely the same degree as is human nature itself.

And even man's physical environment—in so far as this has relevance—changes but little in its fundamentals. The stony face of the earth, the heat of the sun, the cold of the winter, the hills, the mountains, the rivers, are for us what they were for our remotest ancestors. True, man's mastery over these things and forces has been enormously increased. But the discoveries of science have not radically changed the central themes and purposes of his life on the earth. He lives at a higher pitch—but still with the same ends in view. He travels faster—but still in search of the same kinds of satisfaction. He makes his voice heard across oceans instead of, as formerly, across a few yards of space. But still what he says concerns the same perennial problems of life. For his fundamental needs, physical, mental, and moral, are the same—the needs of food, clothing, and shelter, the needs of friendship, of the love of women and children, the needs of occupation and amusement, the need of social intercourse. His life is a battle to obtain these things. It was always thus; and it is so now.

But it is time to turn to the consideration of the second objection which was raised to our proposal. Even if we could discover universally applicable rules of human conduct, it was said, the suggestion that these alone should be labelled "morality," and that all others should be excluded from that title, would be entirely arbitrary.

It will be admitted, of course, that a philosopher—or indeed anyone else—is entitled to define his terms as he pleases, provided he explains what he is doing, and provided he sticks as consistently as is humanly possible to the same use of his terms throughout his discourse. Nevertheless definitions are objectionable if they purport to define real objects and yet are based upon boundaries and distinctions which do not exist in the real world. They may also be thought objectionable if they involve anything which could reasonably be called a misuse of language. You can define man as a four-legged animal with horns if you want to. But this is an abuse of language. And if you write a book about "man" in that sense, you will simply not be discussing what most people understand by that term. You will certainly not be contributing to the science of anthropology. So too, if I were to define the rules of morality in such a way that they turn out to be, on my definition, identical with the rules of football, I might be logically within my rights, but I should be perverting language. And I certainly should not be contributing to the subject of ethics.

It cannot be said, however, that the proposal to limit the term morality to those rules of conduct which are of universal application is arbitrary in the sense that it is not based upon any real distinction. For if it be the case that there *are* some rules which are universal in their application and others which are not universal, then this distinction is a real one. The boundaries and distinctions upon which the definition relies will in that case be boundaries and distinctions which exist in the real world.

Nor is our proposal arbitrary in the sense that it will result in a conception of morality so far removed from what most people understand by that word as to constitute an abuse of language. Of this, of course, I can hope to convince the reader only when he has before him our fully developed concept of morals. He will then see, I hope, that it maintains intact the essentials of morality as commonly understood by enlightened persons.

Certainly there are bound to be discrepancies between the philosophical concept of morals, when clearly defined, and the numerous vague, incoherent, and mutually inconsistent ideas which may from time to time be taken by different sets of people to represent the meaning of the word. There will be cases in which what some people would include under the head of morality will be excluded by us. There may perhaps be cases in which we shall include what others would exclude. Indeed examples of discrepancies of this kind have already made their appearance. For we do not think that the rule against the use of pig-flesh as food is a moral rule, while many people would assert that it is.

But what would you have? There *is* no universally admitted, clearly defined, meaning of the word morality. Popular notions, and even the notions of philosophers, are utterly confused. Some give to morals a wider extension, some a narrower. And some conceptions are inconsistent with others. Therefore any attempt to clarify the subject, to settle upon a concept with determinate boundaries, is bound to leave out what some men would include, and to include what others would leave out. This, I say, would be true, not merely of our theory of morality, but of any clear philosophical theory of it whatever. Therefore it cannot be made a ground of complaint against our theory. We have in fact the choice between two alternatives. Either we must swallow wholesale and undigested the entire confused, half inarticulate, inconsistent, chaotic jumble of ideas which is found in the popular consciousness. Or we must be prepared to differ in our view from many widely accepted notions of morality. And if we are to attain to any clear ideas at all, we have to accept the latter alternative.

The question is really one of degree and of emphasis. How *far* shall we differ from commonly held opinions? If the divergence is too great—if, to quote our previous example, morality in our theory should turn out to be what most people call football—we should certainly stand condemned. Again, will that which we select out of the whole confused mass be that which humanity at large—or at least the most advanced sections of it—would admit to be the most vital part of morality? Or will it turn out that we are emphasizing some trivial and unimportant rules of conduct merely because they happen to have universal application? In the latter event too we should stand condemned. Now these questions cannot be answered before the actual outcome of our enquiries is visible. When our concept of morals has been developed in its fulness, let the reader judge for himself whether, in either of these directions, we have erred. Until then let him not raise the objection that our views are arbitrary.

One word more regarding the question how the word morality should be used. The matter is to some extent a purely verbal one. Suppose we should find it to be the case that there actually is an inner core of universal rules of conduct and an outer fringe of variable rules. So far this is not a matter of words but a question of fact. But my suggestion is that the inner core be called morality, and that the outer fringe be regarded as extra-moral. For the reasons given I do not believe that this procedure can be accused of being arbitrary in any objectionable sense. But suppose that the judgment should go against me on this point. Suppose it should be decided that it would be better—for some reason of convenience or linguistics—to call the whole sphere, the outer fringe as well as the inner core, by the name "morality." Would my position be in any vital way affected? I think not. I should say "Use the word morality as you please. Call by that name all the rules of conduct ever devised including all those that are the most utterly variable. I am not in the last analysis concerned with the use of words, but only with facts and realities. It has been shown to be a fact that some rules of conduct have a permanent and universal application. This alone is sufficient to overthrow the ethical relativist. For his position is that *all* rules of conduct are variable and relative. And in this he is wrong. If you use the word morality in your wide, loose, way to stand for all rules of conduct whatsoever, you will still have to admit that not all morality is relative. You will still have to say that part of morality is permanent and universal, though part is relative and variable. And I believe that in the end you will have to admit that the permanent and universal part is the only really important and vital part, that it forms the inner essence of what most people have all along thought to be morality. And with this result I shall be perfectly satisfied."

If our suggestion is carried out, it will consist in a *narrowing* of the circle of morality so that it covers, not all rules of conduct, as Professor Dewey would apparently have it, but only those rules which, because they are based upon common and permanent elements of human nature, are permanent and universal in their application. But even the formula "all rules which are universally applicable" will prove to be too wide. The circle will have to be still further narrowed. For there are rules—such as that men must eat at least some organic matter—which are universal but yet not moral. This particular rule, as we saw, belongs to the sphere of dietetics. It will be found in the end, I believe, that only those rules are moral which govern the mutual relations of human beings. Morality, as has often been said, is essentially social. So that our formula will assert that *morality includes only those universally applicable rules of conduct which seek to control the relations of men with one another.* It does not include other rules of conduct, such as those of diet, even though they may be universal in their application.

Finally let me re-emphasize that it is not my purpose to argue that there exists an absolute standard of morality which will *never* change. The race of men may some day be superseded by a race of supermen. It is not suggested that any human standard of morality must apply to such beings. I do not profess to know what morality, if any, would apply to the men on Mars or to the future supermen of this earth. Martian morality will presumably grow out of the nature of the beings on Mars, which may be quite different from the nature of man. I speak only of man as we know him. An "eternal" morality is not to be found. Surely it will be enough if we can discover a morality permanent in the sense that it has lasted many thousands of years, and that it will probably last as many more, universal in the sense that it is capable of being made a measure for all men of our species in any age or country with which we are ever likely to be concerned.

CHAPTER 4

THE UNITY OF MORALS

IN the last chapter we saw that one of the main obstacles to the recognition of the existence of a universal morality is the indiscriminate inclusion within the sphere of morality of every possible precept or rule of human conduct. From the chaotic mass of human customs and habits we have to isolate out what is genuinely moral. Only then can we hope to discover a universal morality—if such a morality exists. Gold is of identical mineralogical nature whether it is found in the Urals, in Alaska, in Africa, or anywhere else on the earth. But gold, as it is found in its natural state, is mixed with baser materials of many various kinds. If one is to discover the uniform nature of gold, one has to separate it out from these other materials. If one included under the heading "gold" the various unsifted mixtures of gold as found in their natural state in various parts of the world, one would inevitably be led to the conclusion that the nature of gold is variable. One would be led to a doctrine of the "relativity" of gold. It is the same with morals. Amid all the confused and contorted habits of mankind in different countries and ages it is possible that some of the pure gold of morality is everywhere discoverable. But one cannot expect to discover its uniform character so long as one declines to distinguish it from that with which it is mixed. Our next problem, therefore, is to isolate from adventitious accretions the pure concept of morality.

But before we attempt to do this we must briefly take

note of another source of confusion which has powerfully helped the cause of the ethical relativist. Traditionally morality has always been supposed to consist in a *plurality* of particular prohibitions and commands. It will be my contention, on the contrary, that morality is a *unity*, or in other words that there are not a number of different and independent duties but only one duty, or at least only one general principle of duty from which all particular prohibitions and commands can be deduced. We shall have ultimately to give a positive account of this single principle of morals. But to do this is not the purpose of the present chapter. My immediate purpose is to show that the inadequate conception of morality as consisting essentially in nothing but a multiplicity of independent particular maxims of conduct has been in the past, and still is, widely influential; that it colours all popular thinking on moral subjects; that it has deeply infected philosophy. Further I wish to show that its inevitable result is ethical relativity; and that the only way of avoiding this result is to seek for the source of morality in a single principle.

That this conception of morals colours all popular thinking on the subject needs, I think, very little proof. Consider any well known code of ethics, the code of the ancient Hebrews, that of Christ, that of the Buddha, that of Confucius, that of the Stoics, or that of any savage tribe. As set forth by its founders and followers any such code will always be found to consist of immense numbers of particular precepts relating to the common affairs of daily life. The morality of Moses was summed up in *ten* commandments, that of Jesus Christ in the far more numerous maxims of the sermon on the mount. Popular morality everywhere expresses itself in a multiplicity of rules directed against lying, thieving, murder, and so

forth. We are to do this and this and this, and to refrain
from doing that and that and that. The details of these
various moral maxims do not concern us. It is to the almost universal habit of regarding morality as split up into
an infinity of special rules that I am now directing the
reader's attention.

The opposite suggestion, that morality may be reducible
to a single universal moral principle, has of course been
common among philosophers. According to Kant the
sole law of morals is the categorical imperative. Special
rules against lying or thieving, special obligations to help
the needy and the poor, are in Kant's opinion deductions
from the categorical imperative. They are applications
of it to particular cases. The utilitarians likewise thought
that all morality could be reduced to a single principle,—
the duty to act in such a way as to achieve, as far as
possible, the "greatest happiness of the greatest number."
But the philosophical conception of morality as consisting
essentially in some one general principle has never penetrated the popular consciousness. It has never found
expression in the ethical codes by which human beings
have in practice regulated their lives. The popular mind
has always conceived morality as being nothing but an
indefinitely large variety of particular rules.

For this there have of course been excellent reasons. In
the first place the masses of men cannot rise to ideas of a
very general character. They understand in the concrete
but not in the abstract. They demand to be told by their
moral or religious leaders what to do in each specific set of
circumstances. The more precise the instructions the
better—from their point of view. Hence the plurality of
maxims which make up all the ethical codes of the world.
Even these particular maxims are in fact generalizations.

The rule "thou shalt not lie" does not tell anyone precisely what he ought to say on any particular occasion. It is, of course, impossible for any moral code to descend to the concreteness of the individual case. But the tendency of leaders is to go as far as possible in that direction in order that the masses of men, for whom their codes are intended, may comprehend.

In the second place, even if a man is capable of intellectually grasping an abstract generalization, it is likely to be in practice very difficult to apply it successfully unless he has at his command a variety of more or less ready-made applications. The actual problems of life often come upon us swiftly and unexpectedly. They demand immediate action. There is no time to think out in each case how some remote and abstract general principle should be applied. If a man is faced with a complicated, perplexing, and urgent situation, it is of no use to tell him to act so that the maxim of his action might without self-contradiction be made a universal law of nature; or that he ought to try to achieve the greatest happiness of the greatest number. But it may be of use to remind him that he should not solve his problem by lying, cheating, or murder. These more precise rules may in reality be nothing but deductions from some moral first principle. But whether they are or not does not matter to the practical man faced with an immediate problem. Nor will it help him at all to know that they are. Even if they are, he will still require them as rules of thumb capable of swift aplication. And this is, of course, just as true of the philosopher as it is of the unreflective man. The philosopher too, when not in his study, stands in the same need as do his neighbours of particular moral maxims to enable him to deal quickly and effectively with the practical problems of his life.

In the third place, it is in specific moral rules that the moral experience of mankind is stored and made available to posterity. Even if in reality the only moral rule is to act so as to bring about the greatest happiness of the greatest number, yet it is very useful to have discovered that lying is, as a general rule, not a good means to this end. And it is of great value to have enshrined this discovery in a maxim which can be remembered and passed on. If all special rules could be wiped out of the human consciousness, and if for them could be substituted in all men's minds the consciousness of some one universal principle of morals, the only result would be to deprive humanity of the benefit of its accumulated past experience.

Thus the conception of morality as a multiplicity of special maxims is not only natural but is a practical necessity. Nor is it, if properly understood, a false conception. There *are* these many moral rules. Even if there does exist a single universal principle of which they are specific applications, it is still true that there *are* these applications. But although the conception, thus interpreted, is not false, it is philosophically inadequate. And it becomes actually false if it is taken to mean that morality is in its essence *nothing but* this heterogeneous collection of particular rules. For it is then taken to imply that each rule is an independent, self-contained, and absolute moral truth. This, I think, is the popular view. And there is danger in it. For if the philosopher falls into the trap of taking over the popular concept uncritically, the effect upon moral theory is likely to be disastrous. For the inevitable result of taking this concept as not only practically necessary (which it is) but as also theoretically sufficient (which it is not) is ethical relativity. And a great

many of the common arguments in favour of ethical relativity depend solely upon the fact that those who use
them *have* fallen into this trap.

This can be most easily made clear by drawing a parallel
between ethics and physical science. If scientists had
argued in the same naive way as some ethical philosophers
do, we should now believe that there is no universal law
of gravitation, but that various different and mutually
inconsistent laws are in operation in different parts of the
physical universe. We should be committed to a doctrine of "gravitational relativity." For some astronomers,
observing planets, would have formulated the law that
bodies within the gravitational influence of the sun move
in ellipses. Other astronomers, observing certain comets,
would have framed the law that bodies within the gravitational influence of the sun move in parabolas. When
these two sets of astronomers met and compared notes,
they would have been forced to the conclusion that there is
one law of gravitation for planets and another for comets.

Again, men of science might have framed the law that
"heavy bodies fall to the ground." On its being pointed
out that balloons and aeroplanes ascend, although they
are heavy bodies, a separate and special law might have
been framed to cover these cases. So again we should have
had one law for apples blown from trees, chimneys blown
from houses, ballast thrown from balloons; and another
opposite law for balloons, aeroplanes, and birds.

In reality, of course, there is only one gravitational law.
And this one law, when applied to different kinds of bodies
in different sets of circumstances, gives rise to different
and apparently opposite effects. But if astronomers had
failed to look for the single underlying law, if they had
taken each separate little uniformity of nature to be an

absolute and independent law of nature, they would have been led to believe in gravitational relativity. The world of physics would have been as lawless and chaotic as is the world of morality according to the ethical relativists.

The law of gravitation is not relative, does not vary from age to age, from place to place, from one set of circumstances to another. It remains everywhere universally and always the same. But as applied to different sets of circumstances it results in varying forms of physical motion. Is it not possible that, in the same way, the many apparently different moral laws which obtain in different countries and ages—and which form the basis of the stock arguments of ethical relativists—are merely applications to different sets of circumstances of one single moral principle which itself does not change?

Let us suppose for the moment, and merely for the sake of illustration, that the single principle of morals is, as the utilitarians supposed, "the greatest happiness of the greatest number." Is it not perfectly conceivable that the general happiness might be better served in England and America by monogamy; but that in other countries, such as Arabia and India, having regard to their totally different circumstances, polygamy might be better calculated to minister to the general happiness? If so, not only would it be the case that monogamy is *thought* right in the former set of countries, polygamy in the latter. It would even be the case that monogamy *is* right in the former, polygamy in the latter. And yet the doctrine of ethical relativity would be false. What then becomes of the stock argument that since monogamy is considered moral in one country, polygamy in another, we have to believe in ethical relativity? It is seen at once that the conclusion simply does not follow from the premisses.

How is it that such arguments would be thought child-ish in physics, but are taken perfectly seriously by philoso-phers in the sphere of ethics? The answer is that in science it has long been the custom to seek for the explanation of special and local uniformities of nature in higher and more general laws; whereas morality has traditionally been regarded as nothing but a mass of little special rules of conduct, each ultimate and absolute in itself, and none of them deducible from any higher principle. If moral philosophers take their departure from the popular concep-tion of morality, instead of from the philosophical concep-tion, they inevitably become ethical relativists; just as men of science, if they had been content to take their departure from popular conceptions of nature, from popu-lar views about the habits of apples, aeroplanes, and balloons, would have been led to the belief that the laws of nature are variable and capricious.

Nothing in this chapter has any tendency to prove that there actually is a single first principle of morals from which all particular duties can be deduced; or that the application of this principle to varying circumstances is the actual explanation, or a part of the explanation, of the variability of particular maxims of conduct in differ-ent ages and countries of the world. Whether or not this actually is true is a question for our further investigation. But our argument in this chapter does show that many commonly used arguments in favour of ethical relativity are involved in a gross fallacy. I may find that in France a certain action is thought wrong, whereas in China the very same action is thought right. Facts of this kind are con-stantly relied upon by ethical relativists in attempting to prove their case. Yet they do not prove the truth of ethi-cal relativity because there is another hypothesis by which it is often possible that they may be explained. This alternative hypothesis is that a consideration of the different circumstances which exist in France and China respectively might resolve the seeming contradiction. In both cases there may be only one single moral principle involved, but, when applied to different sets of circumstances, it may result in apparently opposite duties. To argue in the way in which the ethical relativist does argue in such cases may be precisely as if the man of science were to argue that, because lead sinks in water and wood rises, therefore there are two different and mutually inconsistent physical laws at work in the world.

Indeed we do not need to go to places as far apart as France and China to see the force of this. We can see the same principle at work by looking under our noses. For all that has been said amounts in the end to no more than this, that circumstances alter cases. Without going further afield than our own homes it is surely obvious that while in most cases it is immoral to cause pain to one's fellow beings, yet in some circumstances—frequently met, for example, by the physician and the surgeon—it may be a duty to do so. Are we going to argue that this is an example of the variability and relativity of the moral law?

It is not, of course, suggested that these simple considerations are alone sufficient to explain all the contradictions which exist, or seem to exist, between the different moral codes of the world. There certainly may be in the world mutually inconsistent ideas of what is right and what is wrong which no poring over the different circumstances will ever serve to resolve. To deny this would be, I think, to shut one's eyes to facts. But it is suggested that many so-called contradictions among moral ideas can be explained in this way. And it is clear that the mere fact that a certain action is thought right here and wrong there does not prove the truth of ethical relativity—as some people naïvely seem to think it does. For it is always at least possible that a full consideration of the circumstances of each case might resolve the apparent contradiction.

The upshot of our argument, then, is twofold. Negatively, it points to a possible fallacy in the arguments sometimes used by ethical relativists, a fallacy so obvious that one feels almost ashamed to dwell upon it, yet one which is, I am afraid, often implicitly and unconsciously relied upon by ethical relativists themselves. Positively, the considerations which have been here adduced point us to the road which we ourselves ought to follow. We must not seek for a universal moral code in the particular maxims of conduct which men ordinarily apply in their daily lives. Nor must we look among so-called "moral customs," since these are all concerned with the particular details of life. If we do this, we are likely to discover nothing but a mass of mutually inconsistent maxims and customs. We have to penetrate deeper, to look below the surface. We must seek for a single general law of morals from which particular maxims can be deduced. If we do this, we shall at least be able to claim that we are more "scientific" than some of our friends with all their store of anthropological facts and their insistence on empirical method. For we shall be doing, in the moral sphere, what men of science have done in the physical sphere, and what alone has reduced that sphere to order. It is along this path that we shall attempt to proceed.

I will conclude this chapter by offering some remarks upon the method to be followed in the enquiry which is before us. We are in search of a first principle of morals which shall be applicable to all men in all countries and ages of the world. And from this principle the commonly accepted maxims of conduct which we attempt to use in our daily lives must be deducible.

It will be plain from the first that our method cannot be deductive. For we have no hope of reaching a self-evident "axiom," an *a priori* truth, upon which morality could be based. Whatever the first principle is to be, it will have to be reached by empirical and inductive methods.

But this does not mean that what we propose to do is to examine all the moral codes of humanity in the hope of finding some common or universal element. That, I suppose, is the first idea that would occur to one. Go to Guatemala, Trinidad, New Guinea, Timbuctoo, the South Sea Islands, Siberia, Japan, France, England, and America; study all the moral ideas to be found in these and other places of the globe; search in the same way the past history and pre-history of moral ideas; and see finally whether in all this you can find a core of universally accepted morality. This perhaps is what some of my empirically-minded and scientifically-minded friends would recommend to me. This, it would seem, would be the genuine empirical and scientific method. This, however, is not at all my idea of the way in which I ought to proceed. I hold that such an enquiry—even if it were carried out by someone possessed of the vast and encyclopaedic knowledge which it would require—would be utterly useless.

What do we *mean* by a universal morality? We do *not* mean a moral principle which is, as a matter of empirical fact, believed and accepted by all men. We mean a moral principle which is *applicable* to all men in the sense that, even if they do not accept it, they *ought* to do so. What we have to show is that the same moral obligation in reality falls upon all men. We do not have to show that all men know what this obligation is, or that there is among them any agreement about the matter. We have to show that what really *is* right is the same for all men. We do not have to show that what men *think* right is everywhere the same. Consequently it would not serve our purpose to prove that all the apparently contradictory ideas and opinions of men upon moral subjects have a universal element, a common core.

I shall therefore decline the kind of empirical enquiry which was suggested above. If it succeeded, it would not bring us what we want. And if it failed, its failure would in no way disprove our contention. For even if it were the case that not a single moral opinion could be found upon which all men were in agreement, it might still be true that there *is* some principle which is in reality binding upon all men in the sense that they *ought* to accept it and act upon it.

This, it will be said, does not sound at all like empirical ethics. For what can be meant by talking about a possible moral principle which all men merely "ought" to follow but which is not actually to be found in men's moral ideas? And even if this idea had any meaning, how could such a principle be discovered by any kind of empirical or inductive method? *Where* could we look for the actual evidence of its existence if not in the history of men's moral ideas? How could such an idea ever be empirically verifiable?

These are indeed weighty questions. And we shall have in due course to provide satisfactory answers for them. This cannot be done at the present stage of our enquiry.

But for the moment I will say this. I have already clearly and explicitly recognized the justice of the challenge thus posed and my obligation to meet it. I have pointed out that we shall have in the end to give a purely empirical meaning to the word "ought." We shall have to show that what it means is not in reality something which merely ought to be, but is not—but something which actually is. I hope to do this by reducing the moral law to a statement of the following form. "All men, because of their common humanity, have certain universal needs in common. There is only one way of satisfying these needs, and that way is the same for all men. It is the way of morality. Morality is therefore the same for all men." To say that all men ought to accept the same first principle of morals is, in that case, to state an alleged matter of *fact* —and of fact which is empirically verifiable. It means that *as a matter of fact* all men have certain needs in common. And it means that as *a matter of fact* those needs can only be satisfied in one way, that is, by following the moral principle. These matters of fact will be empirically verifiable by reference to actual experience.

This will explain too why in the last analysis we are not deeply concerned with what men *think* moral in this, that, or the other remote corner of the world. For if by morality we mean the road which all men must follow if they are to reach a goal which they all desire, is it anything strange that men should have different and even mutually contradictory ideas about it? All or any of these ideas may easily be wrong. Some of them, or one of them, may be right. Our problem is not to show that all men think alike about the means they ought to adopt if they are to reach a certain end. We ought not to expect this. Our problem is to show that as a matter of fact there is only one set of means by which it can be reached, and that this is true whether men happen to agree in their opinions about it or not.

As a matter of strict logic it is no concern of ours whether men agree in their moral ideas or not. Yet I believe that in the end we shall find that there is some measure of agreement. I believe it will be possible to show that even among quite undeveloped peoples there are to be found, buried doubtless under chaotic piles of moral falsehood, some rudimentary beginnings of the moral truth which is more clearly recognized in the ethical codes of advanced peoples. But I must not, in this matter, anticipate any further.

Although our view rejects absolutism, yet it will be seen that it retains the distinction, which absolutists make, between what is right and what is merely thought right. This distinction is essential. For to identify the two is precisely the root of all that is objectionable in ethical relativity. It is this which renders it impossible that any one morality should be truer than any other, since there cannot be any truth in ideas for which there is no referent in the world of fact. Hence even if it could be discovered that all men agree in thinking certain things morally right, this discovery could be of no use to us unless we could show that the moral ideas on which they agree are *true*. It would still be the case that, unless there is some set of objective facts which corresponds to their universal thinking, and which makes it true, this thinking might be mere universal delusion, or else a mere meaningless play of ideas. And it would still be the case that, if certain individuals or tribes should arise with moral ideas which differed from those up to that time universally entertained, they would have as much right to maintain that *their* ideas were true as had the holders of the previously universal ideas. Or rather, neither would have any such right at all. For the whole question of the truth or untruth of ideas, whether about morality or anything else, has no meaning unless those ideas refer to, and can be brought to the test of correspondence with, some objective state of affairs.

What was objectionable in the view of the absolutists was not the distinction between moral ideas and their objective counterpart. It was the belief that the objective counterpart was something mysterious and transcendental, something beyond the reach of experience. It was this which rendered their views incapable of any kind of verification—which rendered them in the end meaningless. The mere fact that they insisted that moral ideas, like other ideas, might be true or false, and ought to refer to something objective, could have no such effect, and is not open to any objection. Now the very purpose of our view is to make morality objective while yet bringing it down to earth and rendering it empirical. For us therefore moral ideas must have an objective reference. But the objective state of affairs to which they refer, and by reference to which they are to be judged true or false, will have to be plain facts of experience which are open to the inspection of all.

These facts will be, first, that all human beings have certain universal needs in common; and second, that these needs can only be satisfied by leading the kind of life which is called moral. For us, therefore, any set of moral ideas which mistakes the means which should be adopted to satisfy these needs, or which denies the existence of the needs themselves, is a false set of moral ideas. It is false in exactly the same sense as a fairy tale is false, in the sense, namely, that it does not correspond to the facts. And for us, accordingly, it is essential to insist upon the distinction between what people think right and what actually is right. But the distinction does not carry with it any of the non-empirical implications with which perhaps the reader has been accustomed to associate it.

As to the question where we are to look for evidence of the existence of a universal morality, if not in the moral ideas of different races, the answer to this question has already been in principle given in the foregoing paragraphs. What is it that we require evidence of? Not of anything beyond the sky, not of anything non-empirical, transcendental, outside space and time, but only of certain plain facts—or what I believe, and hope to prove, are plain facts—about human life. They are the two facts that men, because their minds exhibit a common psychological structure, have universally certain needs; and that obedience to the moral principle is the only way in which those needs can be satisfied. The evidence for the first of these facts will be, in a broad sense, psychological in character. The evidence for the second fact will not indeed be found in any recognized branch of science, but rather in the practical wisdom which men have gathered by actually living their lives. It will not be discovered in written books, but rather in the book of the world. Such evidence is none the less empirical, for it has been gathered in men's experience of living their lives. It is empirical unless to that term there is given some very narrow professional interpretation.

And it is in this sense that our method will be inductive. It will be so because our case will rest in the last resort upon the evidence of actual facts discovered in the course of human experience.

CHAPTER 5

THE ENDS OF MORAL ACTION

AFTER what was said at the close of the last chapter it will perhaps be expected that I should first of all set out in detail the facts which are relevant to our enquiry, and that I should thereafter proceed, by the ordinary methods of induction, to derive from them the single general principle of morality. The material at my disposal would, I think, admit of being treated in this manner. But I believe that it will conduce to greater clearness if I proceed in the opposite order. I shall therefore begin by framing, *as an hypothesis*, what I believe to be the first principle of morality, and I shall thereafter attempt to show that it explains and is verified by the relevant facts. The essential logic of the matter, the inductive character of the hypothesis, will not be affected by this procedure. The procedure is dictated only by considerations of convenient exposition.

I do not mean that I am about to excogitate an hypothesis *ex nihilo*, or *a priori*, and then apply it to the facts. Of course the hypothesis has been empirically derived, i.e., suggested to me personally by *some* of the relevant facts. No intelligent hypothesis on any subject comes into a man's mind simply out of the blue. The method of hypothesis consists in trying out an idea which has been suggested by *some* of the facts and seeing whether it explains all the others. Newton's gravitational hypothesis is popularly supposed to have been suggested by the falling apple, i.e., by *one* of the facts to be explained. My ethical hypothesis is actually suggested by the set of facts which is constituted by the moral codes of the most advanced peoples. But that is merely a matter of my personal biography. My method of exposition will consist in first putting forward and explaining the hypothesis, and then applying it to the facts which are to verify it.

This procedure may give to the exposition a certain appearance of dogmatism. For it means that we must begin by stating conclusions without the reasons which support them. I shall perhaps appear to be saying dogmatically "The principle of morals is thus and thus. And it is this principle which is universally applicable to all men in all ages and countries." And the reader, while understanding what I say, will perhaps fail to see why he should accept my statements. Especially he may fail to see why he should suppose that this principle is in any sense universal. The morality which I expound may very well be (he may say) *our* morality, the morality of the European races, the morality of specifically Christian peoples. But why suppose that it is in any sense applicable to Chinamen, South Sea Islanders, or Patagonians? These questions will certainly appear puzzling to him. But if it is remembered that I am pursuing the method of hypothesis, that I am explaining my hypothesis first and am reserving my reasons for a later page, the reader will perhaps consent to delay his judgment. And I trust that before I reach the end of the book I shall have succeeded in showing that there are at least some good reasons for thinking that my hypothesis may be true.

The view of the first principle of morality which I desire to express is not, of course, new in any of its essentials. Seeing that all men—at least all civilized men— possess the notion of morality in their minds in some shape or other, a totally novel principle, one which had never been heard of before, would almost certainly be false. The task of the ethical philosopher is not to discover anything which men did not know before, but to *analyse*, to make explicit, to make clear, the notion of morality which men already in some sense understand, albeit vaguely, incoherently, and perhaps half unconsciously. In science one discovers new facts. Even in metaphysics it is at least arguable that there may be new truths to be discovered—though many philosophers believe that here too the task of philosophy is simply the clear analysis of what is already known. But in ethics it seems indisputable that it is not the business of the philosopher to discover some moral principle which is unknown to men at large, to men who consciously pursue a moral life and must surely have some understanding of what they are doing.

Nor is it likely that all the philosophers of the past have failed entirely in their attempts to analyse the notion of morality. For they too, being themselves moral beings, knew in a sense what morality is before they began to analyse it—knew it in the same sense at least as other men know it. True, there have been widely different philosophical conceptions of morality. And some of these seem actually to contradict one another. So that some of them at least—it may be said—must be false. But it would seem to me more probable that all are true, though some or all of them may possess the kind of falsity which is characteristic of half-truths. Opposite half-truths may seem to contradict one another. They are in reality complementary. Each seizes and emphasizes some one aspect of the full truth. In so far as they are false, it is because of what they leave out, or because their emphasis is wrong. And in ethics it seems probable that one school has emphasized as central what is really—though true in itself—aside the true centre of morality; and that other schools have in similar manner over-emphasized other elements. If this is so, then it will hardly be the case that one of the historical schools of ethics is wholly right, the others wholly wrong. It will be rather that one approximates nearer the truth than does another. And to me it seems that the nearest approximation to the truth yet attained was the theory of the utilitarians. Consequently the theory here to be advanced will resemble utilitarianism more than it resembles other ethical philosophies. It will be a *kind* of utilitarianism.

But it will differ in very important respects from the classical utilitarian theories of Bentham and Mill. Classical utilitarianism suffered from very serious defects which subsequent criticism has exposed with crushing effects. The justice and force of at least some of these criticisms can hardly now be denied by any competent philosopher. Consequently there can be no question of simply reviving the utilitarianism of Bentham and Mill, or of vainly seeking to defend it from these criticisms. It does not at all follow, however, that the fundamental insight of utilitarianism was false. My position will rather be that this insight was true, but that Bentham and Mill expressed it in a hopelessly untenable form. What they were *trying* to say was true, although what they actually succeeded in saying was largely false. My task accordingly will be to try to restate the principle of utilitarianism in a new form which will not be subject to the criticisms which, since the time of Mill, have so severely shaken it. This is a very difficult task. And the attempt to carry it out will occupy me not only in the present chapter, but in several succeeding chapters as well.

Two at least of the propositions about morality which were maintained by the utilitarians were, I shall urge, definitely true. The first is that actions are not right or wrong in themselves, but that their moral quality depends ultimately upon their consequences. Those actions are good which have, or tend to have, good consequences; and those are bad which have, or tend to have, bad consequences. Moral action is not an end in itself, but a means to further ends. The second true belief of the utilitarians was that all the good consequences to which morality is a means can be summed up,—very vaguely, no doubt—in some such phrase as "human happiness." In the last analysis, I shall argue, human morality is a means to human happiness. The kind of actions which tend to increase human happiness are the kind of actions which are called right; while those which tend to increase human unhappiness are those which are called wrong. And I believe that this is what we *mean* by such terms as right and wrong; and that we mean nothing else, nothing in addition to this.

The above statements are intentionally vague and are couched in the most general terms. In order to become philosophically respectable they would have to be carefully analysed. Various qualifications would have to be inserted. We should have to explain precisely what we mean by such words as "happiness" and "unhappiness." The whole idea would have to be elaborately overhauled, examined in detail, and precisely set out with all its implications in exact language. The statements made in the last paragraph are nothing but rough and crude approximations to a genuine philosophical position.

The reason why I have purposely used rough and vague language is that I think that utilitarianism, so long as it remained entirely vague, was true. So long as it confined itself to telling us in the most general terms that moral action is the kind of action which conduces to human happiness, it was expressing a perfectly true insight. It was only when the utilitarians began to try to tell us exactly what their idea meant, when they tried to analyse it, and to express it in precise language, that they went astray. It was not the central idea of utilitarianism which was at fault, or which brought down upon it the violent criticism to which it has been subjected. It was the detailed *analysis* of the idea which was so defective that it aroused protests from all sides and brought discredit upon the central idea itself. The criticisms which have been passed upon utilitarianism are all, in my opinion,—so far as they are valid—criticisms of the analysis, not of the idea.

The task of restating the utilitarian position in tenable terms is therefore, in the end, a task of re-analysis. But before we begin upon such an attempt it will be wise to dwell a little upon the two propositions mentioned above, retaining them still in their vague unanalysed form.

The first proposition gives expression to the idea that the moral character of an action depends in some way upon its consequences. This, of course, has often been denied. There are ethical theories which insist that morality is an end in itself, and that it is not, or ought not to be, a means to any end beyond itself, such as happiness. And in accordance with our principle that ethical philosophies of the past are not likely to have been simply false, we may conjecture that there must be some element of truth here, though there may also be mistaken emphasis.

That morality ought to be regarded as an end in itself does, I think, express a relative truth. There really is a sense in which we say truly that a man ought to do his duty for its own sake, and not for the sake of any ulterior end.

This means, in the first place, that he ought not to do it merely because it subserves some selfish purpose of his own. One ought in all cases to be honest, even if, in some particular case, honesty is not the best policy. One ought not to make honesty a mere means to one's own advantage, so that one is ready to throw it overboard the moment it becomes disadvantageous. The doctrine that morality is an end in itself has the merit that it expresses a valuable protest against ignoble views of morality, views which would make it subservient to the selfish interests of individuals, views which would identify it with low-grade or merely "commercial" morality.

In the second place, it is very important that it should be pointed out, from time to time, that the actual consequences of our actions are largely incalculable; that we cannot ever really be sure whether they will in the end produce more good or more bad consequences; and that it is therefore wiser in our practical lives to keep our eyes pretty steadily fixed upon the character of the action itself—or at least upon its generally recognized character as good or bad. I cannot know what are in the long run going to be the total consequences of my telling a lie. There may well be cases in which it seems to me that no harm will be done, or even that good may accrue, not only to myself but to others also. But to allow my mind to be in this way entangled in the endless ramifications of future circumstance, in the maze of all possible, probable, or improbable consequences—this is a profoundly dangerous proceeding. It is so fatally easy to twist such considerations into an excuse for doing what I want, a justification of myself for deviating from the straight and narrow path. It is better to avoid all this, to keep my eyes fixed upon the safe rule "Do not lie" and to turn them steadily away from all else. It is generally better to do what the rule tells us is right, and to let the consequences be what they may.

Such considerations are, I think, very salutary, very important to be kept in mind. And theories which make morality an end in itself perform the office of pressing them home, of holding high the moral standard as against all attempts to lower it. But they cannot really, in the end, convince us that the morality of an action has nothing to do with its consequences. It may be true that we cannot know what the total consequences of our actions will be. But this only proves that we cannot know for certain whether in the end our actions are more good or more bad; we can only act upon probabilities. It does not prove that the goodness or badness of actions does not depend upon consequences. It may be true that the doctrine of the dependence of morality upon consequences is capable of being twisted by bad men into an excuse for their badness. But this does not make the doctrine false. For in one way or another almost any truth can be put to bad uses. It may be true, finally, that for most people it is safer to follow a well tried rule of thumb such as "Do not lie" than to attempt to think out for themselves whether a particular action will have good or bad consequences. But although this may be good practical advice it has no bearing upon ethical theory.

The utilitarians perceived that a view of morality which dismisses consequences as irrelevant to moral valuation is remote from reality and from the considerations upon which all men, in the actual affairs of life, base their moral judgments. It is the kind of view which one would expect to be maintained by academic persons who are completely out of touch with life and with the real doings of real people. It would seem obvious to those who are involved in the hurly-burly of life that the reason why it is, in general, immoral to be untruthful is that—as shown by all experience—lying usually causes pain and trouble to all concerned, including the liar himself. That is to say, it is wrong because of its bad consequences. It would seem obvious that to oppress the poor is wicked because of the misery which it produces, and for no other reason. And in actual life men are judged either by the results of what they do or at least by those of the results which they might reasonably have been expected to foresee. To deny these plain facts is surely to live in a world of academic dreams.

There are, of course, those who emphasize the importance of intentions as against actual consequences. A man's moral character must be judged, they say, by what he intends to do, or at least by what he makes serious effort to do, and not by the actual outcome of his deeds. For the actual outcome is not within his control. And with the best will in the world our most earnest efforts to do right often have unfortunate consequences which we could not possibly be expected to foresee, and for which we cannot be held accountable. No one would wish to deny this. But it does nothing to shake our belief that in the last resort the good or bad character of an action depends upon consequences. For what can an intention be if it is not an intention to produce consequences? And how judge whether an intention is good or bad except by considering whether the intended consequences are good or bad? If I say that a man is to be judged by his intentions and not by the actual results of his actions, what I mean is that he ought not to be held accountable for consequences which he could not reasonably be expected to foresee, but only for those which he intended. But to judge a man by intended consequences is still to make consequences the criterion of morality. It amounts to saying that although good and bad actions are those which have good and bad consequences respectively, yet we cannot take credit for a good which we did not intend nor be blamed for an evil which we did not and could not know would result. It amounts to saying that a man may unintentionally, and even in spite of his best efforts, do the wrong thing, and that in that case he is not to be blamed. But this is not to say that what he did was not in fact the wrong thing to do. His action was bad, although it did not proceed from a bad character, but rather from ignorance.

Moreover the view which would make consequences irrelevant to morality is based upon an abstraction which cannot be maintained. For how can we ever separate an action from its consequences? The consequences of an action are part of the action itself. My will sets in motion a train of events. The fiat of my will (if there is such a thing) and the subsequent events which flow from it constitute a strictly continuous series of changes. It is perfectly arbitrary to draw a line somewhere across this continuous flow and call what comes before it the "action" and what comes after it the "consequences." Thus if I shoot a man, is his death in a hospital the next day a consequence of my action or a part of the action itself? If I say that it is only a consequence, then at what point in the continuous series of events which led to his death did the action end? At the pulling of the trigger? Shall I say that this was part of my action, but that the explosion of the powder, the motion of the bullet, the hole made in the man's body, and finally his death, were merely consequences? Or shall I push the line of division further back still and say that only the fiat of my will was my action and that the subsequent discharge of nervous impulses leading to my finger, and the closing of the finger itself on the trigger, were only consequences? Is it not plain that all such attempts to draw a line of division are unreal and arbitrary, and that therefore the whole attempt to distinguish between an action and its consequences is impossible? And if so, the view that the consequences of an action are irrelevant to moral judgment is impossible to carry out.

This is universally recognized in practical morals. Stealing, we think, is morally unjustifiable. But what *is* the action of stealing? If I remove your goods to my house, the movement of my hands causes the translocation of your property. No one would admit that this change of place is merely a consequence of my action and not part of the action itself. The act of stealing, which is what is considered morally bad, includes the consequences of the movements of my hands. Indeed, it is not the movement of my hands which is morally bad, but precisely the consequences, the loss to you of your property.

Will it be said that this argument cuts both ways—that if it is impossible to distinguish between action and consequence, then it is impossible to say that the moral character of an action depends upon its consequences? If anyone likes to score this purely verbal point, he is welcome. But it does not express the true conclusion. What we ought rather to say is this. Strictly speaking it is impossible to distinguish action from consequence. Yet we do in our ordinary conversation make such a distinction, and we are quite justified in doing so. For the distinction is a convenient one which has practical uses, although it is theoretically indefensible. What we do is to draw a line more or less arbitrarily across the continuous movement of events and to call what lies on the hither side of the line "action" and what lies on the further side "consequences." The point at which the division is made is fixed by convention and by considerations of practical convenience. Thus we should ordinarily call the removal of your goods to my house a part of the action. But the fact that there accrues a hundred years hence some remote and unforeseen effect upon our descendents would not ordinarily be called part of the action, but one of its consequences. Now the ethical theory which I am maintaining can be expressed in two ways. I can either say that the moral character of an action depends upon its consequences; and in that case I am making use of a convenient, though strictly inaccurate, mode of expression. Or, if I aim at greater accuracy, I can say that what we have to take account of in a moral judgment, what fixes the moral character of our deeds, is the nature of the *whole action*—the whole action being understood to include what would ordinarily be called the consequences of the action. It follows that I can express my theory without making use of the distinction between action and consequence; and therefore that the theory is independent of that distinction, and that if the distinction is not theoretically justifiable this makes no difference to the theory. But the opposite theory, which says that consequences are irrelevant to the moral character of an action, cannot express itself without making use of the distinction, and is therefore absolutely dependent upon its validity. For it is essential to it to distinguish the consequences from the action in order that it may be able to say that the former are irrelevant, the latter relevant. This theory, therefore, collapses as soon as it is pointed out that the distinction is not valid.

I shall not hesitate to continue speaking in terms of action and consequence and saying that the moral character of an action depends upon its consequences. For it will be much more convenient and more readily intelligible to speak thus than to say that the whole action must be taken into account, meaning by the whole action both what a man does and all the effects of what he does for the rest of time. To use the word "action" in this sense would be a very wide departure from the ordinary usage of language, and would, I think, involve constant risk of serious misunderstanding. And I do not think that I shall be misunderstood if I speak, as men ordinarily do, of actions and their consequences. And I do not think that anyone who brings to the reading of what is to be written here a modicum of good will and a measure of good sense will accuse me of inconsistency because I point out that there is no real distinction between action and consequences and yet continue to say that the goodness or badness of an action depends upon its consequences.

The second true belief of the utilitarians was that the consequences which determine the moral character of an action are its consequences for human happiness; and that in general those actions are good which increase human happiness, and those bad which decrease it. It is true that it is exceedingly difficult to know what is meant by "happiness." It is an exceedingly difficult idea to analyse, and I think that the utilitarians made egregious blunders in their attempts to analyse it. It is also true that the notions of "increase" and "decrease" as here used are difficult to understand. For the increases and decreases spoken of do not seem to be in any ordinary sense measurable quantities. But these words "happiness" and "unhappiness," "increase" and "decrease" do undoubtedly mean *something*. And there is a sense in which it is true to say that *everybody knows what they mean*. For everyone—or at least nearly everyone—knows whether he is happy or not, and knows that he is happier at some times than he is at others. He knows in his own experience that certain things or events increase his happiness and that other things or events decrease it. So long, then, as we remain at the level of everyday common sense conversation, so long as we take these terms to mean what everybody (in a sense) knows them to mean, so long as we do not attempt the difficult and slippery task of philosophical analysis, it seems to me that we can believe it to be quite true, and even obviously true, that happiness, the happiness not only of ourselves but of others, of society at large, is the end at which moral activity aims. And this, of course, is just what the utilitarians did say.

I do not think that anyone ought seriously to object if I were to say that the essence of morality lies in unselfishness, that is, in having consideration for the happiness of others. The saying "Do unto others as you would that they should do unto you" is often taken to express the quintessence of Christian morality. And this saying might not unfairly be translated into the words "Consider the happiness of others as you would have them consider yours."

If lying is immoral because it brings evil consequences, because it brings upon people trouble, pain, and sometimes disaster, cannot all this be roughly summed up by saying that it is immoral because it increases, or tends to increase, human unhappiness? If an unselfish deed is morally good because of its good consequences, does this not mean in effect that it is good because of the happiness which it yields to those who come within the sphere of its influence?

To all such statements it can rightly be objected that we do not know exactly what they mean, that they are not clear, and that they stand in need of careful analysis to make them clear. But then this will be true of almost any common sense statement that one makes. And it has no tendency to prove that the statements are not true. And my only contention at the moment is that the statements made in the preceding paragraphs about the relation of morality to happiness are true. I certainly would not assert that they are clear.

And now, having outlined the true, if vague and unclear, insights which characterized utilitarianism, I will proceed to examine some of the mistakes of analysis which it made with a view to seeing whether there is any way in which they can be rectified.

The first criticism of utilitarianism which I will discuss concerns a well known fallacy of Mill's. Mill, it will be remembered, attempted to argue that because every individual man in the world desires his own happiness therefore all men desire the happiness of all men.[1] He apparently thought that this showed that every man desires, not only his own happiness, but the happiness of all other persons. And this, of course, is a very gross fallacy. For it may very well be true that "all men desire the happiness of all men" in the sense that each desires his own, while being false that "all men desire the happiness of all men" in the sense that each desires the happiness of himself and of all others.

Now what this means is that the utilitarians—and in

[1] J. S. Mill, *Utilitarianism*, Chapter 4.

particular Mill—were bankrupt when it came to an attempt to solve the problem of the basis of moral obligation. Mill apparently thought that he could, by means of this fallacious argument, show that the moral end, "the greatest happiness of the greatest number," was something which was as a matter of fact desired by all men. And if this were so, there would be no need to seek any further for a basis for morality. For if all men do as a fact desire the greatest happiness of the greatest number, then there would be no point in asking why they *ought* to do so and why they ought to strive for that happiness. The difficulty of the problem of the basis of moral obligation is precisely the difficulty of seeing why I ought to do something which I do not desire to do. Why should I strive for an end which I do not desire? Why should I concern myself about the happiness of any person other than myself? No one would think of asking what is the basis of my obligation to try to make myself happy. Or at least I personally should think such a question pointless. Why I should seek my own happiness is obvious. It is simply because I desire my own happiness. But why I ought to try to make *you* happy, especially if by so doing I decrease my own happiness, is not at all obvious. And to find an answer to this question is, as I understand it, precisely the point of the problem of the basis of moral obligation. To this question Mill had absolutely no answer to offer. He had nothing to say except that as a matter of fact all men do desire the happiness of all other men, and that therefore the question does not arise. And there does not seem to be any reason to suppose that this is true. There seems every reason to believe that many men care nothing at all about the happiness of the greater number of their fellow beings.

This criticism of Mill is, I think, quite unanswerable. What we can do, however, is to discard what was worthless in his teaching and retain what was good. Suppose we put it in this way. There are two quite distinct and independent questions which the moral philosopher has to answer. The first is "*What* ought men to do?" The second is "*Why* ought they to do it?" The first question asks for a *description* of what morality is. The second asks what the *basis* or *foundation* of morality is. Now it is quite possible that a philosopher might have a very good and a perfectly true answer to the first question, and yet might not be able to give any answer at all to the second question, or might give a quite false answer. And this, I think, is precisely what is the case with Mill and the utilitarians generally. I should accordingly maintain that Mill's failure to solve the problem of the basis of morality, perhaps one might almost say his failure to understand it, has no bearing upon the truth of utilitarianism in so far as utilitarianism is taken as being simply a *description* of what men's moral duties actually are. And I think that utilitarianism actually is, if only its general insights are considered, true in this way. That is to say, it is a good description of what I ought to do to say that I ought to strive in all my actions for the greater happiness of humanity. But to say this does not, of course, throw any light upon the problem of the *basis* of moral obligation.

Now it will be remembered that the question with which we are actually concerned in the present chapters is precisely the question of what morality is, what its first principle is; we are not at present concerned with the problem of its basis. That question is quite a separate one, and it will not come to be taken up until we reach a very much

later chapter in this book. We can therefore ignore it altogether for the present. And in our search for the first
principle of morals, it is a matter of no importance to us
that the utilitarians had no solution of it to offer. In other
words, this first criticism of utilitarianism which we have
considered, though perfectly justified, is irrelevant to our
present enquiry. It was, however, all to the good that it
was brought to our attention at this early stage. For it
is extremely important that we should keep quite separate in our minds the two questions "What ought men to
do?" and "Why ought they to do it?" and that we should
fully realize that it is only the first question that we are
at present trying to answer.

The results reached in this chapter are certainly very
slight. What we have concluded is that morality is not
an end in itself, but is a means to something called "happiness." But we do not ourselves profess yet to know—
except in a vague unanalysed way—what the word "happiness" means. And we have Aristotle and Bradley at
our elbow to remind us, if we need reminding, how utterly
meagre this result is. Speaking of the question what is
the highest of all goods achievable by action Aristotle
says: "Verbally there is very general agreement. For
both the general run of men and people of superior refine-
ment say that it is happiness. . . . But with regard to
what happiness is they differ." [1] And Bradley: "Happiness is the end? Yes, happiness is the end which indeed
we all reach after. . . . Alas! the one question, which no
one can answer, is, What is happiness?" [2]

[1] *Nichomachean Ethics*, Book I, Ross's translation.
[2] *Ethical Studies*, Essay 3.

CHAPTER 6

HAPPINESS

WHAT, then, is happiness?

And in the first place, does there really exist such a thing as happiness at all? For there have been those who thought that, though pain and unhappiness are real and positive existences, pleasure and happiness are merely "negative."

Even if this were true, it need cause no embarrassment to the philosopher who believes that happiness is the end at which moral action aims. He will need only to redefine his terms. Happiness, defined now as the absence of pain and unhappiness, will become for him the end of moral action. The good man will aim at mitigating the pain in the world, at destroying the unhappiness.

But it is not necessary to make these pessimistic admissions. What meaning is to be attached to the statement that happiness is merely negative? We certainly do experience states of consciousness which we call joy, happiness, delight. These actually *are* experiences which human beings do have. They are *existent* experiences. And if anyone says that happiness is negative in the sense that it does not exist at all, he says what is simply false. Negative, therefore, cannot be interpreted to mean non-existent.

Does the statement mean, then, that though we sometimes think or feel that we are happy, yet in reality we are not so? But this suggestion is incoherent. For to be happy means nothing else than to feel happy. And therefore if one feels happy, one *is* happy.

Perhaps the statement means that, although we do have

experiences which we call being joyful, delighted, happy, yet we mistake their character. We take them to be positive when they are really negative. But in that case we shall have to ask again what we mean by "negative." We cannot mean non-existent, mere nothingness. For you cannot take nothingness to be anything. There is nothing to take. In order to mistake one thing for another, the first thing must be some kind of positively existing entity. You can mistake a white sheet for a ghost. But you cannot mistake absolute nonentity for a ghost or for anything else.

It seems to follow that in order to give any coherent meaning to the view that happiness is really negative, you have got to take the terms "positive" and "negative" as both being (in some sense or other) words which apply to actually existing things. You have got to suppose that some existing things are positive while other existing things are negative. We often do use the words "positive" and "negative" in this way. For example, we speak of positive and negative electricity. Or we may—for some special purpose—call the west positive and the east negative. To say that in this sense two things are respectively positive and negative simply means that they have opposite or contrasting characters. And in this sense we can of course say, if we like, that happiness is negative and unhappiness positive. But this will only mean that happiness and unhappiness have opposite characters— which nobody ever doubted, and which is not worth saying. Moreover it will be indifferent whether you call happiness negative and unhappiness positive, or whether you call happiness positive and unhappiness negative; just as it is indifferent whether you call the west positive and the east negative, or *vice versa*.

I conclude that the statement that happiness and pleasure are negative is either false or meaningless. The fact is that by writers like Schopenhauer it is used "emotively." It constitutes a deft stroke of the brush in the painting of the sombre picture of human misery which Schopenhauer delights to exhibit. But it has no cognitive meaning.

What, then, is happiness?

This, says Bradley, is what *no one knows*. I do not deny that in a sense Bradley is right. And yet his statement is at best only a half truth. And I will now place over against it the other half of the truth which he omitted, namely, that *everyone knows what happiness is*. For everyone knows in his own experience the difference between being happy and being unhappy. He knows whether he is happy or not now at this moment. He knows whether he is happy or unhappy in his relations with his wife. He knows that in some periods of his life he was happier than in other periods. He knows that he is happy today, and was unhappy yesterday. And how can he have all this knowledge if he does not know what happiness is?

If this is so, why should I proceed any further? Why should I try to explain to the reader what happiness is, since he already knows this as well as I do, or perhaps better? There is indeed no compelling reason. It would, I think, be perfectly legitimate to say, as we already have, that morality aims at happiness, and to give no further account of the nature of happiness, but to rely upon every man's innate understanding of the meaning of the word. And in that case we might pass on without further ado to the next heading of our ethical theory.

And yet it would be unwise to do this. We might be accused of relying uncritically upon an unanalysed common sense notion which the philosopher ought to analyse.

And apart from this, so many false notions have been connected with the concept of happiness—especially by utilitarian philosophers—that it becomes a positive duty at least explicitly to repudiate these.

As to analysis, I do not think that I can do much. To analyse a concept means to split it up in thought into its simple elements. But I am not sure that happiness has any simpler elements of which it is composed. Certainly it was a mistake of the utilitarians to imagine that it is composed of "pleasures," or that it is a simple collection of these. And yet I should hesitate to say that happiness is an unanalysable simple ultimate entity like a colour. That is too easy a solution. The truth is that I doubt whether the simple antithesis of either "analysable into simple elements" or "unanalysable ultimate" applies to such a thing as happiness. That is the kind of dichotomy which we find a valuable instrument in dealing with physical things. We split something up into sense-data and their relations, and we say that the sense-data are unanalysable. And it seems legitimate enough in the material sphere to present the dilemma that everything must either be capable of analysis or be itself a simple ultimate. But happiness is not a physical object. And I am more than doubtful whether these categories of physical analysis have any application to it at all. I certainly know that the only analysis of happiness ever attempted, that which makes it an aggregate of "pleasures," is false. And I suspect that any other attempted analysis would be false too.

At any rate I shall not attempt a formal logical analysis of happiness. My efforts will be much more modest. In the end, no doubt, I shall be relying upon the common sense notion of happiness which everyone has. But there are two additional things which I can do. I can try to study some of the conditions upon which happiness depends. And I can try to point out some of the mistakes which philosophers have made in their descriptions of happiness.

Let us start from the utilitarian conception according to which happiness is a complex, or collection, of pleasures. I am sure this is a false notion, and yet there is in it a sufficient grain of truth to make it a good starting point for discussion. Perhaps we can, by a process of paring away some of its errors and crudities, reach a juster conception.

I will begin by making a point which is, perhaps, only verbal. The word "pleasure," as used in the utilitarian analysis of happiness, is singularly unfortunate. Instead of "pleasures" I propose to speak of "satisfactions." For the notion of pleasure arouses prejudice. Historically it has been especially associated in men's minds with the grosser pleasures of the body. If we think of satisfactions as constituting a kind of scale of "lower" and "higher"—a conception which, of course, must later be justified—then we may have, perhaps, the satisfactions of the body, such as those of eating and sex, at the bottom. These, we shall say, are the "lowest" kinds of satisfaction. Higher up we shall get the satisfactions of the mind. And perhaps at the top we shall get the satisfactions of the religious consciousness. (I am merely giving this as an example of a possible scale, not asserting that it is the true scale.) Now the word pleasure seems thoroughly suitable to the lowest kinds of satisfactions, but seems to become progressively less and less suitable as we mount the scale. To speak of intellectual and artistic "pleasures" is indeed allowable, and yet seems to most people hardly to do justice to the exalted character of the things of the mind and the spirit. And it would seem to be altogether out of place to talk of religious "pleasures," or to describe the mystic's vision of God as one of his pleasures.

This objection to a particular word may be mere prejudice. But such considerations have undoubtedly caused much of the repugnance which many minds feel towards utilitarianism. It was partly because of this that utilitarianism was described as a "pig-philosophy." But the word "satisfactions" is, I think, neutral in this respect. It is less weighed down with ignoble associations. We can perhaps speak of the satisfactions of men's intellectual, artistic, and religious natures without arousing prejudice. And I shall as a rule use this word, although I shall not entirely forego the use of the word pleasure. I shall sometimes use it if the context seems to make it unobjectionable.

Next, I am quite prepared to admit that the notion of a *calculus* of satisfactions and dissatisfactions is impossible. But I cannot conceive why any philosopher should want to have one. It is sometimes assumed that the breakdown of this conception involved the breakdown of utilitarianism. For it is said that if you cannot make a calculation of the relative amounts of pleasure and pain which your actions will produce in the world, you cannot know which actions are good, which bad. This, however, is a very shallow argument. In the first place, even if you cannot measure pleasures and pains, this does not prevent you from knowing that some pleasures or pains are greater than others. A man does not need a thermometer to know that he is being frozen to death or boiled alive. And without any such instrument he can detect the difference between a hot day and a cold one. So too a man knows that some pains are terrible, some slight; that some pleasures are great, some small; although he cannot measure either the pleasures or the pains. And a man knows when he is slightly unhappy, more unhappy, very unhappy. Hence we can often foresee pretty clearly that our actions will cause much or little happiness or unhappiness. I am likely, in general, to produce more unhappiness by killing the sole bread-winner of a family than by stealing his dog. We can sometimes see that one action will affect, for good or ill, the lives of many, and that another action will affect only the lives of a few. We can take into account the various factors involved, including the characters and tastes of the people to be affected, and so try to discover what will make them happy, what unhappy. If we are not sure whether a man whom we propose to benefit will be made more happy by an increase of salary or by a change of climate, we can ask him. It is true that he may not be sure himself, or that he may judge wrongly. But that is inherent in the human situation, and we simply have to do the best we can in the circumstances.

In deciding which of several possible courses of action we ought to pursue, we can take into account, to the best of our ability, a great number of factors—the number of people who will be affected by what we do, the extent of the benefits we are likely to confer on each or of the damage we are likely to inflict, the length of time over which these benefits or damages are likely to last, the tastes of the persons concerned, the strength and ability of one person to bear suffering, the weakness and inability of another. To each of these factors we can do our best to attach the proper weight. By such methods we can roughly balance one action against another and assign to them degrees of moral excellence or heinousness. Nothing more than this is, or ever will be, possible. The idea that we could ever assign to actions their precise places in a numerically ordered scale of moral values is ridiculous. And the idea that any conceivable criterion of morals could ever enable us to know with absolute certainty what it is morally best to do in all the complicated circumstances of life would only occur to an utterly academic mind.

Whatever ethical philosophy we espouse there is, and always must be, a vast amount of doubt about the moral character of this or that particular action. And with this doubt we have got to put up. Morality lies in the region of the empirical, the variable, the doubtful, the human—not in the region of logic and mathematical calculation. And the fact that we cannot always be sure, by applying the utilitarian criterion, which of two proposed actions it is morally better to perform, does not show that the criterion is false. It only shows that morality is not arithmetic. The good man is he who strives most and succeeds best, in these very difficult conditions, in doing the best he can for suffering humanity. Who but a fool would deny that it is often, indeed usually, extraordinarily difficult to know what is the best thing to do in life? And why should this difficulty be charged up especially to the debit of utilitarianism?

A juster complaint against utilitarianism is that it tends to institute a false separation between happiness or pleasure, on the one hand, and the things which yield happiness or pleasure, on the other. It thus cuts off happiness and pleasure from concrete things and makes of them mere abstractions or else inward and subjective feelings. And it represents men as seeking happiness and pleasure as ends, while all concrete things are treated as mere means to these abstractions.

This is psychologically false. Men do not desire things for the sake of, or as means to, something called pleasure. They desire the things themselves. What men desire are always concrete things, states of affairs, or situations. They do not desire these things because they give pleasure. On the contrary, they give pleasure because they are desired. Suppose that I find it pleasant to play tennis. The pleasant game of tennis is something concrete. It is absurd to break it up into two parts, the game and the pleasure, and to say that the game is a means and that the pleasure is the end. Pleasure cannot be separated from the pleasant activity. Or if it is so separated, it becomes an abstraction which no man desires. What in this case is desired and what is therefore the end is not pleasure but simply the pleasant game of tennis. It is therefore false to say that there is only one end at which all human activities aim, namely pleasure. And it is equally false to say that the one end is happiness in the abstract. Human activities aim at countless different kinds of ends. These ends are such concrete things as games of tennis, wealth, houses, power, wives, and children.

Nevertheless this criticism can be met by a most trifling verbal modification of the utilitarian formula. All we have to do is to substitute for the word pleasure some such round-about phrase as "pleasant things, experiences, and activities." We shall then be able to proceed precisely as before. We shall say that morality is that kind of action which tends to yield to the greatest number of human beings the maximum number of pleasant things, experiences, and activities. And we can make a similar substitution for the abstract word happiness. What we aim at, we shall say, is not *happiness*, but "a happy life." This is a concrete idea. And by it is meant a life full of happy activities and experiences, a life replete with the things which bring happiness.

Indeed, when we have proceeded thus far, we begin to see that the criticism of utilitarianism which we are considering is more verbal than real. When people say "happiness" do they not in fact *mean* "a happy life"? And when they say "pleasure" do they not in fact *mean* the concrete things, activities, and experiences, which are pleasurable? And is it necessary to use these cumbersome and round-about phrases every time we wish to speak of these matters? Cannot we, for short, use the word "pleasure" to mean the concrete things, and the word "happiness" to mean a happy life? This, in fact, I shall do henceforth. I shall not hesitate to speak as before of pleasure and happiness. Only the meaning of the words must be taken in the concrete.

Nor need we fear that, if once we admit that human ends are many, and not one, this will get us into trouble. There is nothing sacred about the number one. Nor can it be urged that, if the one end, happiness, is seen to split up into an indefinite multitude of ends, this will involve us once more in ethical relativity. It is true that the sort of concrete things which make me happy are not the same as the sort of concrete things which make you happy— and in general that different people are made happy by different things. And it is true that one might argue from this to ethical relativity. If morality is, one might say, simply a means to happiness, and if happiness is, when concretely considered, utterly different for different people, then the means to be adopted to reach it (i.e., morality) will differ with different people.

But to argue thus would be quite fallacious. Even if it were true that no two men ever had a single identical end in common, even if it were the case that no two men ever had the same needs, it would not follow that there could be no single moral rule for them all. The bare fact that all men *have needs* is itself something which all men share in common. It is a common element of their natures. And on it a common morality could be founded. For one could still say that morality consists in so acting as to increase to the utmost of one's powers the total of human happiness by satisfying, so far as possible, the differing needs of each individual man. Even as it is, no one supposes that making our neighbours happy means giving them all the same identical things or preparing for them all the same identical situations. It means giving to each man what *he* needs and preparing for him the kind of situations which make *him* happy. It includes taking into account the special wants of each man. Mr. Bernard Shaw's remark "Do not do unto others as you would that they should do unto you. Their tastes may be different" is no doubt a smart saying. But it seems to overlook the fact that "doing as you would be done by" includes taking into account your neighbour's tastes as you would that he should take yours into account. Thus the "golden rule" might still express the essence of a universal morality *even if no two men in the world had any needs or tastes in common.*

But this is not, of course, the actual state of affairs. Men have innumerable needs in common. Here, as elsewhere, we tend to exaggerate differences. No doubt it is true that the needs of individuals differ. But men are after all made on a common pattern; and in spite of all differences it is possible to say in general terms what constitutes the happy life for man *as man*. There are certain fundamental needs which all men share. And these can be made the basis of moral rules which are universally applicable and which are more specific and detailed than the bare golden rule.

Thus it is not impossible to say, in general terms, what constitutes the happy life for man. Or at least one may point to some of its general conditions without pretending that one's account of them is at all complete. One may list a few of the more obvious conditions. One may begin by observing that health, the absence of physical pain and mental worry, the possession of a reasonable sufficiency of wordly goods are, for most men, a necessary pre-condition of happiness. A man cannot be happy if he is starving, has no roof over his head, or is in constant physical torment. Those who say that the good man is happy on the rack are, as Aristotle observed, talking nonsense.[1] If a man is in these respects sufficiently well situated, it is probable that the next most important essential is that all his powers, both of mind and of body, should have opportunity for their regular activity. The activity must be regular but not excessive in amount. Otherwise fatigue supervenes, and other equally important activities are crowded out. A proper *balance* of activities is profoundly important. For if there be too much of one and too little of others—as happens for example where a man is kept drudging all day and every day at a single constantly repeated mechanical operation in a factory—then these others are starved. It is the personality as a whole which has to be exercised, now in this part now in that, to make a well balanced and truly happy life. Nevertheless different personalities differ in respect of the development of their different faculties, some being by nature more suited for one activity, others for another. And if a man

[1] *Nichomachean Ethics*, Book VII, 13.

possesses some special gift in which he excels, the exercise of this is for him above all necessary. The blocking of any normal activity leads to some degree of unhappiness. But if a man possesses a faculty in the exercise of which he is preëminently fitted to shine, it is in the exercise of this that he is likely to find his greatest happiness. And the blocking of this will be for him the greatest unhappiness.

That there are many other conditions which make for happiness goes without saying. A reasonable portion of amusement, relaxation, "pleasure." The ability to command leisure hours. Freedom from anxiety and overwork. A measure of independence of the wills of others. And if there is any condition which can rival the exercise of special gifts as the chief source of man's happiness, I would say that it lies in the affection of friends and in the love for one another of the members of a family. For when all else turns in a man's mouth to dead sea fruit, when advancing years bring disillusionment and disgust with the will o' the wisps which men for the most part pursue, then these things—the attachment of a few friends, the love of a child, a wife, a brother,—are seen as goods more abiding and more satisfying than all others. And when all other "pleasures" are seen as false and hollow shams, or at least as things of which the spirit wearies, these are seen to remain solid and real and not to fail. Moreover while only the few can have riches and power, friendship and affection, in more or less degree, are open to all save the most unfortunate. Friendship is the poor man's riches; and it is a happier lot to be rich in human affection though poor in gold than to be king of half the world but without a friend.

These, then, are some of the concrete ends which should, in our view, replace the abstract notion of "pleasure" in ethics. And they are *common* ends, ends in which all men find satisfaction. True, there are differences between men even in these fundamental matters. Some men have more need of one end, others of another. There may even be exceptional men who have practically no need at all of certain of these ends, or who at least contrive to be happy without them. But these differences are not to be exaggerated. On the whole these are common *human* needs, not the special ends of peculiar individuals. And the relatively trivial differences between men in respect of them need not prevent us from founding upon them a common morality. And if, instead of saying in abstract language, that morality is a means to "the greatest happiness of the greatest number" we say that the supreme end of morality ought to be to see that as many men as possible in the world have health, a sufficiency of material means, opportunity for the proper exercise of their faculties, a measure of relaxation and leisure, a home, a family, and friends—we shall surely not be advocating either a false or an ignoble view of morality. Certainly this will not be a "pig-philosophy."

I come now to the most difficult of all the questions which we have to face and the one in regard to which the utilitarians went most seriously astray. This is the question of the *relation* which holds between satisfactions (or pleasures as the utilitarians called them) and happiness. The utilitarians were clearly right in thinking that satisfactions *have something to do with* happiness. That is perhaps the vaguest statement which it is possible to make regarding the relation. We may even be a little more precise and say that satisfactions are among the *conditions* upon which happiness depends. For whether a man is happy or not does obviously depend in some degree upon the satisfactions which enter into his life. Up to a point he may be made happier by the possession of friends, of family affection, of opportunities for intellectual culture, even of material goods. And he may obviously be made unhappy by the absence of these things. But the utilitarians made a gross and fatal blunder when they jumped from these facts to the conclusion that satisfactions are the *parts* of happiness, the elements of which it is composed, and that happiness is analysable into satisfactions. Their error lay in supposing that happiness is nothing but a *collection* of pleasures, an *aggregate* of satisfactions. They thought that the relation between pleasures and happiness is the relation of parts to a whole or of members of a collection to the collection. This is not, indeed, the language they used. I am interpreting, not quoting or paraphrasing. But obviously this was the spirit of their philosophy.

The probability is that the utilitarians thought as they did because their ideas of analysis were formed on the model of the kind of analysis which is successful in the case of physical existences. They thought that pleasures bear to happiness the sort of relation which sense-data bear to material objects. Hence pleasures became for them the simple and ultimate data into which happiness is analysable.

The view that happiness is merely a collection of pleasures or satisfactions is shown to be false by some of the most elementary facts in man's moral experience. For it is notorious that one man may be happy although he has very few pleasures or satisfactions; while another whose life is replete with pleasures and satisfactions may be relatively unhappy. And this may even be true when the first of these men has, along with the paucity of his satisfactions, a considerable load of dissatisfactions; and when the second has, to detract from his happiness, very few positive dissatisfactions. The happiest men are often those who have little; while those who have much are often the most unhappy. It is a commonplace that to give men all they want, even if all their wants are quite legitimate, is no sure way of making them happy. There is a story that one who was in search of happiness was told that he could obtain it if he could but find a truly happy man and wear his shirt. He searched the whole world and at last found a truly happy man. But the man had no shirt. Now if happiness were a whole with pleasures for its parts, then to increase the amount of the pleasures would necessarily result in enlarging the happiness. If happiness were a collection of satisfactions, then to increase the number of the members of the collection would be the same as increasing the size of the collection, i.e., of the happiness. But this is not the case. Therefore a man's happiness cannot be simply the sum-total of his satisfactions. It is a rule of the part-whole relation that the whole is equal to the sum of its parts. But a man's happiness is by no means necessarily equal to the sum of his pleasures.

This mistake, again, was one of the causes of the persistent prejudice against utilitarianism. If this view were true, then what every man ought to do would be to pursue and capture every possible pleasure within his reach. He should spend his life amassing vast quantities of satisfactions. He would then ensure his own great happiness. Now everyone knows in his heart that this is not the formula for happiness, although it is true that most men act as if it were. Everyone knows that the relentless annexation of all possible pleasures and satisfactions for one self defeats its own end, leads to disillusionment and even disgust. To preach this doctrine was to preach a low and false ideal. It went counter to man's deepest moral intuitions. It rang false to his moral experience. The antipathy which utilitarianism aroused in the most sensitive minds was largely due to this cause.

In part, no doubt, the facts can be explained, and made consistent with the view that happiness is a sum-total of satisfactions, by the simple consideration that appetites become jaded and satisfactions pall. Increased beyond a certain limit they yield a diminishing return. We might try to retain the opinion that happiness is a mere collection of satisfactions by pointing out that, as you keep on increasing the number of the members of the collection, these members, so to speak, decrease in size, so that the size of the whole collection is not perceptibly increased. The hypothesis would be that as pleasures increase in number they, as it were, shrink in dimensions, and so fill a smaller volume. Thus happiness might still be a collection of satisfactions, and yet it would not be true that to increase satisfactions is necessarily the same as to increase happiness.

I do not doubt that this is a part of the explanation. But it is quite insufficient. For if this were all, it would still be true that *up to a point* increase of satisfactions would always and necessarily result in increase of happiness. It would still be true that man's best course would be to pursue and amass satisfactions, being careful only not to pass what one might call the point of saturation. But this too rings false, and does not accord with the facts. This indeed is the philosophy of the cautious and cultured Epicurean, so careful only to taste pleasures so far as they do not pall. But the epicure too defeats his own purpose. He is no happier than another. There is something radically wrong with a life planned on these lines. And the epicure does not earn the respect, but rather the contempt, of other men. For though men cannot give the reason, they divine instinctively that this philosophy is false, and does not lead to happiness. The Epicurean too commits the error of thinking that happiness is a collection of satisfactions. His mistake is less crude in that he allows for the law of diminishing returns in pleasure. But it is still the same mistake.

It is not merely that a man who, as it were, too greedily piles on his satisfactions fails to attain happiness. It is that even among those who are perfectly moderate, whose appetites are unjaded, who retain the capacity to "enjoy" to the utmost the satisfactions which they have, it still remains true that many who have few satisfactions are happy, while others who have many satisfactions are less happy. One cannot, on the hypothesis suggested, explain how it is that a poor man without even a shirt may be truly happy, while one who lives in comfort and security, without any special cares, may fail of happiness.

There is, I think, only one way out. We must make a distinction between satisfactions or pleasures on the one hand and happiness on the other.[1] The mistake of the utilitarians was to *identify* happiness with pleasure, or at least with a sum of pleasures. We must say, on the contrary, that happiness is one thing and that satisfactions are quite another thing. Satisfactions may be in part the

---

[1] This is, of course, a very ancient distinction. But I think that in the past the distinction between happiness and pleasure has usually been confused with the distinction between higher and lower satisfactions. The tendency has been to identify happiness with the higher satisfactions and pleasure with the lower. But the view which I am about to develop in the text is different from this. On my view the highest satisfactions, say those of religion, are no more to be identified with happiness, than are the grossest sensual pleasures. Happiness is distinct from all and every satisfaction.

conditions upon which happiness to some extent depends. But it is not true that the happiness simply *is* the satisfactions. Once we get clear in our minds the conception that we may have in our souls on the one hand a certain set of satisfactions; and on the other hand a state of happiness; and that these two are quite distinct; and we shall have made an enormous stride forward towards the understanding of a number of ethical problems.

If this view is taken, it becomes at least *prima facie* comprehensible how a man's satisfactions may be very great, and yet his happiness small; and how his satisfactions may be very small, and yet his happiness great. For the happiness being distinct from the sum of satisfactions does not have to have what one may call the same "volume" as they have. This was entirely unintelligible, and indeed self-contradictory, so long as we believed that the happiness and the satisfactions are simply identical.

But still this does not explain what is the actual relation between satisfactions and happiness. It only tells us that they are different. Now we have admitted that satisfactions *have something to do with* happiness, and even that they are among the *conditions* of it. I shall adopt what is doubtless metaphorical language and shall say that satisfactions "contribute to" happiness, and dissatisfactions to unhappiness. And this is indeed obvious. I can certainly be made unhappy by pain, worry, displeasure. And my various satisfactions bodily and mental, my friendships, loves, artistic enjoyments, religious feelings, also my bodily feelings of health and the like, do certainly contribute to my happiness. And even on this basis one would expect—what we have seen is not the case—that the extent of a man's happiness would vary directly with the extent of his satisfactions. A number of rivers flowing into a lake contribute to the lake, and the size of the lake will be proportional to the volume of waters contributed. But somehow it is not in this manner that satisfactions contribute to happiness. The volume of the happiness is not necessarily proportional to the volume of the satisfactions. And this has somehow to be explained.

This is indeed a very great mystery. I do not believe that I can fully explain it. Arithmetic will not help us. Perhaps all this talk about volumes, sizes, quantities, of satisfactions and happinesses is mere metaphor taken from the physical world and applied woodenly to the things of the spirit. Perhaps satisfactions and happinesses are not really quantitative at all, and the laws of quantity do not apply to them. I will not pursue that suggestion here. I will instead offer two considerations which I hope may throw light upon the paradox with which we are confronted.

In the first place, there is something in the individual personality of each man which determines the degree of his happiness independently of any satisfactions which he has or does not have. Some men seem to be born happy, others to be born unhappy. We use vaguely such words as temperament, disposition, here. A man who has a happy temperament simply *is* happy, and will continue to be so even with the minimum of satisfactions. A man who has an unhappy temperament simply *is* unhappy, and will continue to be so though you give him all the satisfactions which the world holds. It is no part of my present business to explain this. There are those who will attribute it to purely physical causes, the state of the bodily organs and their functioning. And while I do not doubt that this has something to do with the matter, I do not think that this is the last word. The mind itself contributes something here. But whatever the causes of the fact, the fact itself is certain; and it helps to explain our paradox. Happiness is not proportional to satisfactions because, although satisfactions are among the conditions of happiness, they are not its only conditions. Satisfactions are what come to a man from the outside, and they do in part determine happiness. But what is within the secret chambers of the man's own soul determines it too. Therefore however many satisfactions a man has, he will not be happy if the internal conditions of happiness are not present in him.

There is, however, a second consideration which, though much less obvious, is far more profoundly important. Some satisfactions, I shall say, contribute more to happiness, others less. The question then arises what determines which of two satisfactions, A and B, contributes most. On the answer to this question hang all-important consequences. I hold that the utilitarians, and also most ethical philosophers of the empirical tradition, as well as practically all ordinary men and women, have made the fatal mistake of supposing that the *intensity* of a satisfaction is one of the factors which determine the quantity of its contribution to happiness. They have supposed that the more intense a satisfaction, the more it contributes to happiness. As against this I maintain that *the intensity of a satisfaction has nothing whatever to do with the quantity of happiness which results from it*. A very intense satisfaction may, and indeed usually does, contribute less to happiness than a less intense satisfaction, even though the two might be considered in all other respects (such as duration, etc.) equal. For example, the satisfaction of sex is perhaps the most intense in human experience. And yet considered in itself—i.e., taken apart from such satisfactions as friendship and companionship which are often entwined with it

—it contributes very little to happiness. On the other hand, the esthetic character of one's surroundings, whether in the way of natural scenery or artifacts such as buildings, contribute a very great deal to happiness, even though the feelings produced by them may often be so faint that a man may not even notice their presence and may—especially if they are his habitual surroundings—take them entirely for granted.

What then does determine how much a given satisfaction contributes to happiness, if its intensity does not? I hold that the amount of its contribution is determined, either wholly or at least in by far its greatest part, by the *specific nature* of the satisfaction. By the specific nature of a satisfaction I mean that character of it which distinguishes it from other kinds of satisfaction. Thus the specific nature of sexual satisfaction is just that it is sexual. The specific nature of the satisfaction of friendship is just that it is the satisfaction of friendship, and not some other satisfaction such as that of sex. (In just the same way the specific nature of blue is its blueness, of green its greenness, and so on.)

No law can be stated which helps us to understand *why* a satisfaction of one specific nature yields more happiness than a satisfaction of another specific nature. We simply find in experience that it is so. It is a brute fact. Thousands of years of experience have taught the wisest of men to distinguish those satisfactions which contribute much to happiness from those which contribute little, and to arrange them roughly in some sort of order which constitutes a scale of values. For example, it has been found by long and bitter experience that the physical pleasures of eating, drinking, and sex, in spite of their intensity, bring little happiness; while the satisfactions of religion and friendship bring much more. The essential point is that it is upon the specific character of our satisfactions that the greatness of our happiness depends, and *not upon their intensity*. The mistake of supposing that it depends upon their intensity is the source of the great illusion which lures men on to pursue phantoms of pleasure instead of true sources of happiness; and which leads to disillusionment, cynicism, and disgust with life.

As I said, no "reason" can be given why a satisfaction of one specific nature should yield more happiness than a satisfaction of some other specific nature. The determination of this is entirely empirical, and the great moral teachers of the world are the men of genius who have made important discoveries in this sphere. When we begin to ask such detailed questions as what is the relation between happiness and particular satisfactions, such as those of sex, art, friendship, intellectual endeavour, religion, we find a mass of information awaiting us in their writings and sayings. Most of the maxims and moral precepts of such men as Jesus Christ, Buddha, Confucius, Marcus Aurelius, Epictetus, Plato, are essentially attempts to answer questions of just this kind. Thus the impressive array of warnings uttered by all the great moralists against over-indulgence in bodily pleasures means, in effect, that the universal experience of men—finding its utterance in these men of genius—is that bodily satisfactions, however intense, however great their own "size" or "volume," add extremely little to the "size" or "volume" of the happiness into which they enter. Of course these warnings are also based in part upon the more obvious fact that such over-indulgence leads to disease, pain, and positive dissatisfactions of various kinds. That is the meaning of them which lies blatantly upon the surface. Their deeper meaning is that, quite apart from these painful consequences of over-indulgence—even if they could be miraculously obliterated—satisfactions whose specific natures are bodily are poor contributors to happiness. Their intensity does not cure this. They are like coins of copper or lead, which may be large and heavy, but add little to one's wealth.

Again the saying that "It is more blessed to give than to receive" means that the satisfaction of giving adds more to happiness than the satisfaction of receiving. "Blessed are the pure in heart" means that purity of heart is a greater source of happiness than impurity. The great moral teachers of mankind are those who have made it their business to set before men *a true scale of values*, that is, a scale showing what satisfactions by their specific natures contribute more to happiness, what satisfactions contribute less. And it never occurred to any of them to suppose that this depended upon the intensity of the satisfactions. They were men of genius just because their vision penetrated through the great illusion which possesses the minds of common men.

These considerations should help us to understand better the apparent paradox that the greatness of our happiness does not necessarily correspond to the greatness of our satisfactions. For by a "great" satisfaction we usually mean an intense one. This is at least the most important part of our conception of the "amount" of a pleasure. The duration of it no doubt enters into our calculation, but it is the intensity which we mostly have in mind. And if we allow—as I think we must—that this is a perfectly reasonable concept of what is meant by the "quantity" of a pleasure, then we see at once why the quantity of a pleasure bears no relation to the greatness of our happiness. Those who with few and small pleasures are yet very happy will usually be found to be those who choose as sources of their happiness, not the intenser pleasures, but those satisfactions which, though themselves small (in intensity) yet yield great happiness. That is why a poor man rich in friendship is happier than a rich man with no friends. Friendship contributes more to happiness than riches do. Again the man who is loaded with satisfactions and is yet unhappy will usually be found to be he who chooses as sources of his happiness intense pleasures which have little happiness-value. For example, if a man makes the mistake of sacrificing his friendships for the sake of his "business"—which means in the end for the sake of money, motor cars, large houses, luxurious eating, jewelry for his wife—he loses his happiness because he gives up a source of great happiness in order to obtain intenser satisfactions which bring little joy.

I will now attempt to show that by adopting the view of the relation between happiness and satisfactions which I have advocated it is at last possible to give a complete solution to a problem which was, for the utilitarian, utterly unintelligible. The problem is well known, and may be presented here in the form of a dilemma. Utilitarianism implied that the criterion of the moral character of actions is solely the *quantity* of pleasure which they produce. But if so, it follows that no one pleasure can be regarded as *qualitatively* superior to any other. For this would be to introduce into the grounds of moral judgment a criterion other than quantity of pleasure. Hence if utilitarianism were to be self-consistent, it would have to take the view that there is nothing as such finer or nobler in the satisfactions of the mind or spirit than in the grossest pleasures of the body. All satisfactions must be for it on a dead level of equality, the only differences between them being differences of quantity. But this conclusion, so the critics of utilitarianism urged, is utterly repulsive to man's moral consciousness. It reduces utilitarianism to a "pig-philosophy" by putting even the noblest satisfactions of the mystic, the saint, the artist, the scientist, on no higher a level than the most animal pleasures of the body.

This is one horn of the dilemma. Now let us turn to the other. If, in order to avoid the unfortunate results just described, utilitarianism tried to find room within its borders for the idea of *qualitatively* higher and lower pleasures, if it admitted that some pleasures are morally of higher quality than others, then it contradicted its fundamental hypothesis. For if some pleasures are higher, others lower, there must be some *standard* by which they are judged higher and lower. What is this standard? It cannot be pleasure itself. It can only be some standard which is *outside* the pleasures themselves. But to admit this is to give up the primary article of the utilitarian faith, which is that things are to be judged better or worse solely by the standard of pleasure.

The upshot of the matter is that the consistent utilitarian cannot admit the existence of higher and lower pleasures. He is forced to put them all on the same level. And this— it is suggested—is a revolting and ignoble conclusion, a conclusion which the universal moral experience of mankind will repudiate.

How does our view of happiness solve this problem? I will say at the outset that in my opinion it is unquestionably true that some satisfactions are of intrinsically higher quality than others. No desires, no satisfactions—I should hold—are in themselves bad or immoral. It is always their context of circumstances that make them so. Hence the desires of the flesh are perfectly legitimate. They have a right to satisfaction. And they have their proper place in the economy of human life. But it does not at all follow that all satisfactions are equally good. The overwhelming consensus of the opinions of the great and wise men of all ages and nations testifies to the contrary. The satisfactions of the mind and spirit, in art, in science, in philosophy, in religion, are higher and nobler than the satisfactions of the flesh. To deny this is to fly in the face of deep human instincts which cannot—in the interest of a mere theory—be ignored.

In all the great religions and ethical systems of the world that which pertains to the mind (or "soul") is thought to be more noble than that which pertains to the body. This is an almost universal human belief—universal, at any rate, among all peoples who can make any claim to culture and civilization. At times, of course, it suffers distortion and exaggeration. It gives birth to puritanical or ascetic doctrines which, by the extremes to which they run, bring about their own downfall. Human nature protests against this violence, insists as against the extremist on the recognition of the proper claims of the body and its satisfactions to a place in the sun. At times, too, belief in the more noble nature of the mind becomes entangled with ideas which many think superstitious, with possibly fantastic claims regarding the soul's importance in the cosmic scheme, its origin and its destiny. We can discount all these exaggerations and perversions. We do not need to countenance them. But we must take seriously the fundamental belief in the superiority of the mind to the body from which these exaggerations and perversions are outgrowths. It is a deep and true intuition, an ineradicable human feeling, that in *some* sense, in *some* way (let the philosophers explain it how they will), *the mind is more noble than the body*. And from this it follows that the satisfactions of the mind are "higher" than those of the body. This is part of the wisdom of the ages; that is to say, it is the distillation of the moral experience of the most finely sensitive minds of the world. Somehow or other this practical ethical wisdom has to be incorporated into theoretical philosophy. To leave it out, still more to deny it, is to cut philosophy adrift from its roots in the soil of human moral experience. Such a procedure results in the sterility of mere *a priori* theorizing. And an ethical philosophy which does this, because it is divorced from man's actual moral experience, is radically *un*empirical.

I have said before that a certain weight is to be attached to the *feelings* of humanity—especially in regard to matters of value—inchoate, confused, and inarticulate though they be. Beware of the philosopher who thrusts aside all ideas which are based, as he expresses it, on "mere emotions." He has not learned that the intuitions of men (which, owing to his naïvely over-simple psychology, he miscalls emotions) often contain an inarticulate wisdom which points the way to a truth which it is the business of him, the philosopher, to extract, to articulate in concepts and logically justify. The men of wisdom are wiser than the men of intellect. It is the clever fool with his logic chopping who derides or ignores the vague intuitions of the masses of men.

The question for us, however, is, what does this belief— the belief that the mind is "higher" than the body— *mean?* As it issues from the lips of religious leaders and practical moralists it is a mere incomprehensible moral dogma. This is because it is the expression of feeling or instinct, the inner import of which no one understands, the rational justification of which is—so far as the religious leaders and practical moralists are concerned—utterly lacking. It is for philosophy to illuminate with thought the blind obscurity of mere feeling. If the feeling is right, is true—as I hold that in this case it is—it is for philosophy to mediate it, to compel it to assume cognitive form, to exhibit the rational structure which is potential within it. And in the present case this is to be done by asking and answering the question by what *standard* are the satisfactions of the mind judged "higher" than the satisfactions of the body? And for us in particular the question presents itself in the following form: By what interpretation can this belief be made consistent with a philosophy which finds happiness itself to be the supreme standard of moral value? How, in short, can satisfactions be higher and lower if there is no outside standard to judge them by, if satisfaction (or happiness) is itself the only standard of judgment?

The attempt to interpret philosophically the belief that some satisfactions are higher, some lower, has been historically the source of much metaphysical moonshine. It has been held that the obvious necessity for a standard outside pleasure, by which pleasure is to be judged, points to some criterion of judgment outside of experience altogether. We can only understand this mystery, we are told, in terms of the Absolute, only if we accept some such philosophy as that of absolute idealism. Or else—it has been asserted—we must introduce a teleological conception of the universe at large. The satisfactions of the spirit are higher because of the spiritual nature of the whole universe, because they forward the cosmic plan in which the movement towards spirit, and away from matter, is the leading idea.

I do not assert that there is no cosmic plan. I only assert that I do not know whether there is or not, and that if there is I have no understanding whatever of what the plan may be. And I am certain that those who talk big about the Absolute and about teleology are as completely ignorant of the matter as I am. And for this reason, if for no other, it is futile to make either the cosmic plan or the Absolute the standard of higher and lower satisfactions. Nor is it necessary to attempt to do this. For the explanation of the riddle, I should say, lies under our noses in quite ordinary, empirical, and mundane considerations. It is capable of an entirely naturalistic solution. It is therefore unnecessary to seek for an explanation beyond the stars.

How, then are we to make the belief that some satisfactions are higher than others consistent with the view that happiness is the sole end of moral action? My contention is that this was impossible for the classical utilitarians because of their faulty analysis of the idea of happiness, but that the conception which we have advanced renders the solution easy.

It was impossible for the utilitarians because for them a man's happiness was *identical* with his pleasures—identical in the same sense as a whole is identical with the sum of its parts. (The utilitarians could, of course, in one sense distinguish happiness from pleasure. They could distinguish it in the sense in which we distinguish a whole from its parts—an orange, for example, from any individual segment of the orange. I shall say, simply for the sake of brevity, that the utilitarians identified happiness and pleasure. When I do so, I am not to be understood as having overlooked the obvious point that the whole can be distinguished from any one of its parts.)

What is required to justify the assertion that some pleasures are higher than others is some standard of judgment *outside* the pleasures themselves. This contention of the critics of utilitarianism is irrefutable. Now for the utilitarians happiness was the final and absolute criterion of moral value. But as pleasure was (in the sense explained) identical with happiness, this meant that pleasure (or a sum of pleasures) was the final and absolute criterion of moral value. Therefore there could not be, for them, any standard of value outside pleasure by reference to which pleasure itself could be judged. To admit the existence of such a standard would have been to destroy the foundations of their philosophy.

But for us *happiness is not identical with pleasure* or, in our language, with satisfaction. It is not identical either with any particular satisfaction or with any sum of satisfactions. It is, therefore, open to us, as it was not to the utilitarians, to make *happiness* the standard by which satisfactions are judged higher or lower. Happiness, for us, lies outside satisfactions. It is, therefore, capable of performing the office of a standard by which satisfactions can be judged. The solution of our puzzle is, accordingly, this. *Those satisfactions are higher which are found in experience to contribute more to happiness. Those satisfactions are lower which are found in experience to contribute less to happiness.* This is the conceptual articulation, and the rational justification, of the confused human feeling that the things of the mind are nobler than the things of the body, and that the mind itself is nobler than the body.

It may be objected that this solution does not accord with the empirical evidence afforded by man's moral experience. Happiness is the standard by which pleasures are judged. But is this really what the moralists mean when they say that some satisfactions are higher, some lower? Our solution purports to be an interpretation of human feelings and intuitions regarding this matter. Is it really an interpretation of them, or is it not rather the substitution of a quite different idea?

I believe that it is a genuine interpretation. That the satisfactions of the body, although they have their place in life, do not yield true happiness, that the things of the mind and the spirit are the only possible bases of a happy life—this seems to me to be the hackneyed theme of the world's wise men in all ages. Is not the whole burthen of their impeachment of sensual pleasures simply this, that however "intense" may be the satisfactions of sex, food, drink, and the like; however strongly men may *think* and *expect* that they will find in them the happiness of which they are in search; yet actual experience shows that men who think thus are under the spell of a powerful delusion, that their thinking is false and their expectations mistaken, because *in fact* these things yield very little happiness? And when the things of the mind, the pleasures of art, of science, of philosophy, or the satisfactions of love and friendship, are praised by the wise men, does not this praise in effect mean that these things, in contrast with animal pleasures, yield a more solid satisfaction, a truer and more lasting happiness? Is not happiness in all these cases the real standard by which pleasures are judged higher or lower? If so, there lies behind our solution the solid support of man's actual moral experience. The solution is truly empirical.

Vaguely, confusedly, it is recognized by most men that happiness is not the same thing as pleasure, that there is somehow and somewhere a difference, however difficult it may be to explain where the difference lies. Men know

this because they know that to increase satisfactions is
not necessarily to increase happiness; and that many men
are happy who have little, many men miserable who have
much. These obvious facts stand in glaring contradiction
to the smug utilitarian conception of happiness as a mere
aggregate of pleasures, and cause men to turn away in
disgust from a philosophy which is so false to their moral
experience. Our view of happiness seeks to take account
of these facts, and to interpret them conceptually. And
it finds that by doing so it is easy enough to understand
what is at the back of the universal human feeling that
some pleasures are better than others. One has only to
make the distinction between pleasure and happiness to
see that those pleasures are better which yield more
happiness.

This solution of the problem of higher and lower satisfactions is really already contained in what was said on an
earlier page about the *specific nature* of satisfactions.
Whether a particular kind of satisfaction contributes
much or little to the happiness of human beings depends,
we saw, upon its specific nature. This is no different from
saying that certain specific kinds of satisfaction contribute
more to happiness than do certain other specific satisfactions; and that this is so independently of the "quantities" or intensities of the several satisfactions. Satisfactions are therefore "high" or "low" by virtue of their
specific natures (their qualities) and not by virtue of any
quantitative aspect which they may possess.

We must not, of course, fall into the mistake of supposing that the higher or lower quality of a satisfaction
is the *same thing as* its specific nature. This would be like
thinking that the pleasantness of green is the same thing
as the green. One specific nature carries with it one degree

of value, another carries another degree of value; just as one colour carries one degree of pleasantness, another another. Nor must one think that the higher or lower value can be found in the specific nature of a satisfaction by analysis, or that it can be deduced from the specific nature. The connection between *this* specific nature and *this* value is not a connection of implication or logical necessity. We have to "wait on experience," as Hume would have expressed it, to discover what value is attached to what specific nature. It is simply a fact that bodily satisfactions yield little happiness (that is, are of low value). And this fact had to be discovered in experience by long generations of men. The men who discovered these facts were the moral geniuses of the world. There is no ascertainable reason why the facts should be as they are. Thus the mind is nobler than the body, not because it is "divine" or immortal or shines like a star, not because it is ethereal or non-substantial or can be in two places at once, but simply because its peculiar sensitivities yield men more happiness than do the sensitivities of the body. And why this should happen to be so, no man can tell.

CHAPTER 7

THE GENERAL LAW OF MORALS

WE have been in search of a single principle of morals such that all particular duties could be deduced from it—a general law which should bear to particular moral maxims somewhat the same relation as the law of gravitation bears to the laws of Kepler or to the particular uniformities of motion observed to be pursued by particular heavenly bodies. We do not, of course, expect the same kind of mathematical precision and accuracy either in the formulation of the moral law itself or in the deduction from it of particular duties as we find in the case of the law of gravitation. For we are in the region of the concrete and human, not in the region of mathematical abstractions. But apart from this there is no reason why the analogy should not hold good. There is no reason why it should not be at least sufficiently valid to be helpful.

It might be supposed that we have now discovered the general law of morals in the idea that men ought to increase the sum-total of human happiness to the greatest possible extent. This is no doubt unprecisely expressed. But if it were given accurate formulation, would it not be the law of morals of which we are in search? The answer, I am afraid, must be, No. This is not the moral law at all. It is only part of it.

For according to the view of morality which I wish to unfold, not every activity which tends to increase human happiness is a specifically *moral* activity. Every moral activity is an activity which increases, or aims at increasing, happiness. But not every activity which increases happiness is moral. In other words actions which increase happiness constitute a *genus*, within which we shall find moral actions as one *species*. There are two other characters, besides the character of producing happiness, which an action must have if it is to be morally good. These are the characters of *unselfishness* and *justice*. These are the *differentiae* which distinguish distinctively moral actions from other happiness-producing actions. We will say that there are three concepts which have to be introduced into the definition of morality, the concepts namely of (1) happiness-production, (2) unselfishness or altruism, and (3) justice. Neither of the two latter can be reduced by analysis to happiness-production. In the end we shall discover that the concept of unselfishness can be reduced to that of justice. So that strictly speaking only two concepts, those of happiness-production and justice, are necessary for the definition of morality. But we shall find it advantageous to proceed for the present as if all three concepts were necessary. We shall treat unselfishness as if it were independent of justice. At a later time in this chapter we will correct this by reducing the former to the latter.

What we have to show, then, is that the mere fact that an action produces, or increases, human happiness is not by itself enough to make that action morally good. To be morally good the action must exhibit the further characters of altruism and justice. In order to demonstrate this I shall talk in terms of the classical utilitarian theory, and I shall even go the length of talking about *units* of happiness. Admittedly such language is metaphorical and inaccurate. But it is extraordinarily convenient for purposes of simple exposition. Without it I should have to use many cumbersome and round-about phrases. And if the essential ideas are grasped in a simple manner by this means, allowance can afterwards be made for the inaccurate and metaphorical character of the language.

Firstly, then, we have to show that the concept of unselfishness must be introduced into the definition of morality, and that it is independent of the concept of happiness-production and cannot be reduced to it. Suppose that there were only ten people in the world, and that I, who am one of them, perform an action which produces ten units of happiness; but that all these ten units accrue to myself, none of the other nine persons getting any. (It should further be supposed that none of them is injured by my action.) My action has then increased the sum-total of the world's happiness by ten units. But is it a morally good action? I think the answer is that although it is not morally bad—since I have a perfect right to increase my own happiness, as long as I injure no one else—it is yet in no way specifically good. It possesses no positive moral value. It is neither moral or immoral, but merely non-moral.

The view I am taking is that not every happiness-producing action possesses *ipso facto* any positive moral value. Only those actions possess such value which aim at increasing the happiness *of others*. By increasing my own happiness I may be increasing the sum-total of the happiness of the world. But I am not thereby doing anything which is specifically moral. My action is perfectly legitimate, provided I do not decrease anyone else's happiness. But it fails to sound the specific note of altruism which is a necessary ingredient of a morally good act. If this were not so, one might have to admit that an utterly selfish man, who succeeded in amassing for himself an enormous wealth of satisfactions while helping no one else, was a better man morally than an unselfish person who amassed less but gave generously to all. For the former would be increasing the sum-total of the world's happiness more than the latter.

It is true that pedants have sometimes introduced "duties to myself" into their classifications of duty. It is also true that one may, if one pleases, *define* the word morality in such a way as to make it cover actions which increase one's own happiness, while not increasing anyone else's. It is further true, of course, that logically one is entitled to define morality either in this or in any other arbitrary way. But to define it thus renders pointless most of the questions which one can ask about morality. For example, the question "Why should I be moral?"— which is the problem of the basis of moral obligation—has point if it is taken to mean "Why should I increase the happiness *of other people?*" For it is not self-evident why I should do this if it in no way benefits me. There is a real problem here. But there is no point whatever in asking why a man should increase his own happiness, since no one would wish to do anything else. The ideas of duty and obligation only arise where there is at least a possibility of a clash between inclination and morality, a clash between what I want to do and what I ought to do. This is not to preach the dismal doctrine that duty must always be contrary to inclination. On the contrary, the morally best men are those in whom duty and inclination coincide. They are those blessed souls who seem to be good by nature and without effort. But to render the idea of obligation meaningful at all it must at least be *possible* that inclination should be opposed to duty.

If these arguments do not sufficiently convince, let us adduce another. Go back to the imaginary case of the human society consisting of only ten persons. Suppose now that I, who am one of them, have the choice between two actions A and B; and that action A will produce ten units of happiness all concentrated in myself, while action B will produce ten units which will be distributed in such a manner that I have only one, or only some, of them, while the rest go to benefit my fellow mortals. Which of these two actions will be judged morally better? Obviously action B. Why? Not because it produces more happiness in the world than action A. For both actions produce the same amount, namely ten units. The reason is that action B possesses the character of unselfishness which is absent from action A. If quantity of happiness were the sole criterion of moral value, then both actions would have to be judged equally good. Therefore unselfishness is a criterion of moral value quite distinct from, and independent of, quantity of happiness-production. It cannot be reduced to happiness-production because an unselfish action does not necessarily produce more happiness than a selfish one. In fact it is quite possible that it may produce less. A man may give up a great happiness for the sake of some one else's lesser happiness. The quality of altruism has not primarily to do with the *quantity* of happiness produced. It has to do with its *distribution*.

The notion of unselfishness, as I have used it in the above passages, is vague and undefined. I shall return to the matter of its more accurate definition later. I have established the necessity of introducing the concept into the definition of morality. And I have also established its independence of the concept of quantity of happiness-production, that is to say, the fact that it cannot be reduced to the latter concept. I will now attempt to do the same for the concept of justice.

Let us provisionally define justice as the fair and equitable distribution of satisfactions. The definition is doubtless open to various objections, for example, that it is both ambiguous and circular. For the present that does not matter. It places the idea before our minds, and we can attend to niceties of definition later.

Imagine, as before, a human society of ten persons. This time I am not a member of it. But I can by my actions affect the happiness of its members. I am some sort of outsider—an angel perhaps. Or if you prefer it, there are really eleven persons in this society, of whom I am one, but my actions only affect the other ten, and not myself. Now suppose I have the choice of two actions, C and D. Each of the actions will produce ten units of happiness. Since by hypothesis my actions are not to affect myself, it must be supposed that I do not in either case get any of the ten units. But action C will concentrate all ten units in one single member of the society. Action D will distribute them equally, so that each member gets one. Which of these two will be the better action morally?

Perhaps you will say that it depends on how "deserving" the members are. It might be the case that the one member who in action C got all ten units deserved them (whether by having helped me to produce them or in some other way) whereas the other nine deserved nothing. In that case action C would be the better. In another set of circumstances action D might be better. Without further information you could not tell.

There are two ways out of this difficulty. One is to point out that by introducing the question of "deserts" we are introducing an unnecessary complication which obscures the real point. Suppose, if you like, that all the ten persons concerned are equally deserving (or undeserving). In that case, it will, I think, be clear that action D will be morally preferable to action C. Why? Not because it produces more happiness. For both actions were to produce the same ten units. Therefore the criterion by which you are judging that action D is better than action C is distinct from, and independent of, the criterion of quantity of happiness-production. Why then? Is it because action D possesses the character of altruism, while action C does not? No. This cannot be the reason because, by hypothesis, I myself was not to benefit by either action, so that either action will be equally unselfish. Therefore the criterion of judgment in this case is distinct from, and independent of, the criterion of altruism. It is accordingly a third criterion. And I think it is clear that you are judging action D better than action C simply because it distributes the units of happiness more fairly than does action C. In other words it is more just. Justice, therefore, is an independent criterion of moral value which cannot be reduced either to happiness-production or to altruism.

The same results will be reached if we take the other way out of the difficulty which you raised about the respective deserts of the different parties. This way consists in accepting your statement that whether action C or action D is to be judged better depends upon the merits of the parties. For if this is so, it must be pointed out that you have admitted that either C might be better, or D might be better. You have admitted that one might be better than the other. But by what criterion? Not by that of the amount of happiness produced, since that in both cases would be the same. Not by that of altruism, for that too is equally present in both cases. So that you have admitted a third independent criterion. And I do not think you will dispute any longer that this criterion to which you would yourself appeal is justice.

We are now drawing nearer to a possible definition of the general law of morals. It is not anything so simple as to contain nothing but the bare obligation to increase to the maximum possible extent the amount of happiness in the world. It must contain as well these other factors of altruism and justice. We can say, so far, that to be moral a man must do three things. He must try to increase the happiness of the world. He must do this unselfishly, that is, it is the happiness of others that he must try to increase. And he must do it justly, that is to say, he must see that the happiness which he gives to others is justly distributed among those others. All this is, I think, true. But unfortunately it is full of ambiguities, some at least of which we must try to clear up.

Let us begin with the concept of unselfishness. What does this mean? What actually does the command "be unselfish" oblige me to do? And here the chief difficulty, I think, is this. The mere command to be unselfish does not apprise me *how far I am to go* with this unselfishness. No doubt I am to minister more to the satisfactions of other people, less to my own. But how much more, and how much less? Am I to give up everything I possess to other people? Am I to deny myself all satisfactions, keep none for myself, give all away? Does unselfishness mean absolute self-sacrifice, absolute self-abnegation?

Perhaps there are some who would say that this is what it does mean. Self-sacrifice, they would assert, is an absolute end in itself. But I cannot think that this is a rational answer. To follow such a precept literally would simply be to commit suicide. A man who literally denied all his own desires and interests in order to benefit other people—allowed himself no food, for example, but gave it all away to the poor and hungry—would be dead in a few days. And this cannot be what the moral life demands. Therefore there must be some sort of compromise between my attention to my own satisfactions and my attention to those of other people. There must be some sort of compromise between the principle of altruism and that of egoism. "Be unselfish" must mean "be more unselfish than you are now, or than most men usually are." It cannot mean "Be so completely unselfish as entirely to disregard your own interests."

But if once this is admitted a fresh problem immediately springs out of the admission, namely, on what *principle* is the "how much more" or "how much less" to be decided? We have to find the proper compromise between absolute altruism and absolute egoism. By absolute altruism I mean the complete and suicidal obliteration by a man of every single one of his own interests and needs in order that he may act solely on behalf of the needs and interests of others. By absolute egoism I mean egoism which is entirely unmixed with even the slightest trace of altruistic feeling or action. Both extremes are, of course, abstractions. They are not found, so far as I know, in any actual human being—at any rate in any sane or normal human being. If cases of either kind do occur, they are pathological. These, then, are the two poles somewhere between which lies all human action, and somewhere between which lies the point of proper compromise. Between the two extreme points we have to find the point at which a right, proper, or moral balance between altruism and egoism is located. The problem now before us is—by what *principle* is this point to be determined?

There must be *some* principle. Or at least to suppose that there is none is equivalent to supposing that there is in reality practically no such thing as a moral law at all. Morality tells me to be unselfish. But what does this mean? It means at any rate that absolute egoism is barred. But is that all? Would a man who lived three score years and ten and who in all that period did only one trifling altruistic action—say gave a penny to his own son—every other action throughout his entire life-span being completely selfish, would such a man be obeying the moral law? Would he be what we should call a good man? Yet he would, by means of his one good action, have removed himself some distance—perhaps we might say an infinitesimal distance—away from the point of absolute egoism, and along the line which joins that point to the other extreme point of absolute altruism. He would be somewhere on the line between the two extremes. Morality, if it is to be a reality, must in some way specify the *right* point on the line for a man to occupy. A moral code which told a man only to occupy a point somewhere between the two extremes, but specified nothing further, would be like a Government department which ordered a light-ship to be anchored somewhere between New York and Southampton, but gave no further directions. In other words it would be entirely useless.

Either the law of morals must contain within itself some principle by which this question is to be decided, or the matter has to be left to the arbitrary caprice of each individual person. And this, of course, would spell moral chaos. What, then, can the principle be?

It is futile to reply, aping Aristotle, that what we have to do is to find the happy mean, and that where the mean lies will depend upon the particular circumstances of each person and each case. All this is no doubt quite true, but it is not helpful. It only states the problem over again without doing anything towards solving it. To say that we must find the mean is only to say that we must find the proper point between the two extremes. This is what we already know, and the question remains unanswered how we are to find it. When we said that morality involves some sort of a compromise between altruism and egoism, we have said in effect that it is a mean between the two. "Compromise" and "mean," in this context, are simply two words for the same idea.

As to the statement that the proper compromise will be different for different people and in different circumstances, this is also true, but not to the point. We have seen all along [1] that the law of morals will be a general law which will give different results according as it is applied to different cases—just as the law of gravitation results in parabolic orbits in some cases, elliptical orbits in others. We have not only admitted this, but insisted upon it, because the failure to understand it is one of the breeding grounds of ethical relativity. Thus the mere fact that the point where the mean is held to be will depend upon persons and circumstances in no way avoids the necessity of discovering a principle in the matter. In fact it is precisely this which makes a general principle necessary, just as it is the various different kinds of orbital behaviour of the different heavenly bodies which necessitates our looking for some universal law under which they can all be subsumed. Suppose that, in the moral field, we know all the circumstances of a particular case and a particular person, we still require a principle to

[1] See especially Chapter 4.

decide where, in *that* particular case and for *that* particular person, the proper mean is. The very fact that we think it will lie at different points in different cases itself implies the existence of some principle. For if none existed, the decision would have to be arbitrary, and there would be nothing to prevent it from being arbitrarily decided that the mean should lie at the same point in all cases. And this is probably what men would decide, if it were possible, since it would be so simple and convenient. What renders this impossible is precisely the presence of a principle to which all particular decisions have to conform.

We have discovered three distinct criteria of moral value, namely happiness-production, altruism, and justice. Now I suggest that the principle of which we are in search is none other than the principle of the third of these criteria, namely justice. We have defined justice provisionally as the fair and equitable distribution of satisfactions. This is vague enough. But even leaving the definition as it stands, we can see that the idea is relevant here, and that it contains, in essence, the solution of our difficulty. The essence of the solution is this. Suppose that we require in a particular case to know where to take our stand between the two extremes of altruism and egoism. Suppose we have to decide between advancing our own interests and advancing those of some other person which are inconsistent with ours. In these circumstances the question which we ought to ask ourselves is: what action will lead to a fair and equitable distribution of satisfactions as between ourselves and that other person? The proper degree of unselfishness for me in my dealings with you is that degree which will result in both you and I receiving a fair and equitable share of the available satisfactions. In short my duty is simply to be fair to you while also having the right to be fair to myself. The unselfishness which morality commands is the unselfishness of treating all other people with as much consideration as I treat myself. The selfishness which morality condemns is that of treating myself as a special case, or as a privileged person. It is that of taking more than my proper share of satisfactions, and giving other people less than theirs. It is that of making exceptions in favour of myself.

In all this, of course, we are using terms such as "fair," "equitable," and "proper share," of which we do not as yet know the exact meaning. Give myself my proper share, and no more. Yes, but what *is* my proper share? Unless I know that, the problem is not solved. This means simply that we are operating still with the undefined notion of justice, or at least with the notion defined only in the vaguest way. But I cannot solve all parts of the problem at once and in one breath. Give me time. I will come to all that in due course. But in the meanwhile I want first to make another point. And for the moment I shall continue to operate with the still vague notion of justice.

I will attempt to support the suggested solution of our problem by asking the question: by what principle, if not by that of justice, is the question of the proper mean between altruism and egoism to be decided? If the reader is disposed, for some reason, to reject the principle of justice as the criterion which ought to be used here, what other principle can he suggest? Some principle there must be, otherwise the ship of morality will be adrift without anchorage on the wide sea which lies between the far distant points of extreme altruism and extreme egoism.

The question is therefore urgent. It cannot be left unde-
cided. It is not open to the objector to reject the suggestion of justice and yet to put nothing in its place. Criticism, to be valuable here, must be constructive.

Could the required principle be that of happiness-
production? Could one, that is to say, urge that a man
in deciding how far he ought to advance his own interests
and how far he ought to give way to the adverse interests
of his neighbour, should determine this question by asking
what division of satisfactions between himself and his
neighbour will give rise to the greatest total quantity of
happiness? (This might refer either to the total quantity
of happiness of himself and his neighbour, or to the total
quantity of happiness of humanity. For our immediate
purposes it does not matter which is meant. But presumably the final criterion would have to be the happiness of
humanity.) This is a very natural suggestion to make.
It seems to fit in very well with the general principles of
utilitarianism or of any other happiness philosophy. And
no doubt it is the answer to our question which many
would give. They would, that is to say, attempt to justify
the principle of justice by treating it as a means of advancing the happiness of humanity in general. And they
would point, in confirmation of their views, to the un-
doubted facts that the failure of justice among mankind
does in general lead to an increase of unhappiness, while
its firm establishment leads to an increase of happiness.
The view, therefore, is a very plausible one. But it will
not work.

For without denying any of the facts to which appeal
is made, it should be obvious from considerations adduced
in the earlier part of this chapter that this cannot be the
final analysis of the matter, nor the final justification of

justice. For it is inconsistent with the proof we already gave of the proposition that the concept of justice is independent of the concept of happiness-production and cannot be reduced to it. No doubt in many cases—perhaps even in the vast majority of cases—the doing of justice does increase the total quantity of human happiness. But as we showed before, there are possible cases in which this would not be true, but in which we should *nevertheless* value justice and think it morally good. Thus if there were ten units of happiness to be distributed among ten persons (all supposed to be equally deserving) we should think it morally better to distribute them "fairly" than to concentrate them all on one of the ten persons. Justice, or fairness, therefore, is something which we think to be morally good *even when it does not increase the total of human happiness in any way*. And from this it follows that our thinking it good cannot be because—or at any rate not wholly because—it increases the total amount of happiness in the world. Justice is something good quite apart from its tendency—a tendency which it undoubtedly has—to increase happiness. It is an independent value.

Happiness-production, therefore, is not the principle by which the proper mean between egoism and altruism is to be determined. It is an absolute necessity that we find some principle. I suggest that of justice. And I am at a loss to know what other feasible suggestion could be made.

It will be noticed that the result of our procedure is to define altruism in terms of justice. (By altruism I mean here the proper or moral degree of altruism. And I shall use the term in this sense in future. If I wish to refer to that maximum degree which is the extreme pole of the egoistic-altruistic opposition I shall call it absolute altruism.) Altruism consists in being fair and just as between myself and all my fellow human beings. And it is in this way that—as we forecast at the beginning of this chapter—the concept of unselfishness is reduced to the concept of justice. Altruism, as now appears, is merely a particular case of justice. Justice in general means—still sticking to our vague provisional definition—the fair and equitable distribution of satisfactions among all persons. Altruism means the fair and equitable distribution of satisfactions as between *myself* and other persons. I am just when I divide satisfactions up among different persons in a fair manner. I am altruistic when one of the persons among whom the satisfactions are justly divided by me is myself. Altruism means doing justice in a cause in which I am both the judge and also one of the parties. Justice is a genus. Altruism is one species of it. The notion of justice is therefore more fundamental than the notion of altruism.

We have defined altruism in terms of justice. But we have not yet defined justice in any satisfactory way, and to do so would seem to be our next task. We have seen that it is equivalent to fair and equitable distribution of satisfactions. But what is fair? And what is equitable? These are only synonyms for the word just. Hence to substitute them for the word just as we have so far done is not to give any analysis of the idea of justice.

Now the notion of justice is, in its bare essence, I should say, very simple and easy to define. It is true that there are, connected with it, a variety of very difficult and complicated problems. But I believe that a careful analysis of these problems would show that they are all in reality practical in their nature. That is to say, they are not concerned with the nature of the concept of justice itself, but with the problem of its application to the com-

plexities of actual life.   Many, perhaps most, political
problems are of this kind.   What divides political parties
is not a number of different conceptions of justice, but a
number of different views as to what in practice conforms
to the notion of justice.   Thus the socialist will argue that
the present distribution of wealth is unjust.   The indi-
vidualist will argue either that it is just, or at any rate
that it is less unjust than the socialist thinks and more
just than the kind of distribution the socialist wants.
They both profess to march under the same banner of
justice.   In practice, of course, neither party is ever quite
honest.   The theories of both are to some extent governed
by their interests.   But we have to discount that, and
assume that both are intellectually honest and have
regard only for the truth.   And if so, or in so far as it is so,
it is not at all clear that different conceptions of justice
are involved in their opposing political views.   What is
much more likely is that the immense tangle of facts with
which the politician has to deal renders it exceedingly
difficult to know what measures and what institutions will
work out justly in practice; and that differences of political opinion are really differences of view on this question.
We, of course, are not concerned with any of these problems of practical application.   They do not belong to the
domain of the philosopher, but to that of the statesman.

Justice, then, is a simple idea.   And it may be defined
as *the recognition* (I mean, of course, the recognition in
practical action, not merely theoretical or intellectual
recognition) *of the intrinsic equality of all persons as persons*.   Another way of stating the same idea is to say that
it is the recognition of the truth *that I = I*, i.e., that
every I is intrinsically, or as an I, equal to every other I.

Actually, of course, men are unequal in all kinds of different ways—in ability, in goodness, in the extent and character of their needs, in the nature of their surrounding circumstances. But all these differences are *extrinsic*, that is, they do not arise from the essentials of the persons as persons, but from the fact that each person is this or that particular sort of person. One man is hungry, another sated (difference of needs). One is good, another bad (difference of merits or deserts). One is stupid, another clever (difference of ability). One is fortunate, another unfortunate (difference of surrounding circumstances). But all these differences are extrinsic, because none of them is of the essence of personality. To be a person, a man need not be hungry. And he need not be sated. And so of the other differences. None of them are essential to being a person. None of them are intrinsic to personality.

Now justice does not deny any of these extrinsic differences between persons. Nor does it deny that persons must be treated differently on the basis of their extrinsic differences. It does not deny, for example, that a hungry man may justly be given more than a sated person, nor that a good man may deserve more than a bad man. It can fully admit that both needs and deserts should be taken into account in the distribution of satisfactions. What it does deny, however, is that there ought ever to be any difference of treatment between different persons *except* on the basis of extrinsic differences of circumstances, character, or what not. It denies that there ought to be any different treatment of different persons simply as persons. It says that *intrinsically* all persons are equal.

This, it might be said, is self-evident, and therefore pointless, since there *are* no differences between persons other than extrinsic differences. According to the account just given, all differences whatever between persons are

extrinsic, and no such things as intrinsic differences exist
at all. And this would indeed be a very good way of expressing the principle of justice. The principle simply
states that there are no intrinsic differences between
persons. This, in fact, is the same as saying that they are
all intrinsically equal. And since this arises from the mere
definition of extrinsic, it is a pointless analytic proposition
without content. No one could possibly deny it, and
therefore there can be no point in asserting it.

And yet people do deny it—in their *actions*, if not
theoretically and intellectually. *Practically* to deny it is
in fact the root of all injustice. And we can best see this,
and see at the same time the point of the principle, if we
take for examination that particular type of justice which
we have called altruism. Suppose that there is a question
how certain satisfactions are to be divided between me
and my neighbour. And suppose that I alone have the
power to decide this question. I can take all, or give all,
or divide as I please. This is the sort of situation which
tests whether a man is selfish or unselfish, just or unjust.
Now justice does not necessarily ordain that I ought to
make an equal division. If all our respective needs, deserts, and other relevant circumstances were identical,
then the just division would be an equal division. But if
either my needs or my deserts are greater than my neighbour's, I may be acting justly and with perfectly proper
altruism if I assign to myself more than I do to him. Injustice and selfishness will only arise if I give myself
more, not on the basis of any extrinsic differences, but
*because I am attaching to my own personality an intrin-
sically higher value than I attach to his*. I am unjust
and selfish if I give myself more, on no proper grounds
such as deserts or needs, but simply because *I am I*. I am

then forgetting or denying that he is also an I and, simply as such, is entitled to as much as I am. The root of all selfishness, and indeed in the end the root of all evil, lies in the fact that each man tends to prefer himself simply because he is himself, and apart from any question of needs or deserts or any other circumstances. This is the denial of justice. And justice simply means the principle that, apart from such special needs, deserts, qualities, circumstances, all men are entitled to the same treatment. Intrinsically—and the word intrinsically simply means "apart from such special needs, deserts, qualities, circumstances"—all persons are of equal value and are entitled to identical treatment.

This principle is embodied in jurisprudence in the maxim that all men are equal before the law. This is not a denial of the obvious differences and inequalities which exist among men. Nor does the law divide up things equally between all men. It takes account of extrinsic differences, and bases upon them its differences of treatment. But it insists that, apart from these extrinsic differences, no differences of treatment are justified. It insists that no one can claim *privilege*, none can claim that, apart from special superiorities in his deserts, his abilities, or his circumstances, he is entitled to more consideration than other people. The equality of all men before the law is thus the juridical expression of the philosophical principle of the intrinsic equality of all persons as persons.

Another way of expressing the same idea is to say that justice is *impartiality*. And it may be useful occasionally to refer to it in terms of this concept.

We are accordingly now in a position to formulate the general law of morals. We began by pointing out that it must embody the three concepts of happiness-production, altruism, and justice. But we reduced altruism to justice, so that altruism can be left out of the definition. The moral law is: *Act always so as to increase human happiness as much as possible. And at the same time act on the principle that all persons, including yourself, are intrinsically of equal value.* The words "including yourself" are really redundant. But they are inserted in order to emphasize that the duty of justice includes the duty of altruism.

CHAPTER 8

SOME COROLLARIES

IN the last chapter I showed that altruism can be reduced by analysis to justice. In consequence the moral law was defined in terms of happiness-production and justice, and the concept of altruism disappeared altogether from the final statement of it. It is now desirable to reverse this process and to state the law in terms of altruism, leaving out the concept of justice. For *theoretically and logically* the notion of justice is more fundamental than that of altruism; and we have so far been concerned with logical analysis. But *practically and psychologically* the notion of altruism is far more important than that of justice. And it is very important for the further development of the views for which I am contending that this should be made clear. It is important that the law should be statable in terms of altruism, because it is by the mark of altruism, rather than by the mark of justice, that morality is commonly recognized. All the great ethical codes of the world stress altruism as the essence of morality. "Do unto others as you would that they should do unto you." This is commonly thought to express in a sentence the essential spirit of Christian morality. And the spirit which it stresses is simply the spirit of unselfishness, of caring for the happiness of others. Now it is certainly important to realize that the analysis of morality which was given in the last chapter is not really at variance with the implicit account of it which breathes through the great ethical and religious systems of the world. For we are not inventing a new morality, but attempting to interpret philosophically that morality which is as old as the world. Superficially there may appear to be a discrepancy here between morality as taught by the wise men of all ages and as interpreted in the last chapter. For they have laid the emphasis on altruism, while we have made justice central, and treated altruism as a mere case of it, and therefore as less fundamental and essential than justice.

If, however, the matter be properly examined, it will be seen that there is no real discrepancy. For in practice injustice is always caused by selfish motives, and justice always implies altruistic motives. In spite of their logical relation of genus and species, justice and altruism are, *in practice*, convertible terms.

The simplest way of showing that this is so is to take some such case as the following. Suppose that I am to judge between two persons, A and B; I am to divide between them certain satisfactions. Suppose that I do this unjustly, giving to A more than his share, and to B less. So long as no question is asked about my psychology, my motives for doing this, it might appear that we have here a case of injustice which is not a case of selfishness. For it would appear on the face of it that A and B are receiving between them all the available satisfactions and that I myself am getting nothing. But suppose it be asked, *why* did I favour A? Assuming, of course, that this was not a case of mere mistake on my part, assuming that I knew well enough what I was doing, then it will *invariably* be found that my favouritism was impelled by some selfish motive. Perhaps I was bribed. Or if nothing so crude is suggested, still it may have been the case that A was my son, or my friend, or my friend's son. Or perhaps it was merely that A was, like me, an

Englishman, while B was a foreigner. I must have had *some* reason of my own for wanting A to have more than B. What I was doing, then, was to indulge my own personal and selfish desires. My judgment was determined by considerations of *my* satisfaction. I was selfish. I was interested when I ought to have been disinterested. It is only when we leave out the practical and psychological point of view that it appears possible that there should be cases of injustice which are not cases of selfishness. In practice there cannot be such cases, because a man must have a selfish motive for being unjust. To be selfish is always in concrete cases to be unjust, and to be unjust is always to be selfish. It is therefore really indifferent whether we say that the essence of the moral law is to forbid injustice, or whether we say that it is to forbid selfishness. And it follows that it is indifferent whether we say that it commands justice or that it commands altruism. The two modes of expression are in practice convertible. There is accordingly no discrepancy between our abstract analysis of morality which places the emphasis on justice, and the accounts given by religions and practical moral codes which place the emphasis on altruism.

Why, then, the difference of emphasis? The answer is obvious. The purpose of philosophy is as a rule logical analysis. It therefore emphasizes the concept which is logically prior and more fundamental. The purpose of religions and moral codes is practical, and they therefore emphasize that concept which is for practical purposes the more important. And there can be no question that this is altruism, and not justice. For in the first place ninety-nine out of a hundred moral conflicts are directly concerned with the antagonism between a man's own interests and those of his neighbour. It is in only a comparatively few cases that men are called upon to act as judges between other persons. But this is not really the decisive consideration. For of course it cannot be denied that there are many cases in which men are called upon to be judges. Parents have to judge impartially as between their children, employers as between their employees. And a practical moral code cannot afford to leave these cases without regulation. The really decisive consideration, therefore, is not that which has just been suggested— though that does undoubtedly carry some weight—but the following. What a man has practically to fight against is always his own self and the persistent attempts of that self to grasp more than its proper share of satisfactions. This is true in all cases whatever of moral conflict, even in those in which a man is called upon to act the part of impartial judge. For if in this latter kind of case a man has any temptation to depart from the path of impartiality, it must be because some selfish interest of his own is attempting to force an entry upon the scene. Hence for the practical moralist there is no point in making a distinction between cases which call for altruism and cases which call for justice. Since in all cases alike the real moral conflict of a man is with the aggressive greediness of his own self, it is here that the practical moralist puts the emphasis. Battle against your own selfishness—this becomes his watch word. And for him altruism becomes the central idea of morality.

If a man is unjust, the psychological root of the evil lies always in his *egoism*. Extirpate that, and his injustice will disappear. Make a man genuinely unselfish, and he cannot be unjust. Practical moralists and religious teachers therefore put their fingers on the right spot when they condemn selfishness as the essential evil and laud self-sacrifice as the supreme virtue. The notion of justice seems to us a cold and pale intellectual abstraction. But a man's struggle with his egoism is fervent with the heat of battle, and it is of this struggle that his concrete moral existence is made. This is flesh and blood. It is no abstraction. It touches the red-hot centre of human life. It is of this, then, that the moralist who wishes to move men practically—and not merely, as the philosopher does, to convince their intellects—will speak. But the philosopher and the moralist are not saying different things when they respectively make justice and altruism central. They are saying the same thing, speaking of identically the same moral law. Only they are speaking in different languages. There is no inconsistency.

Moreover it is altogether desirable that now, once we have accorded proper recognition to the fact that justice is in the abstract the logically prior idea, we should nevertheless ourselves think in future in more concrete and practical terms. And I shall in the following chapters very largely turn my back upon the abstractions of logical analysis. I shall turn towards a more concrete and practical view of morality. I shall view it as being essentially altruism. I shall say that, for all practical purposes, the supreme law of morals is "Be unselfish." And when I come to examine the question of the universality of morals; when I come to ask whether in civilizations remote from, and lower than, our own, there are to be found any traces of a recognition of the same morality which we ourselves profess to follow; I shall not look for recognition of the abstract idea of justice, but I shall look for the concrete idea of unselfishness. I shall take altruism, not justice, to be the essential mark of morality and of the moral man. Whatever the abstract analysis of morality may be, the practical spirit of it lies in caring for the happiness of others, in attempting to increase that to the maximum possible extent. In short, there is but one moral evil—selfishness. And there is but one moral duty—unselfishness.

After having formulated the general law of morals, our next step would naturally be to show that all particular moral duties and maxims can be deduced from it, just as the particular uniformities of planetary and stellar motions can be deduced from the law of gravitation. It is, however, more or less obvious that this is so, provided that proper allowance be made for the differences of subject matter. We do not, of course, expect in morals the kind of accuracy of deduction which is found in mathematical astronomy. But that deduction of duties can be made is clear. Stealing, murdering, raping, lying, are all obviously unaltruistic, and they all decrease human happiness. Honesty, integrity, gentleness, kindness, truthfulness, and the rest of the commonly recognized virtues are, directly or indirectly, altruistic and tend to increase human happiness. To expatiate upon such themes would be wearisome, and I shall accordingly turn my attention elsewhere.

In an earlier chapter I pointed out that many of the commands and prohibitions which have been regarded traditionally as belonging to morality have in fact nothing *moral* about them. Rules of conduct which have their fountain-head in all sorts of considerations irrelevant to morality have been mixed up indiscriminately in the popular consciousness with genuinely moral requirements. Some of these considerations were sensible and rational—those, for example, which were concerned with health and sanitation. Others were based upon irrational prejudices, superstitions, and false ideas. Others again have been founded upon mere dislikes which proceed from physiological causes having nothing to do with morality. For there is always a tendency to confuse any strong dislike with moral disapprobation. Whatever men strongly dislike they tend to label forthwith as "immoral," "wicked," "bad," making no discrimination of the grounds upon which their dislike is based. There are, in fact, various grounds upon which a thing or an action may be pronounced objectionable. It may be thought so on grounds of health, on sanitary grounds, on esthetic grounds, on grounds of sheer physical disgust (such as nauseation), and finally on genuinely moral grounds. And to lump all such grounds of objection indiscriminately together as moral grounds is, we saw, a fatal, if natural, mistake. It leads among other things to ethical relativity, since in all this strange hotch-potch of human aversions, superstitions, prejudices, physical dislikes, and idiosyncrasies, it is obviously impossible to discern any uniformity. And we saw accordingly that it is necessary to isolate the pure concept of morality. Only if this were first done could we intelligently go on to enquire whether morality is in any sense universal. It is upon this isolation of the moral concept that we have been engaged in the last few chapters. And it is this isolation which we finally completed in the last chapter. Our conclusion—to put it in a word—is that the essence of morality is unselfishness. The essence of immorality is selfishness. And therefore any objection which anyone may urge against any course of action on any ground other than that it is selfish is not a *moral* objection.

Our procedure is similar to that which Kant adopted in the realm of esthetics. Kant sought, among other things, to investigate the question whether the esthetic judgment possesses any claim to be universal or binding on all men. And he rightly saw that the first thing to do is to isolate the genuinely esthetic element from other elements which are apt to be mixed up with it in any concrete work of art. This is the significance of his distinction between beauty and charm. Something may charm us by its colours, its soft velvety feel, its fragrance, its sweetness of sound. But the charming is not the beautiful. The charming varies from person to person, and has no claim to universality. But the beautiful may have such a claim. If it has, it will be fatal to confuse the two together. For the relativity of the charming will obscure and even, obliterate altogether the universality of the beautiful. Only if we first isolate the latter shall we be able to discern its universality. Whether Kant was right or wrong in his esthetic analysis we need not enquire. The point is that his procedure was parallel to that which is being followed here in the case of ethics. Here too we seek to disentangle the *moral* rule of conduct from other rules of conduct in order to ascertain whether the former, when taken pure, may not possess some kind of universality. That this is the right procedure to follow in the case of ethics I have no doubt.

It will serve to illustrate some of the points which I have been making if we apply to a concrete ethical problem the criterion of morality which we have laid bare in this and the preceding chapter. And I will take for this purpose the problem of sex—or rather some of the problems connected with that difficult subject. Remembering that the criteria of morality and immorality are respectively unselfishness and selfishness, we may lay it down as a corollary that *nothing can be morally wrong which does not cause, or tend to cause, injury (unhappiness or decrease of happiness*) *to a fellow being.* Actions which do not do this may often be objectionable. But they are not *morally* objectionable. They may contravene perfectly reasonable rules of conduct. But these cannot be moral rules.

Bearing this in mind, let us ask the question whether it is contrary to morality to have sexual intercourse outside marriage. The view taken by practically everyone fifty years ago in Christian countries was that any such intercourse was absolutely and unconditionally immoral. And this is the view taken by very large numbers of people even today. But no such unqualified opinion can be deduced from the general law of morals. Obviously the view we must take is the following. There is only one kind of action which is *in itself* immoral, namely the kind of action which is selfish. Sexuality, animality, and the like are not marks of immorality. (If animality were a mark of immorality, then it would be immoral to eat.) Selfishness is the only mark of the immoral. Therefore no problem about sex relations is *as such* a problem about morality. To have sexual intercourse either inside or outside marriage is not in itself either moral or immoral. But any sexual act becomes immoral *if* the circumstances in which it occurs make it selfish, if, that is, it causes unjustifiable injury or unhappiness to any of one's fellow beings. Thus it is immoral to have intercourse even within marriage in some circumstances—for example if serious injury will be done by it to the health or happiness of one's marriage partner. On the other hand, it will be morally innocent to have intercourse outside marriage if no unhappiness will be caused thereby. If a man and a woman, being unmarried, choose to indulge in the pleasure of sex, and if the circumstances are such that there is no likelihood of either thereby injuring the other, or of any injury arising to third parties, then I cannot think that they deserve the slightest condemnation.

But the proviso that no unhappiness must be caused to others is all-important, and saves the principle from being—what it might at first sight appear to be—a justification of universal license. The circumstances must be such that the man, in thus acting, causes no unhappiness to the woman; and that the woman causes no unhappiness to the man; and that their joint act causes no unhappiness to third parties. But the circumstances very seldom *are* of this character. And I will now proceed to point out some of the factors which render the principle less "loose" than might be supposed. In the first place—to make a very obvious point—a man who "seduces" a girl in circumstances which are likely to bring serious unhappiness to the girl herself, is acting with gross selfishness, and is open to the gravest condemnation. Nor does it matter through what channels such unhappiness is likely to come. It may be through damage to her prospects, through damage to her reputation, through the narrow-mindedness and petty persecutions of her circle of associates. In as much as the man, to gratify his own desires, ignores these things and selfishly risks the happiness of his partner, he commits moral wrong. Nor can he justify his act by arguing that it was she who took these risks upon herself, knowingly and willingly, that it is "her affair"—the usual excuse of the seducer—and that he is therefore blameless. The truly unselfish man, the good man, will safeguard the happiness of others, when he can, even against their own foolishness or weakness. He must not use that foolishness or that weakness to gain selfishly an advantage for himself to their detriment. Nor can the man, in such a case, argue that the unhappiness which his action brings upon his partner is really due to

the unreasonable prejudices and superstitions of society—
that if people in general thought intelligently on these
matters, they would not pursue the woman with persecutions and unhappiness—and that consequently her mis-
fortunes will be *their* fault, and not his. In the first place,
we cannot admit that the views of society in this matter
are mere prejudices and superstitions. As we shall see in
a moment there is a great deal of reason in them.[1] But
this is not really to the point. Suppose we admit, merely
for the sake of argument, that society is in this matter
wholly unreasonable, still the prejudices and superstitions
of the world are facts which a man is bound to take into
account in estimating the consequences of his actions in
terms of the happiness or unhappiness of other people.
An unselfish man will not expose others to these things.

Such considerations as these are indeed obvious. But
there are other more imponderable factors, which are
likely to be forgotten, but which must certainly be brought
into the account. It is the almost universal experience of
mankind that indiscriminate indulgence in the gratification of sex, without any accompaniment of affection and
companionship, coarsens and brutalizes human feelings
generally. Sex itself is thereby spoiled and cheapened. In
this respect, no doubt, the sexes differ. Men can, as a rule,
indulge in sex unaccompanied by affection with less injury
to their general emotional set-up than can women. To do
this is more contrary to the nature of women than it is to
the nature of men. And to the man, therefore, it probably does less harm. But this is a mere matter of degree.
Men who are accustomed to associate with women solely
for the sake of animal gratification come to ignore their
more specifically human feelings and qualities. In the re-

[1] Cf. Browning's line, "The ways of the world have a certain worth."

sult they tend to ignore their happiness. They use women as mere means to their own pleasures, caring nothing for their inner spiritual, moral, and mental lives. They thus become brutalized and selfish in their relations with women, and this coarseness is bound to extend itself to all their other human relations. The selfishness which is engendered is a centre from which radiate waves of unhappiness among their associates in general.

Thus the older and more conventional views of sex-morality turn out in the end to be capable of a large measure of justification. Sexual gratification outside marriage cannot *as such* be condemned. There may be examples of men and women living happily together and bringing up families without having been formally married.[1] And it is mere superstition to suppose that what they are doing is necessarily immoral (though even here they may be open to condemnation for inflicting upon their children the disabilities which usually arise from such a situation. Each case must be judged on its own merits). Their case may be indistinguishable from that of ordinarily married persons. The absence of a ceremony cannot alter this. Nor can one think that sex indulgence between persons who have no intention of establishing any lasting relation, even of an "irregular" character, is in itself immoral. It may be accompanied by genuinely tender feelings and by the exchange of much innocent, if ephemeral, happiness. It may be for both of them an ennobling, and not a debasing, experience. And yet indiscriminate "free love," since it almost invariably leads to brutality and selfishness, must be condemned. It is

[1] Though even this is very doubtful. See the very interesting article "I Thought I Was Modern" by Evelyn Havens in the *Forum* for October, 1935, in which the authoress describes the unhappiness of such a union.

hard to know where to draw the line. If a man and a woman may innocently indulge their sex desires without marriage, without any intention of forming any kind of lasting union, and with the full knowledge that they may shortly change their respective mates, what is to prevent this from degenerating into universal and indiscriminate indulgence? Nothing indeed except the better feelings of the parties concerned. The older morality cut the knot by drawing a hard and fast line. No sexual intercourse whatever without marriage. And it cannot be denied that there was in this much practical wisdom. If we must have a rule of thumb, this was the only safe one. It was certainly better than "free love." Its defect—and it is the defect of all rules of thumb—was its unintelligent rigidity.

Unintelligent rigidity—not only in matters of sex, but in all matters—was a characteristic mark of the older morality, that is, of the moral views of our immediate ancestors. And it has brought about in due course the inevitable reaction—a flying off to unintelligent and unjustifiable looseness. That, however, is not our concern. What we have to point out is the disastrous results which this rigidity has had upon moral theory. Morality ought to be conceived as a single general principle. A general principle, when applied to particular cases, results in flexibility. But instead of this, morality has been conceived as a multitude of little rules of thumb. Each of these, because it is not deduced from any higher principle, appeared in the moral consciousness of men as something absolute, ultimate, and mysterious. It appeared as irrational. And as different societies adopt slightly different rules of thumb—according to the special circumstances in which they are placed—both irrationality and variability come to be thought of as characteristic of morals. The upshot is ethical relativity, which finds morality to be founded either upon mere local customs or upon entirely irrational emotions. The remedy is to point out the true state of the case. The rigid rules of thumb which have come to be worshipped as if they were sacred mysteries are not morality in its purity at all. And they are neither sacred nor mysterious. They are nothing but crude attempts to apply the general law of morals—the law of unselfishness—to a variety of particular circumstances. To set them up as being, each in itself, a rigid and ultimate moral rule, is to do morality the disservice of making it appear to be a sphere of nothing but irrational caprices and local prejudices.

The matter of sexual perversion is also full of instruction for us. Until recently pederasty and similar sexual perversions were regarded as moral offences so abominable that they vied with murder, possibly even exceeded it, in blackness. In Scotland sodomy is still in strict law a capital offence. But there has been some change of opinion in this matter. Nowadays the tendency is to regard perverts as cases for the doctor rather than for the moral reformer or the hangman. With the pathological aspects of the question I am not concerned. I am inclined to think that modern opinion here is sometimes vitiated by sentimentality as well as by prurience. But what is significant for us is the shift of opinion whereby sexual perversions tend to be removed from the sphere of *moral* categories and listed under other headings, medical, pathological, etc. This removal of the subject from the sphere of morality is, I think, in accordance with truth. And it illustrates the importance of isolating moral disapprobation from other kinds of aversion.

I should maintain that sexual perversion is not, as such,

immoral. In itself it has nothing to do with ethics, and is not a moral problem at all. Why, then, has it been thought immoral? The answer is that this is a perfect illustration of the principle that the popular consciousness tends to label as immoral anything which it deeply dislikes, although the grounds of its dislike may have nothing whatever to do with morality. It is a perfect example of the confusion of moral aversion with other kinds of aversion. Any serious human abnormality, whether physical or mental, tends to cause feelings of disgust in normal onlookers. The sight of a withered limb is to many people so repulsive that they have difficulty in forcing themselves to associate freely with the victim of it. And to persons of normal sexual appetites the very notion of homosexuality is loathsome. It seems to me that what is really involved here is nothing but a kind of *physical* disgust. It is not in kind fundamentally different from nauseation. This physical disgust is mistaken by most people for moral repulsion.

As is well known there are cases of disease in which the patient will eat mud or other filth. This practice undoubtedly arouses in healthy persons feelings of the deepest aversion. But no one would think of condemning the sufferer from such a disease as immoral. I suggest that we have here a parallel to sexual perversion. In the one case we have a perversion of the appetite of hunger; in the other a perversion of the appetite of sex. Both produce disgust, but in neither case are we in the presence of *moral* evil.

But if the cases are parallel why, it may be asked, do we not condemn dirt-eating as immoral in the same way as we condemn sexual perversion? The example, in fact, seems to tell against our thesis. For if the belief that sex perversion is immoral is due to nothing but confusion of

physical disgust with moral disapprobation, why does not
the same confusion cause us to think dirt-eating immoral?
The fact is that popular consciousness does make a clear
distinction.   It regards pederasty as immoral and dirt-
eating as merely a case of physical disease.   Whereas if
our theory were true, it ought to regard both in the same
light.

The difference, however, is easily explained. Dirt-eating
is always associated with other obvious symptoms of illness. Pederasty makes its appearance in men who appear
to be perfectly healthy.   Dirt-eating comes suddenly
upon men who have previously been quite normal in their
eating habits. It comes upon them when their health is
obviously deranged, and it departs when their health is
restored. But sexual perversion is often, indeed usually,
a permanent condition of its victim, and it goes with apparently normal health. Thus dirt-eating must always
have been recognized as a mere symptom of illness and
thus taken out of the category of moral offences. It was
otherwise with homosexuality.

The different attitudes of different societies towards
homosexuality have often been quoted as examples of the
variability of moral ideas. We now see how shallow such
an argument for ethical relativity really is. The Greeks
exhibited in regard to pederasty an attitude very different
from our own. It was fairly openly countenanced. Herodotus speaks of those who introduced this new pleasure from
the Orient into Greece almost as if they were benefactors.
He speaks in very much the same spirit as that in which
we might extol Sir Walter Raleigh for introducing tobacco
from America to England. Romantic love attachments
between grown men and beautiful boys—though not necessarily involving physical acts of sex—were viewed as

ennobling and poetical—much as romantic love between the sexes is among ourselves. The Socrates of Plato's *Republic* condemns pederasty, it is true, but only on the ground of its being *vulgar*, not on the ground of its being immoral. Is, then, this difference of attitude between the ancient Greek and the modern European, an argument in favour of ethical relativity? Obviously not. For it is not a difference of *moral* attitude at all. No moral question is involved. If our feeling of repulsion for pederasty is, as I maintain, a mere physical disgust, then all that follows from differences of attitude on this question is that in certain respects the Greeks had different physical tastes from our own. And this will no more tend to support ethical relativity than will the fact that some men prefer to eat beef, others mutton. We have in such an argument an example of the kind of damage which, as I pointed out in Chapter 3, is done to ethical theory by a too wide and loose definition of morals; an example of the inevitability of ethical relativism if all rules of human conduct, from whatsoever source they are derived, are indiscriminately lumped together as *moral* rules.

Thus sexual perversion, however physically disgusting, cannot be said to be, in itself, immoral. But the case here is exactly similar to that of normal sex activity. Normal sexual intercourse, we saw, whether between married or unmarried persons, is not in itself immoral. But it becomes so when it is selfish, when it threatens to injure human happiness. It is just the same with perverted sexual appetites. They are not immoral in themselves. But they are immoral if indulged to the injury of the happiness of others. And such injury is frequently, if not invariably, done. Thus if a grown man seduces an immature boy in a society such as ours he commits a gravely immoral act for which there can be no shadow of excuse. For he is likely to inflict damage upon the boy's subsequent happiness. He may turn towards permanent homosexuality a child who under other conditions might have developed normally. This, in turn, may result in misery to the victim.

Consider, on the other hand, the case of a man who has sexual intercourse with an animal. His act is at once disgusting and grotesque. It is a question whether he should not be confined to an asylum. Yet in my opinion he cannot ordinarily be condemned for immorality. For, in ordinary circumstances, he injures no one.

In our discussion of the problems of sex there are two aspects of it which I have not mentioned. The first is that of intemperance, or excess, in sexual activity. The second is the fact that sex, because it is physical and shared with the animals, is considered to be a "low" kind of satisfaction. Both these considerations are irrelevant to what we have been discussing, and I only mention them now in order to point out their irrelevance.

If excess is objectionable, it is objectionable in anything, and therefore it has no special relevance to the question of sex. No doubt it is more objectionable in the case of animal appetites than it is in other and higher things. This is because it is low down in the scale of values. And we naturally think worse of a man who pursues inferior things to excess than of one who is excessive in what is in itself nobler. But I cannot see that to be immoderate in sex is any more objectionable than to be immoderate in eating. And all this has, in any case, no bearing upon such a question as whether it is immoral to have sexual intercourse outside marriage. For such intercourse may be perfectly moderate.

Neither is it relevant to the problems which we were

discussing to point out that sexual pleasure is lower in the scale of satisfactions than music, say, or art, or religion. We have already seen why this is so. The "lower" pleasures are lower because they contribute less to happiness. But because a satisfaction is inferior it does not thereby become in any way positively immoral. No desire of whatever kind, whether it be high or low, is as such immoral. It only becomes so when it is selfishly indulged. And therefore the fact that sex is an inferior kind of satisfaction has no bearing upon the questions which we were discussing.

CHAPTER 9

MORALS AND MOTIVES

IT will not have escaped the reader's notice that in our whole account of morality nothing whatever has been said about the motives which inform men's actions. We have defined the nature of morality. We have defined what is meant by a good action. And we have defined these terms without making use of the concept of motive at all. It would seem necessarily to follow that motives are irrelevant to the question of whether an action is good or bad. Such a conclusion will seem to most people to be highly doubtful, to be out of accord with our ordinary moral feelings and with the actual procedures by which our moral judgments of men and their actions are formed. It may well happen that two men perform what is outwardly the same action, but that the motives of one are good, while those of the other are bad. Should we not all agree that in such a case the first man is morally a better man than the second? And if this is so, how can it be right to leave motives altogether out of our account of morality?

I answer this question by making a distinction. There are two kinds of moral judgment. In the first we judge that an *action* is right or wrong, good or bad. In the second we judge that a *man* is good or bad. This latter is a judgment, not immediately of any particular actions, but of *character*. Now motives are irrelevant to the concept of the "good act," but they are relevant to the concept of the "good man." We implicitly recognize this when we say, as we sometimes do, that a bad man, acting from a bad motive, may sometimes perform a good act. I may be charitable from a thoroughly discreditable motive. I cannot then be praised as a good man. Nevertheless the charitable act which I did was a charitable act. It was a good act, considered in and by itself. And the character of the motive which informed it cannot alter this fact.

Most of our actual moral judgments are of mixed character. We tend to judge a whole situation in a lump, not separating action, motive, and character. And for practical purposes we may be perfectly justified in doing this. But there may result a tendency to be confused concerning the place of motives in moral theory. For purposes of theory we must abstract. We must separate the concept of the good act from the concept of the good man.

I shall maintain that the primary concept of morals is that of the good act, and that the question of motives is irrelevant to this; and that the concept of the good man, to which the question of motives is relevant, is secondary and derivative.

The good act is the act which is altruistic, the act, that is, which increases the happiness of other people. If it has this character, if it actually does increase human happiness, then it is, formally and outwardly, a good act, from whatever motive it was done. Suppose that my action is altruistic in the sense that I give up valuable satisfactions in order that another man may benefit. It is quite possible that I do this action from motives which are entirely selfish. I care nothing at all about the other man's happiness. But I see that in the end I shall acquire greater satisfactions for myself. And this is the sole reason why I do what I do. It may be that I, as a man, can claim no credit for this. My character is not deserving of moral praise. But this does not alter the fact that what I did was the right thing to do, and was therefore a good action.

Now if actions, simply as actions, can be finally judged as good or bad without reference to motives, why cannot *men* be judged good or bad in the same way? Why cannot we define the good man simply as the man whose actions are good? Or, since it is true of no man that all his actions are good, why cannot we say that a good man is one most of whose actions are good—or something of that sort? If we could do this, motives need never be introduced into moral judgments of any kind. If a man, objectively and by his outward actions, produced much happiness for his fellow beings, he would be judged a good man. And to this judgment all questions of motive would be irrelevant.

If "intelligent self-interest" could always be relied upon to produce the maximum of happiness for society, then there would be no need to trouble our heads about motives. It would not matter to humanity in the least what a man's motives were. Selfish motives would be just as good as unselfish ones. For motives are in the end to be judged by the same criteria as actions, that is, by their tendency to advance the happiness of humanity. And if intelligently selfish motives could be relied upon to do this, they would be just as good as unselfish motives. We should still be concerned as to whether men were, in their selfishness, intelligent or unintelligent. For unintelligent selfishness would no doubt diminish, not increase, human happiness. But we should think the intelligently selfish man just as good as the unselfish man, for the actual results of their actions would be the same. They would have the same tendency to increase human happiness. Motives would therefore be irrelevant. And no distinction would ever have been made between good and bad motives. The concept of "good motives" would not have been invented.

But the experience of all humanity shows that intelligently selfish motives *cannot* be trusted to achieve human happiness. That they do achieve it in many cases, perhaps in most cases, is not disputed. It is not doubted that the really intelligent man will see that altruistic actions are as a rule to his advantage, and will act accordingly. Mere self-interest will lead the intelligent tradesman to be, *in general*, honest. But it will not lead him to be universally honest. For if a case arises in which he can by dishonesty make a large gain with no risk of discovery, his principles will lead him to be dishonest. The only thing which can save him here is the disinterested desire to be just and to do no injury to others, that is to say, a genuinely unselfish motive. The intelligently selfish man will practice honesty as a general policy in his business, because it obviously pays. But he will make exceptions in special cases if he thinks he can do so without risk. In these exceptional cases his actions will be bad and immoral, since they will work injustice and injury to other people.

However much we may seek to show in theory that intelligent self-interest should lead men to act morally, we know that in fact it does not. Selfish men, however intelligent, are centres of darkness. They are the sources of most of the world's misery. High intelligence may lead them to simulate the outward forms of morality. They may have every appearance of being honest, fair, kind, and charitable. But within them there is darkness because they love only themselves. They are rotten at the core. They are bad men in spite of their outward respectability and success. The inward badness will, sooner or later, express itself in outward actions. Public life provides endless examples of men who being at heart bad—that is, selfish—yet rise by dint of exceptional intelligence to places of high trust and honour in the councils of the nation. They are set over men to rule and judge. And their intelligence teaches them that, though their real aim is only their own advancement, they can best achieve this by an apparently assiduous regard for the public weal. But men in general, even the stupidest men, have an uncanny gift for penetrating disguises and for seeing, as by divination, the inner secrets of a man's character. Instinctively, in a manner infinitely subtle, they perceive the inward darkness or the inward light. And while public men of no character imagine that they are making a great impression, everyone perceives what they really are. They are not trusted. And rightly. For in the end it is not through men of their stamp that happiness comes to humanity. The light—what light there is in the world—comes from those who love their fellow men, not from those who love themselves. It comes from the few rare souls—so rare that those who have made their appearance in historic times can be counted almost on the fingers of one hand—who are genuinely selfless. When they do appear, the millions of the world follow them, worshipping the ground on which they tread. For here too the immediate intuition of men divines the inner light. Those who direct their lives upon the basis of intelligent self-interest are not those whom their fellows recognize as genuinely good men. They are clever bad men, clever enough to simulate goodness up to a point. Good men are those whose actions proceed from a pure disinterested desire to make their fellow men happy, whether it advances their own interests or not.[1]

It is in this way that there arises the concept of the good motive. An action is, outwardly and formally, good, if it tends to increase human happiness—or rather if it tends to increase the happiness of persons other than the doer of the deed. It may or may not proceed from good motives. I confer a benefit upon my fellow man. If I do so simply out of policy and self-interest, my motive may not indeed be positively bad. As the world goes, it may be accounted respectable enough. It will only be thought positively bad if my aim is in the end to do someone an injury greater than the benefit which I have conferred. But in no case can such a self-interested motive be accounted positively good and morally praiseworthy. It will only be this if it is genuinely disinterested, if my act proceeded from the desire to make my neighbour happier, and if this end was desired *for its own sake*, and not for the sake of some ulterior advantage to myself. And such a motive is called good because experience shows that it is only from men who are actuated by such motives that much happiness is in the end likely to accrue to the world. Experience shows that, from men whose sole motive is self-interest, happiness for others does not in the end issue—however "intelligent" they may be, however they may appear to be serving the public good. Their motives, therefore, are not thought to be genuinely good.

It is for this reason that we take motives into account when we desire to estimate the goodness or badness of a man's *character*. If the man who is impelled only by intelligent self-interest could be trusted always to do good

---

[1] The doctrine of ethical egoism holds that no such disinterested altruism exists or is psychologically possible. This opinion is examined in the later part of the present chapter.

acts, the best acts, he might reasonably be called a good man, and all enquiry into his motives would be irrelevant. But in fact this is not so. The selfish man is never truly good in his actions, however intelligent he may be. The inward badness will out—will reflect itself in outward behaviour. Peach fruits do not grow upon nettles. As the root is, so are the leaves, the flowers, the fruit. Therefore we do not call a man good whose only motive is his own advancement, even though in most of his actions he may conform to the moral law. Such a man may be respectable, may be a fairly satisfactory citizen. But only the unselfish man is truly good.

Hence to the question how far, when we wish to form a moral judgment, motives are relevant, the answer is that it depends upon whether we are judging an action or a man. If we are judging an action, if, that is, we want to know simply whether a particular action was right or wrong, good or bad, in accordance with the moral law or not, then all questions of motive are irrelevant. The sole test is the probable effect of the action upon the lives and happiness of other people. The action itself, lifted out of its context of human character, must be compared with the moral standard and pronounced to be in accordance with it or not in accordance with it. But in judging of a man's character these merely external and formal tests are insufficient. We have to look into the man's motives. And our judgment of the man's worth is, or should be, the result of *both* considerations. If his actions are generally, so far as we can see, good, but his motives inferior, we may call him respectable, fairly satisfactory as a man and a citizen. We shall credit him with the moral correctness of his actions. But we shall not accord to him the crown of true moral nobility. He is not what we understand by a good man in the highest sense. But neither, on the other hand, shall we accord the highest place of honour to the man whose motives are good, but whose actions habitually bring more unhappiness than happiness to his fellows. We shall say, perhaps, that he has a good heart, but that he is unwise, foolish, unintelligent, and so on.

We may say, if we like, that there are two senses of the word good—that it means one thing when applied to actions, another thing when applied to men; and that therefore the criteria and tests of goodness will be different in the two cases. We shall judge actions by their consequences, while men will be judged both by the consequences of their actions and by their motives. But in the long view the criterion of goodness is the same in both cases, and the meaning of the word the same. That is good—both the man and the action—which tends to advance the happiness of humanity. But in the case of actions we do not take motives into account. In the case of men we do so because only men of good motives—which means disinterestedly unselfish men—do in the end greatly increase human happiness.

The account just given of the place of motives in morality takes for granted the psychological existence of a state of mind which may be called *disinterested* altruism. But at this point we are brought abruptly to a stand by the assertions of those who deny the existence, or even the psychological possibility, of disinterestedness.[1] They propound the theory of ethical egoism, and they assert that

[1] I use the term egoism in the sense explained in the text. Ethical theories based upon the concept of "self-realization" are sometimes brought under the rubric of egoism; but this is a wider usage of the term than that which I employ. Hence my criticism of egoism is not a criticism of self-realization theories.

morality is, and must be, founded upon egoism. The thesis for which, in the previous chapters, I have been contending—that altruism is the essence of morality—is not necessarily incompatible with this view. For that thesis does not depend upon any question of motives. We have defined morality—meaning the nature of morally good actions—without introducing the concept of motives into the definition at all. And therefore our theory of the nature of morality will stand, whatever may be the character of human motives. And the egoist himself may perfectly well admit that altruism is the essence of morality. Only he will say that this altruism proceeds always from egoistical motives. Intelligent selfishness, he thinks, should lead, and does lead, to altruistic actions. And upon such intelligent selfishness morality is, in fact and of necessity, founded.

Nevertheless the spirit of ethical egoism is out of accord with the spirit of our view of morality. It explicitly contradicts the views developed in the earlier part of the present chapter. And it is utterly inconsistent with what we shall have to say regarding the problem of the basis of moral obligation. It stands as a stumbling block in our way. We cannot avoid the discussion of it.

The exponents of egoism do not deny, of course, that there is such a thing as what is popularly called "unselfishness." What they deny is that it is ever *disinterested*. The altruistic man benefits his fellows, according to the egoist, because he knows that in the long run this is the best way of benefiting himself. He is intelligent enough to see that by a too exclusive preoccupation with his own interests, combined with too great a disregard for the interests of others, he will in the end injure himself. For others will retaliate. Or they will at least ignore *his* interests.

Experience shows that the best way to get what one wants is to have a certain regard for what other people want. Each individual member of a community of men who habitually help one another obtains more satisfactions than he would if all of them fought against one another, each man for his own hand. Intelligence therefore dictates a certain degree of "unselfishness." But this unselfishness is in the end purely self-seeking. Its motive is entirely egotistical. Morality consequently can be nothing but "intelligent self-interest."

There are in reality two distinct theories involved in this, though I have so far lumped them both together under the single heading of "egoism." One of the two theories may more properly be denominated psychological egoism, the other ethical egoism. But ethical egoism is founded upon psychological egoism. Psychological egoism asserts it to be a fact that human nature is so constituted that every man is governed in his actions entirely by the motive of self-interest. It is impossible for any man to act at all except on the basis of an egotistical motive. Disinterested altruism is simply a psychological impossibility. From this follows the doctrine of ethical egoism proper. Since there is no such thing as disinterested altruism, morality must be founded upon egoism. It cannot be anything except intelligent calculation. And intelligent calculation shows that a man benefits himself most on the whole and in the long run by "unselfishness," and in general by the kind of actions called "moral."

As is well known, it was upon an opinion of this kind that Thomas Hobbes based his famous theory of the political state. And nothing is so characteristic of Hobbes's opinion of human nature as the passage in which he analyses what he thinks to be the nature of gratitude. What he calls the "law of gratitude" is to the effect that "a man which receiveth Benefit from another of meer Grace, Endeavour that he which giveth it, have no reasonable cause to repent him of his good will." [1] And he comments: "For no man giveth, but with the intention of Good to himselfe; because Gift is Voluntary; and of all Voluntary Acts, the Object is to every man his own Good; of which if men see they shall be frustrated, there will be no beginning of benevolence or trust; nor consequently of mutuall help." [2]

Hobbes does not think that gratitude is a natural, spontaneous, and disinterested human emotion. It is a kind of commercial calculation. He who does a benefit does it because he expects a return, if only in gratitude. He who receives the benefit gives gratitude in the hope of further benefits to come. And the statement that "of all Voluntary Acts, the Object is to every man his own Good" asserts explicitly the opinion that all human action is ultimately egoistic in motive.

In our own day a similar opinion is expressed in the writings of Mr. E. B. Holt. The difference is that, whereas Hobbes based his view upon the kind of experience of human nature which is open to all of us, Mr. Holt's opinion professes to be "scientific," and to be vouched by the discoveries of the so-called modern science of psychology. In a recent essay Mr. Holt writes "Man addresses himself to nature for what he can get, and he addresses himself to his fellow men with precisely the same intent, and *never* with any other." [3] And again

---

[1] *Leviathian*, chapter 15.   [2] *Ibid.*
[3] Mr. Holt's essay in *American Philosophy Today and Tomorrow*, page 189. The italics are Mr. Holt's.

"Adience means approach and then appropriation. . . . Any individual will appropriate to himself the person, the labour, the possessions, and the life of any other individual if he can, and if he has use for them in any further adient enterprises of his own. Such is the plainest teaching of history; and history further teaches that this propensity has no limit. If any man, other than the ever-voluble moron, seeks to darken counsel by denying this teaching, it is because he has projects of his own which he fears may come under scrutiny." [1] From this we learn that anyone who disagrees with Mr. Holt's opinion must be (in Mr. Holt's opinion) either a rogue or a fool.

Mr. Holt's view is based upon two kinds of grounds. The first is "the teaching of history," that is to say, our general knowledge of human nature—the same ground upon which, as is evident, Hobbes relied. The second is the findings of "science." I will examine the so-called scientific argument first.

This argument, briefly summarized, is as follows. The movements of the human foetus in the womb are at first random movements. But owing to physiological causes which need not be here explained in detail the organism sets up "reflex circles." This means that, if any part of the surface of the body is stimulated, the nerve impulses which are thereby generated tend to pass up through the central nervous system and back to the muscles which control the part stimulated, in such a manner as to cause that part to press out against the object from which the stimulus proceeds, and so to obtain more and more of the same stimulation. Thus if the flexor muscle of the finger contracts, so that the finger is pressed inwards against the palm of the hand, the nerves of both the palm

[1] *Ibid.*, pages 187, 188.

and the finger tip are stimulated. The nerve impulses tend to return, in circular fashion, to the hand, and to cause a further contraction of the fingers upon the palm. It is owing to these facts that at birth a baby's hand will close round a stick, or any similar object, and grasp it tightly. Similar reflex circles are set up in other parts of the body. Stimulation of the soles of the feet will cause the leg to be straightened and pushed out towards the stimulating object so as to increase the stimulation. Again, the child clings to his mother and returns her caresses—that is, he presses any part of his body which is stimulated by pressure against the object which is stimulating him so as to increase the stimulation. Avoidance reflexes are only apparent exceptions. An overstrong stimulus automatically brings into play the muscles which cause a withdrawal of the part of the body which is stimulated. This "adience" is the basis of all learning and of all purposive behaviour. In mature life it develops into acquisitiveness, ambition, egotism, self-interest. All human conduct, therefore, is adient, or in other words, selfish.

It is difficult to think that this is seriously intended *as an argument in favour of* psychological egoism. For if it is so taken, it contains an almost childish *non-sequitur*. Physiological adience is the cause of selfishness. All human organisms are physiologically adient. Therefore all human beings have the character of being selfish. So far the argument is good enough. But if we add that *therefore they can have no other character*, such as that of being sometimes disinterestedly unselfish—which is the only conclusion which will establish egoism—we are falling into an absurd paralogism. This is just as if we were to argue that, since water has always certain physical characters which cause it on occasion to freeze, therefore it can never boil.

If, on the other hand, the considerations adduced regarding the reflex circle are not intended to be taken as an argument in favour of egoism, then what relevancy have they to the subject? They become in that case interesting pieces of physiological information which, however, have no bearing whatever upon the issue whether all human motives are egoistic or whether disinterested motives are ever possible.

Physiological psychology is a science in its infancy. We know, as a matter of fact, pitifully little about the physiological correlates of our different cognitive, emotional, and conative mental states. But let us suppose, for the sake of argument, that all the facts about the reflex circle are fully known and that they constitute the physiological correlate of the grasping proclivities of the human being; and even that they, in some sense or other, "explain" those activities. We have now a physiological explanation of at least the cruder forms of selfishness, those forms which consist in the actual physical grasping of an object. What then? Everyone knew before that human beings are selfish. Have we learned anything new about human nature? To have discovered the physiological correlate of selfishness is no doubt a very great achievement. But it goes no way whatever towards showing that men are incapable of anything *except* selfish actions. To discover the physiological causes of weeping would not prove that men cannot laugh. To ascertain the nervous conditions of seeing does not show that men cannot hear. So it is with the alleged facts about the reflex circle. They exhibit to us the physiological basis of selfishness. And that is all they do. And to argue that because one characteristic of human behaviour has been traced to its physical sources, therefore human behaviour does not have any other characteristics, and is solely governed by the one whose causation physiological psychology happens up to date to have discovered, is so preposterous a *non-sequitur*, that one is astonished that anyone could be so simple as to be deceived by it.

Everyone has always known, without having to wait for physiology to inform them of the fact, that men are selfish. Now physiology tells us that it has discovered the physical basis for this fact. This is excellent. But most people also know that human beings are occasionally disinterestedly unselfish. Now let physiology discover in the nervous system the physical causes of *that* fact. But let them not, for the love of God, tell us that whatever in human nature they do not yet know the causes of cannot exist.

I said a while ago that physiological psychology is a science in its infancy, and that we know pitifully little about the physiological correlates of our mental processes. We know, from ordinary experience, infinitely more about men's psychical states than science can tell us about their physical correlates. For example, we understand quite well the difference between Mr. Holt's ideas and the ideas of Plato. But no physiologist can point to the precise differences of nervous structure or function which correspond to these mental differences. About human motives, thoughts, emotions, desires, hopes, fears, aspirations, ideals, we possess a quite vast body of knowledge which has been gathered, not from any special science, but from what we may call general human experience, during the last several thousands of years. About the correlated nervous processes we possess a knowledge which is, in comparison, utterly rudimentary, not to say crude. Of the correlates of a few of the simpler mental processes a very little knowledge has been achieved. Of the correlates of the finer and more intricate mental processes nothing whatever is known. Consider Shakespeare's knowledge of human nature, and then ask whether the physiologist can "explain," on a physical basis, the intricate psychology of Hamlet, the character of Falstaff, the differences between the thoughts of Macbeth and Lady Macbeth about the same subject. I am not asserting that for these intricate and subtle nuances of human character and thought there are no physical correlates. Probably such correlates do exist, although no one has ever proved that they do, and if we believe it, it is by an exercise of pure faith. But what I am asserting is that if such physical correlates exist, physiology is utterly ignorant of them. Its knowledge of the *physical* side is crude and almost infantile as compared with the knowledge of the *mental* side of human nature which even the most ignorant of men has gathered from general human experience of himself and his fellow beings. Therefore any attempt on the part of physiological psychology to deny the facts of human nature as known by common experience is utterly presumptuous. What would one think of a physiologist who should attempt to dictate to Shakespeare, or to deny that Shakespeare's characters could behave in the way they did, could think the thoughts and feel the emotions which Shakespeare attributed to them, on the ground that he, the physiologist, was unable to discover the basis of such thoughts and emotions in the structure of the human nervous system? It follows that if men, on the basis of their ordinary experience, believe that human beings are capable of disinterested motives and are often impelled by them, it is mere impertinence for any physio-logical psychologist to deny this by virtue of any knowl-edge he may possess of the nervous system. Whether or not such motives do exist and operate, whether psycho-logical egoism is true or false, must be decided by an appeal to men's ordinary knowledge of human nature, including the "teachings of history." The deliverances of physiology on the subject are perfectly worthless.

We may therefore set on one side the pseudo-scientific humbug which purports to prove from the phenomena of the reflex circle that disinterested unselfishness is impos-sible. We have still to meet, however, the argument from the "teachings of history." And this is a very much more serious matter. For this is really an appeal to general experience of human nature. And if that experience does tend to show that disinterested unselfishness is never found, then there is nothing further to be said. We shall have to accept that conclusion. And it cannot be denied that competent observers of humanity have often thought this. The opinion of Hobbes is entitled to great respect. He was certainly a shrewd observer. His writings have everywhere the ring of genuine sincerity, and there can be no doubt that his actual experience of men and of life led him to believe in universal selfishness.

Yet I cannot but think that his view of human nature was false and warped. It cannot be too often reiterated that in a matter of this kind the views of "experts"—psychological or other—count for nothing. It is the view of the man of the world, the man of affairs, which will be valuable here. For the material required for a true judg-ment is simply experience of life, not data gathered in a laboratory or a library. And I think it is a fact that the almost overwhelming majority of men of experience do

believe in the existence of at least occasional acts of disinterested unselfishness on the part of human beings. The
contrary opinion is maintained for the most part either
by very young and inexperienced men who wish to be
taken for men of the world and who think that cynicism
will help them, or by older men who have been soured
by some unhappy experience, or by bad men who judge
all other men's motives by their own. I cannot, of course,
profess to explain the personal idiosyncrasies which led
a man of Hobbes's calibre to take the view he did. Nor
do I suggest that he falls within any of the categories just
mentioned. There may have been something in his personal experience which soured and warped his judgment
of human nature, or there may not. He may have been perfectly impartial and honest. That a few men who are impartial and honest, as well as capable and experienced, should
hold his opinion, is nothing to be astonished at. For there is
scarcely any opinion on any subject which is not honestly
held by some intelligent and admirable person somewhere.

But it is not enough, it will be said, to assert—even if
the assertion is true, which might be doubted—that men
of experience *believe* that disinterested motives exist. This
is mere reliance on authority, and on a very doubtful
authority at that. We ought to offer actual evidence that
this belief is true. The evidence which can be offered is
of two kinds. First, there is the "teaching of history."
And second, there is the evidence of every man's personal
knowledge of men and women, including his knowledge of
himself. All evidence of this kind (except a man's knowledge of himself) is secondary. For we cannot see men's inward motives, but only their behaviour; and this we have to
interpret. But we may waive that point for the moment,
and ask what the actual evidence is.

As to historical evidence, I hesitate to inflict upon the reader the well worn examples of heroic self-sacrifice which are the theme of endless school books and sermons. Yet, if evidence is demanded, what else can one do but refer to these? I will, however, confine myself to certain remarks about the obvious cases of Jesus Christ and Socrates. It is, I think, unsound to argue that a man's motive in sacrificing his life *cannot* be egoistical, since he cannot possibly benefit by his own death. For apart from the fact that he may believe that he is going to reap the reward in another life, he may possibly derive such satisfaction from the circumstances of his own death as to make it perfectly plausible to accuse him of egoism. A man may, for example, develop a sort of morbid desire for martyrdom, and I have no doubt that many historical "martyrs" were so concerned with their own self-glorification that they were prepared to face death in order to wallow in their own egotistical feelings of self-righteousness. The psychology of such men may fairly be described as based upon a species of self-seeking. But my point is that, *in these particular cases*—those of Jesus and Socrates—this is not a reasonable explanation. I think these were examples of disinterested selflessness. Of course, as was pointed out above, this is mere interpretation. If anyone chooses to think that Jesus died to gratify a diseased self-conceit or a craving for notoriety, I am not aware of any way in which he can be proved conclusively to be wrong. I can only say that in my opinion his judgment is warped and that he is strangely lacking in insight into human character. And I shall have to leave it at that. Professor Carveth Read used to say that to attribute bad motives where good motives appear from the evidence to have been as likely, or more likely, is unscientific.

The case of Socrates is perhaps more convincing than that of Christ because his name is less surrounded by sentimentality and superstition. I do not see how any intelligent judge of human character, knowing the facts, could doubt that Socrates sacrificed his interest and his life in the disinterested pursuit of what he considered his duty. He was not governed by egoism, but by a passion for righteousness.

The other branch of the evidence is that afforded by every man's own knowledge of himself and his fellows. Men in general do distinguish fairly readily between altruistic actions which they believe to be impelled by policy and self-interest and altruistic actions which are genuinely disinterested. And they do think that they experience the latter, at least occasionally, both in themselves and in other people. No doubt they are often mistaken in particular cases. What they take to be selflessness may be nothing but calculating policy. But they can hardly be mistaken in all cases. They could hardly have come to make this distinction between interested and disinterested altruism, if no cases of the latter had ever existed in the whole history of the world—which is what the egoist wants us to believe. And I should myself say that almost every day one encounters, among those ordinary associates whom no one would think to be moral heroes, countless small actions which have plainly been dictated by the desire to benefit others without any thought of a return. In general men have kindly feelings towards one another. Men are affectionate and to some extent generous by nature, and prefer to give happiness rather than unhappiness. And most men are warmed by the sight of a child happy, and will go out of their way to make him so if they can. And it is a very shallow psychology which attributes all this to mere policy.

But, it will be said, men know very well that all this is good policy, that it is wise to help others even when no immediate return is in sight. Indirectly it will pay, even if not directly. I answer that human beings for the most part are not actually as calculating as this. One might even say that they are not so intelligent. This is hopelessly to over-intellectualize their motives.

But—it will be argued against me—morals are not the product of the individual, but of society. And even if the individual is not aware of selfish motives, yet he acts unselfishly as he does because he has been trained in that habit by a society which in general knows well what is the best policy to teach its children in their own interests. Habits of unselfishness originate in selfish calculation among the more intelligent members of society, and are then indoctrinated into the others.

Men discovered that unselfishness pays. For this reason, and for this reason only, they began to practice it. The original selfish motive may be forgotten and yet the habit may continue. Thus unselfish actions, even if the actors are unaware of their own egoism, are really based on selfishness. Now I should not myself agree that this is a true account even of the historical origin of morals. But even if it were, it is not to the point. We are not discussing the social *origin* of unselfishness. We are discussing the *present* psychology of individual men and women. We are discussing what they are, not how they came to be as they are. And if any individual now acts from unselfish motives, it makes no difference for what reasons his parents or teachers taught him to do so. *He*, at least, is actually determined by genuinely unselfish motives. And if this is admitted, our point is gained.

The point now reached in our discussion is this. There

actually are actions performed by human beings, which
are motivated by a desire to benefit other people. They
proceed from benevolent impulses without regard to a
possible return in kind either directly from the persons
benefited or indirectly from society at large. But at this
point a new objection emerges. Suppose we admit, it
will be said, the existence of the purely benevolent motives here postulated, yet even actions which are governed solely by such motives are in the end selfish. For a
man performs them ultimately because he himself derives
satisfaction from them. They satisfy *him*, and it is for
the sake of this satisfaction that he does them. Admit,
if you like, that it gives me pleasure to see others happy,
and that I try to make them happy without any hope of
return. But obviously the return which I get, and for the
sake of which I do the action, is the pleasure which I
myself get from seeing them happy. Hence the motives
of my action are entirely egoistic.

The psychology of this objection is, I think, unexcep-
tionable. It is certainly a fact that every action a man
does is done to satisfy some impulse of *his own*. From
the satisfaction of this impulse he doubtless derives
pleasure. And if he found no satisfaction for himself in
his action, he would not perform it. Indeed to deny these
plain facts would be absurd in as much as it would imply
that a man can act without any motives at all. Obviously
all intelligent and voluntary action—I am not here talking
about reflex actions and the like—is motivated. And
I cannot be moved by any motives except *my* motives. In this sense all voluntary action is unquestionably self-regarding. Moreover this objection is very
timely, for it forces us to explain and define what we
mean by disinterested unselfishness. So far we have

been relying on the unanalysed common sense notion. The difficulty may seem very formidable. But the solution of it is perfectly simple. Suppose I do something which confers happiness upon a child. The action need not be vastly self-sacrificing or heroic to make a good illustration of our point. It may be quite trifling. I may do it because I know that he is well off and I hope that he will some day remember my assistance and benefit me in some way. I may do it with no such special aim in view, but because I think it will advance my interests to gain a reputation for kindness. In all such cases my action is dictated by policy and is to be termed selfish. But I may do it because I am the kind of person who finds satisfaction in seeing children (or, in general, other persons) happy. If so my action is disinterestedly unselfish, although it is of course true that it is done because *I find satisfaction* in the happiness of others. In a word, the distinction between interested and disinterested unselfishness is not the distinction between actions done to satisfy one's own nature and actions which are not so motivated. For no one ever acts except to satisfy his own nature. This is the point upon which rests the objection which we are considering, and the truth of which we admit. The true distinction depends upon *the kind of things which satisfy a man's nature*. If a man finds satisfaction in the happiness, or in the satisfaction, of other people, then so far as this operates as a motive impelling him to acts which make them happy, he is disinterestedly unselfish. In so far as he is impelled by any other motive whatever, such as wealth, power, fame, reputation, then his acts, even though they produce, and are intended to produce, happiness in others, are not *disinterestedly* altruistic. This gives us the definition of disinterested unselfishness, and it will be seen that it is perfectly consistent with the facts of human motivation set forth in the objection which we are discussing. The disinterestedly unselfish man is he who finds happiness for himself in the mere fact of making other people happy, and whose actions are influenced by that motive. It would be absurd to demand that he himself should take no pleasure and find no satisfaction in his own altruism. Yet this is what the objection seems to demand.

It is not at all necessary for our case to prove that any action is ever motivated *entirely* by disinterested motives. Personally I believe that some actions may be of this character. But it is not necessary to accept this view. Human motives are ever a tangled skein. And very often a single indivisible action is brought about by a variety of interwoven motives, some good, some bad, some overtones, some undertones. The good motives may predominate, or the bad, or they may be about evenly divided. Thus a man may help his neighbour *both* because it is good policy and also because he genuinely and disinterestedly desires his happiness. He may perfectly sincerely take pleasure in seeing his neighbour's good fortune, while at the same time profiting by it himself and fully intending to do so. Why should he not? And if the cynic, in such a case, denies the reality of the disinterested motive, and attributes the whole action to selfishness, he is merely being stupid. He is picking out one of two or more joint causes of an event, calling it *the* cause, and shutting his eyes to the existence of the others. Complexity of causes is just as much a true principle in human actions as it is in the physical world.

My point is that it is not necessary for my argument against egoism to prove that there ever occur human actions which are *solely* due to disinterested motives, although personally I see no reason to doubt this. For if it is once admitted that disinterestedly unselfish motives exist at all, and operate at all, even as *part* causes of human actions—even if it be true that they are always mixed with interested motives—our case against egoism is won. For what the egoist asserts is that *all* human motives are interested and selfish, and that a disinterestedly unselfish motive is a psychological impossibility. Hence if once it can be shown that, even in a single case, such a motive has exerted even the slightest influence on human action, egoism collapses. The only question then left will be the question of degree. In what degree are men's motives selfish and in what degree disinterestedly unselfish? And if, on this footing, all the egoist is left to contend for is that the selfishness in the world vastly outweighs the unselfishness, we may give him this point without misgiving. For no one, I imagine, would deny it. And this, I take it, is the true "teaching of history." That the record of the human race is dark with cruelty, greed, and selfishness, is what history shows. But it is not true that there never have been, and never can be, disinterestedly unselfish actions. History exhibits many notable examples of such actions. And countless examples of selflessness, which no history ever records, occur in the daily lives of ordinary men and women.

And in the light of these considerations it must surely be apparent what a poor case the believer in universal selfishness really has. For disinterested unselfishness, as our analysis shows, *means* nothing but action motivated, either partly or wholly, by satisfaction gained from the spectacle of another's happiness. Therefore what the egoist has to show is that no human being ever receives, even in the smallest measure, pleasure from seeing others happy, or is influenced in his actions by the desire for such pleasure. And this, I think, will be too much for any impartial and intelligent observer of human beings to believe. The man who, fully understanding exactly what is involved, accepts such a conclusion, must surely be warped in his judgment or the subject of some strange psychological twist or kink. His condition might perhaps yield to the arts of the psycho-analyst. But he is not likely to yield to argument.

CHAPTER 10

THE UNIVERSALITY OF MORALS

THERE were three questions which, at the end of Chapter 2, I undertook to investigate. They were, firstly, what *is* the universal law of morality? Secondly, in what sense is this law universal? And thirdly, what is the basis of moral obligation? Up to the present we have been concerned solely with the first of these questions. In Chapters 5 to 9 I have unfolded my conception of what morality is, and of what commands it lays upon men. I have now concluded that portion of my enquiry. I turn to the second question which has to be faced, that of the supposed universality of this morality. For even if it be admitted that the moral system which has been sketched is, in its essence, the Christian morality which *we*, the peoples of Europe and America, purport to follow —and even this admission is so excessive that many, I fear, will refuse to allow it—what possible justification can I have for suggesting that it is *also* the morality of the Japanese, the Chinese, the Melanesian Islanders, the Iroquois Indians, and the rest of humanity? Ought not the very thought that I am committed to the support of so fantastic a supposition to fill me with shame and confusion? On an earlier page I asked the reader to suspend his judgment regarding this question until I had had a chance to develop in full my conception of what the nature of morality is. This I have now done, and I can ask for the reader's patience no longer. He is entitled to his answer. I must go out to meet the challenge which I have so far contrived, by hook or by crook, to avoid. I must make good my position, or abandon the field, amid laughter and derision, to the ethical relativist. Nor am I unaware of the heavy burden of difficulties and perplexities which lies upon me and of the apparent odds against the successful performance of my task.

I am to assert that this morality, which I have sketched, is, in some sense, universally applicable to all men. I think the most important point is that it should be clearly understood what, in this proposition, really is asserted, and what is not asserted. The greatest obstacle to its acceptance lies in the fact that it will be thought to mean all kinds of things which in fact it does not mean. It is for this reason that, at first blush, it appears so preposterous. This is because it is supposed to contain, or imply, many things which are in truth preposterous, but which, when it is properly understood, it does not contain or imply at all. Our first task must therefore be to clear away these misunderstandings. And indeed a great part of what I shall have to say will consist in carefully explaining what I do *not* mean by the doctrine of the universality of morals. When this process of elimination has been completed, the doctrine may, I hope, appear less fantastic and more acceptable than it does now.

I will begin by making clear a distinction which has already been suggested on an earlier page. By asserting that there exists a universal morality we might mean that this morality is, or has been, accepted as a matter of fact by human beings everywhere now and in the past. The question would then be purely one of anthropological and historical fact. Is it a fact, supportable by empirical evidence, that there exists a morality which is, and has been, universal in *this* sense?

Now I do not entirely repudiate the challenge even when it is put in this form. I shall attempt to show that there is a measure of truth in the doctrine of the universality of morals even when it is understood in this sense. But at the moment I am concerned to point out that this is certainly not the primary meaning of the doctrine which I am preaching. What that doctrine primarily means is that there is a single moral law which *ought* to be accepted by all men, even if as a matter of fact it is not. Hence my main contention is *not* that the Japanese, Chinese, Melanesians, and the rest, all do as a matter of fact have the same ideas of morality; but rather that the same morality is *applicable* to them in the sense that they ought to recognize and acknowledge it whatever their actual ideas of morality may happen to be. I want to show, not that all men *think* the same things moral, but that the same things *are* moral for all of them, whatever they think.

Already our doctrine begins to wear less the appearance of being ridiculous. It is true that we do not yet know what is the empirical meaning of the enigmatic word "ought." To find the meaning of it is the final puzzle which we shall have to solve before our enquiries can be considered closed. But that after all is a matter of philosophical analysis. In some popular unanalysed common sense way we already—so it must be believed—have the meaning of "ought" within our minds. And if, for the present, we are allowed to proceed upon the basis of such common sense meaning, it is surely not on the face of it ridiculous to think that all men ought to agree in what they hold right and wrong. The inhabitants of New Guinea practice upon one another shocking cruelties. Perhaps they think these practices quite moral, although it is really more likely that they do not think about them in those terms at all. Now if what the doctrine of the universality of morals taught were that the inhabitants of New Guinea and ourselves are in substantial agreement in our moral opinions about such practices, then such a view might well be thought, not merely false, but plainly ridiculous in view of the empirical evidence adduced by anthropologists. But if what we are asserting is only that the inhabitants of New Guinea ought to think otherwise than they do, ought to condemn the very practices which they now approve, ought to give up murder and rapine, ought to learn to live together in friendship and peace, then, though this opinion may quite possibly be false, it cannot be said to be simply absurd. It is at least what millions of sensible and educated people have thought in the past and still think today. It is in accordance with what I may call the moral common sense of civilized humanity. On such grounds it cannot indeed be accepted as a philosophically tenable opinion. To make it so acceptable we must first give a philosophical interpretation of the meaning of the word "ought." But we are at present moving on the level of common sense. And what I am concerned at the moment to show is not that the opinion is true, but that it is not to be rejected offhand as too plainly preposterous to merit enquiry. My hope is only that by means of these considerations I may remove some of the initial prejudice against my view with which perhaps the reader began this chapter.

It is plain that to our view, interpreted in this way, evidence of the actual variation of moral codes in different races and countries is largely irrelevant. For what is asserted is not a uniformity of moral opinion, but a uniformity of moral truth. From a strictly logical point of view we might insist that even if it were admitted that no two human beings had ever agreed about a single moral question, this would be irrelevant to the problem of whether there exists a universal morality. For it might logically still be the case that there is a moral truth which all men ought to accept, even though not a single human being knew, or ever had known, what that moral truth is.

But I do not wish to push the mere logic of the matter so far. I do not wish to admit an absolute divorce between men's moral opinions and the truth. I wish to assert, on the contrary, that there really is a sense in which it may with truth be said, not only that men in general ought to acknowledge a single moral standard, but that they actually do. For if there actually is, among human beings of different races and times, such an utter divergence of moral opinions that no means of reconciling them one with another can be found, then, though it might still be theoretically and logically possible to maintain belief in a universally applicable "ought," yet this would become exceedingly unplausible. For it is hardly likely that, if there existed a single moral truth, or set of moral truths, the greater part of humanity should be in *total* ignorance of it or in chaotic and irreconcilable disagreement about it. The case is not here as it is with science. It is nothing extraordinary if there is some scientific truth regarding which all men are ignorant, or which only a very few men know while all the rest are ignorant of it. For science requires special training, special aptitudes, special instruments, special experience. But all men have the experience which is required for the making of moral judgments— the experience of being alive and having relations with other men. No special instruments, no special aptitudes, are needed. And it would certainly be extraordinary if, in the moral sphere, there should be a truth of which men were in total ignorance. Partial ignorances, together with some divergences of opinion, we should expect here too. We should expect that some men would see more of the truth, others less; that some would be morally wise, others foolish. And if we find it to be so, our belief in the universality of morals need not be shaken. But I think it would be profoundly shaken if the different moral opinions of different ages and lands were so completely contradictory of one another, that we could find in them no common core of any sort; if there were no possibility of showing that they were variations upon a common theme; if there were no possibility of reconciling them and mediating between them. To parody a famous saying of Hegel's, we must surely believe that the moral idea is not so impotent that everywhere and always it only ought to be and never is. Even if there were such an utterly ineffectual moral idea—existing perhaps in a world of ghostly essences, nowhere else—it would be too futile a thing to be worth fighting for.

Therefore I think it is undesirable wholly to reject the challenge of the ethical relativist to find amid the varying moral ideas of mankind a universal element. I think that I ought to show that, in some sense, and in some way, all men really do accept, and always have accepted, a single universal morality. That is why I said earlier that the doctrine of the universality of morals means *primarily* only that all men ought to acknowledge the one morality, not that they do. Primarily, but not entirely. There is a secondary meaning of the doctrine which I am also concerned to uphold, namely that, in spite of the variations of moral opinion, there is, and always has been, a sense in which all men acknowledge one morality.

It is with this secondary meaning alone that I shall be concerned in the present chapter. For it is impossible to show that all men *ought* to acknowledge a single universal morality until we have solved the problem of the empirical meaning of the word "ought." Only after we have discovered the basis and nature of moral obligation can we make any headway with our attempt to establish that the same moral obligation falls upon all humanity. Accordingly I reserve that attempt for the next chapter. And in the rest of the present chapter I shall be engaged in endeavouring to support the view that there is a core of universality in the varying actual and empirically found moralities of the world.

But is not this to return once more to the very view which, at the beginning of this chapter, seemed to invest the doctrine of the universality of morals with an appearance of being patently ridiculous? Do we mean, after all, that the morality which has been developed in Chapters 5 to 9 of this book is, not merely *our* morality, but also the morality of all alien civilizations in our own and in all past times, and even of savages and primitive peoples? And in view of the plain evidences of anthropology, how can we save such a doctrine from perishing amid universal derision and laughter?

Once more let us begin by carefully explaining what we do *not* mean, in order that what we *do* mean may appear in its true light. We really do assert that all men at all times and in all lands do subscribe and have subscribed to one and the same morality. But there are many different senses in which this might be maintained. And some of these senses of the proposition really are ridiculous and contrary to all evidence. Let us eliminate these false and absurd senses of the doctrine. And let us then see whether we may not be left with something which can reasonably be believed.

First of all, then, I do *not* mean that all the peoples and races of the world take the same views as we do of murder, stealing, suicide, sex intercourse, truthfulness, courage, honesty. We should look, amid differing moral systems, not for a consensus of opinions upon the *particular* duties of life, or the *particular* maxims of morality, but for some recognition of the *general* law of morals. This general law is the principle of altruism. This is the *essence* of morals. And all that is asserted is that all moralities have this for their essence. There are certain to be many different views as to what particular kinds of action are altruistic. Differences will arise from two sources. In the first place there will be objective differences, due to the fact that the same general law, when applied to different sets of circumstances, will yield different results. It may really be true that in one country monogamy may be the best (i.e., the most altruistic) institution, while in another country polygamy may be the best. In the second place, there will be subjective differences, due to the different ways in which differently constituted human beings will attempt to apply the same fundamental law. The application of a general principle to particular cases is a work of conceptual thought. And human minds, in performing this work, do not operate like calculating machines which, with mechanical precision, always reach the same result if presented with the same data. Human minds are affected by idiosyncracies and failures of all kinds, due to subjective causes. Hence, even in the same country, in the same age, and given the same sets of circumstances, there will always be differences of opinion as to particular duties and maxims of morality. All we can reasonably expect to find, therefore, amid the various moralities of the world, is a certain uniformity of *inner spirit*, not a one to one correspondence of particular details. Failure to understand this is one cause of the widespread acceptance of the doctrine of ethical relativity. We shall look to see whether we can discern amid different moral codes the inner spirit of altruism as their essence.

Secondly, I do not mean that all human beings have always accepted the morality of altruism *in the form or in the words* in which it is expressed in this book. "Act always so as to increase human happiness as much as possible. And at the same time act on the principle that all persons, including yourself, are intrinsically of equal value." It would indeed be ridiculous to maintain that everyone has always accepted *this formulation* of morality. So far as I know, no one except myself has ever expressed the essence of morals precisely in this way. And now that it has been so expressed, ninety per cent of humanity will be incapable of even understanding what the words mean. And of those who do understand it, probably far more than ninety per cent will flatly refuse to accept it.

This is nothing to be surprised at. Certainly it is nothing which should cause us to retract our views. Men in general may often well understand in the concrete that which they are quite incapable of apprehending when stated in the form of abstract principle. Many understand quite well that apples fall to the ground who could make nothing whatever of the law of gravitation even when stated in the simplest possible terms. Moreover, even among highly educated people, many will accept as true a proposition if stated in one set of words, while denouncing as a dangerous falsehood the very same truth expressed in a different way. To ensure rejection of a truth by your audience you have only to include in the formulation of it some word or words which are apt to carry with them associated ideas against which your hearers have a prejudice. To ensure acceptance of a falsehood you have only to include some word or words which carry with them associated ideas which your hearers like, or which flatter them. All orators, and most writers make use of these two principles. They are found to operate even in discussions of philosophy carried on among professional philosophers. How much more then among the masses of humanity. Now I should say that the moral principle of altruism, as formulated on the previous page, means in essence precisely the same as the saying "Do unto others as you would that they should do unto you." But it will doubtless be the case that many of those who are accustomed to exalt the biblical text as the concentrated essence of Christian morality will nevertheless repudiate our principle of altruism as an abominable perversion of Christian morals.

People in general *do not understand what they themselves mean*. They do not understand the meaning of their own most cherished convictions. It is one of the chief functions of the philosopher to tell them what they mean. This is a profoundly difficult task. And if, on rare occasions, the task is successfully performed by the philosopher, people in general do not recognize their own ideas thus restated, but tell the philosopher that he is talking palpable nonsense.

In the light of these considerations we can understand something of the position which the principle of altruism is believed by us to hold in the sphere of men's moral ideas. It is believed to be a fairly accurate statement, in more or less abstract philosophical language, of the general principle which is at the bottom of all moral codes. It is the general spirit which pervades them, nothing more. Moral ideas themselves, as they are found in the popular consciousness, are vague, confused, fumbling, even self-contradictory. They are expressed in all sorts of different shapes and forms of words. As thus variously expressed, they are not commonly recognized as possessing any common principle. The different *expressions* of the same principle are taken for different *principles*. For nothing is rarer among human beings, even among philosophers, than the capacity to penetrate below surfaces. The ethical relativist, who invariably perceives only surfaces and cannot see beneath them, affirms confidently that there is no common principle. And when the common principle is extricated and stated in its purity by a philosopher, the very persons from whose confused ideas it is a distillation, cannot recognize it as their own. It should be no matter of surprise, therefore, if it should be denied that the principle of altruism is, as it is here stated to be, the universal principle of all morals. Because the average Hindu or Japanese might smile, the Melanesian islander simply gape, if told that this principle is the principle of *his* moral code, it does not follow that this is not in fact true. Whether it is true or not has yet to be determined.

Perhaps, when this particular misunderstanding has been removed, our view may appear a little less ridiculous in so far as it applies to civilized nations, even those outside the tradition of Christianity. Even the morality of Confucius, even the morality of Buddha, might perhaps in this way be shown to be simply different expressions of the spirit of altruism. Certainly both Confucius and the Buddha did teach altruism, though it might still be questioned whether this was the essential part of their teachings. But when it comes to savages—it will be said—our view is no longer even plausible. *Their* creeds—their cannibalistic feasts, their head-hunting expeditions, their orgies of pillage and rapine—these certainly are not expressions of the spirit of altruism. What, then, is to be done?

Now one might point out, among other things, that it was never asserted that all actual practices of all actual races are expressions of altruism. It was not even asserted that all the practices which are *approved* in a particular social group are such expressions. For the matter of that one might find, even in America or England today, many generally approved customs which are in truth cruel and brutal. But this does not prove that the essential spirit of the morality which we English or Americans profess to follow may not be in essence altruistic. Nor can any similar conclusion be drawn from the many vile practices of savages.

It will be well to remember this. Yet this is not, on the whole, what I had to say. This is not the main consideration by means of which I should seek to make plausible the view for which I am contending when it comes to the application of that view to savage morals. I will instead draw attention to a third possible misunderstanding of the theory of the universality of morals.

When it is said that the principle of altruism is found everywhere, this does *not* mean that it is found everywhere complete and fully developed. Among primitive peoples, I have no doubt, it is found only in rudimentary, foetus-like, or stunted forms. Logically, no doubt, a person must either have an idea or not have it. Or at any rate this will be true if by an idea one means an explicit belief, a proposition held before the intellect with its determinate parts of subject, copula, and predicate. Either it is asserted or it is not asserted. It may, of course, be merely entertained. But in any case it exists in the mind either full-blown or not at all. But ideas, for the most part, are not propositions. They appear in the human mind, first of all, as vague feelings. It is only after a long evolution that they slowly begin to take on, in the mind's womb, the form of explicit judgments with the differentiated parts of subject, predicate, and copula. Often enough they do not finally take on this form till they are expressed in words to other people. They lurk in dark places of the mind, obscure, unverbalized, formless. Even the owner of them scarcely knows that they are there until, for some reason or other, the searchlight is turned upon them. Ideas are organisms. They proliferate and grow. They develop from rudimentary beginnings. And as a human foetus may be unrecognizable as human, so may an idea in its origins be unrecognizable as identical with what it is to become when it is fully developed.

Now what is alleged regarding the principle of altruism is this. If you take an advanced code of morals, such as that of Christianity, or that of Confucius, you will probably find the principle stated somewhere in its literature, or in the sayings of its prophets, fairly explicitly—though even here you will never find it stated in its abstract form with philosophical accuracy. It will be expressed in literary, as distinguished from philosophical or scientific, language. For it was not intended for philosophers or scientists, but for the masses of men. Thus in Christian literature it appears as the golden rule, and in many other forms too. But if you take some primitive moral code, that of a people relatively savage and uncivilized, you will not find it stated in explicit form at all. Such a people might even repudiate it as ridiculous if it were put to them in its complete and developed shape. And yet it may be there, deeply buried among their chaotic and primitive notions, forming the living principle and root out of which those notions are slowly growing. And it may be there in a form so primitive and crude that it may require considerable penetration and insight to recognize it at all. And as it frequently happens that the more learning a man possesses, the less insight he has, it is not to be wondered at that there are men whose minds are choked with masses of anthropological facts, which are yet barren and useless because they cannot penetrate to the spirit which informs those facts.

The idea of altruism may first appear in the vague and confused *feeling* that one ought to be *fair to one's neighbours*. Those who are moved by this feeling may have the most elementary notions of what is meant by "fair" and also of what is meant by "neighbour." It may appear quite fair to them that a powerful man should claim the right of ravishing the wife of his servant or slave. It may appear fair to put to death an inferior for a trifling affront. The Sinhalese—the only non-European people of whose customs and ways of thought I have personal first-hand knowledge—think it perfectly right that a high caste man should speak to a man of low caste as if he were a dog. Not only does the high caste man think this, but—and this is the essential point—the low caste man thinks it too, and it would never occur to him to resent it. Even among ourselves it is habitually thought fair that one set of men should appropriate to themselves the product of the labour of others. And until recently this was believed even by the victims. And if the notion of fairness is undeveloped among ourselves, how much more undeveloped will it be among primitive peoples. But it is there. I do not believe that there is any race of men in whose minds the idea of fairness as between men does not exist at all. Now this idea or feeling of fairness when it is fully developed becomes the principle of justice or altruism which asserts that the desires and needs and happiness of every man are intrinsically of equal value one with another.

Just as, in the primitive mind, the notion of fairness is undeveloped, so is the notion of one's "neighbour" restricted. For us "my neighbour" means, or ought to mean and is beginning to mean, any fellow human being. Perhaps also it includes animals. For the savage it means only his fellow tribesman. The principle of altruism is present to his mind, in the form of vague feeling if not in the form of principle, but he does not apply it except in the narrowest way. He feels no moral obligations to the inhabitant of the neighbouring village, but only to the inhabitant of his own. But it is one and the same idea, the idea of fairness, justice, altruism, which forms the essence of morality in the savage as in the believer in universal benevolence.

That the progress of humanity has been marked by the continual widening of the circle of "altruistic sentiment" has been noted, and illustrated with much learning, by none other than Westermarck himself.[1] Yet it apparently does not occur to him that this is evidence of the gradual growth of a single moral idea in varying stages of development among different races. All he can see is the differences which result from this growth. I see no reason why Westermarck should not be called as a witness in favour of the belief that a single morality obtains everywhere among human beings.

[1] *Ethical Relativity*, pages 200, 207, and elsewhere.

The ethical relativist is fond of pointing to different levels of moral development and declaring that they exhibit different and mutually inconsistent sets of moral codes. In one age and place, he tells us, it is considered quite right for the inhabitants of one village, or the members of a wandering tribe, to murder, pillage, and destroy the property of people living a few miles away. In another age and place, the same identical acts are considered immoral. Obviously you have here two quite different and mutually contradictory moral codes. And you are supposed from this to conclude to the truth of the doctrine of ethical relativity.

Could anything be more shallow? Surely this is due to looking unintelligently at the dead surfaces of things and having no insight into their living pulsating interiors. If we treat the facts as dessicated museum specimens, we may well arrive at such conclusions. We attach our labels to the dead specimens, and we find that they differ from one another. They are therefore different sets of moral ideas, they have nothing in common, they contradict one another, and consequently they contradict the whole idea of a universal morality. But this is to forget that morals are human and therefore grow. If the biologist were to take the corpses of a human foetus, a child, and a grown man, dry them, and pin them down in glass cases, as we pin down dead butterflies, he might perhaps conclude that he had before him three entirely different species of animals. Their characters might well appear mutually inconsistent. Biologists do not make these silly mistakes because, being themselves living and growing beings, they interpret the facts with the conceptions of life and growth in their minds. But the ethical relativist is apparently determined to interpret living facts as if they were dead ones. He cannot see that the continuous extensions of the application of the sentiment of altruism, its extension from the family to the tribe, from the tribe to the nation, from the nation to humanity, are an example, not of a heterogeneous collection of different and mutually inconsistent ideas, but of a single idea in different stages of its growth.

Even without introducing the concept of organic growth, the same point ought to be obvious. Newton discovered and formulated a law of gravitation. This law was at first applied only to the solar system. Later it was found to apply to the whole material universe. What would one think of anyone who should argue that the law when applied only to the solar system was one concept; that when applied to all other bodies in space it was quite another concept; and that therefore nature is not governed by any universal law but is subject to a gravitational relativity which means that different laws operate in different parts of the universe? Yet this is precisely the way in which the ethical relativist argues. The moral law is the law of altruism. Humanity first discovered that it applied to some small group of human beings, the family or the tribe. Later on humanity discovers that this same law applies universally to all men. And it is thereupon argued that what we have in history is a series of different and mutually inconsistent moral conceptions.

Another frequent source of confusion is the failure to distinguish between means and ends. The moral man aims always and everywhere at one single end, the happiness of others. But in different countries and different ages opinions differ as to the best means of achieving this end. And straightway these differences of means are seized upon as importing different moral standards, although it is plain that it is the end which is the standard, not the means. For example, our forefathers burned witches alive, while we regard such action with horror. This is not, as is commonly supposed, evidence of mutually incompatible moral standards. It is evidence of the existence of different opinions as to how one and the same standard should be applied, and as to the means which should be adopted to achieve the standard. For our forefathers did not burn witches for amusement. Or if any of them were so motivated, they would not have met with general approval. They burned them because they genuinely believed that this was one essential means towards the saving of souls —whether the souls of the witches themselves or of those innocents whom they might delude if allowed to live. That is to say, their action was altruistic. They were therefore guided by exactly the same moral standard as are modern persons who do not burn witches, but who instead endow hospitals or send missionaries to non-Christian lands.

To sum up what has so far been said. There actually is a single universal morality which all humanity has recognized in the past and recognizes today. But this bold statement does not *mean* that men's moral ideas about particular duties or crimes are everywhere the same. It is compatible with the widest differences in such matters. It does not mean that the single moral law is everywhere understood as being the abstract principle which we formulated in Chapter 7. It is compatible with an almost universal refusal to admit that that principle is the true law of morals at all. Finally, it does not mean that the principle of altruism, in any shape or form, appears in all moral codes in an easily recognizable or fully developed form. What it does mean is that the principle of altruism, as formulated in Chapter 7, is the abstract statement of that which, whether as vague feeling or as conceptual idea, is everywhere the moving spirit and the inner life of whatever morality exists. Here it is no more than a scarcely visible seed. There it is a full grown tree. Here it is dim and misty. There it shines out with the purity of a star. Here it is overlaid and encrusted with barbarities. There it is found nearly pure. Wherever there is morality at all, there, in that place, there is altruism in greater or less degree. Where there is no altruism—and there may be, for all I know, tribes of men so low that they exhibit no altruism at all, though I doubt it—there, in that place, there is no morality.

Take any set of so-called moral ideas. First pare away from it the irrational taboos and prejudices, the mere physical dislikes, the local and inessential customs and traditions, with which—in the minds of its adherents (and in the minds of ethical relativists)—it is invariably mixed up. Pare away next those customs which, though not irrational nor of merely physical origin, are based on sanitary, medical, or other non-ethical considerations. Try to get at the *essence* of the morality in question, and you will find that this essence consists in the idea of altruism, that is, the idea of being fair, kind, just, considerate (so far as these terms are understood), to one's neighbour (whoever, at the particular stage of development, is understood to be one's neighbour), of treating him as one would oneself like to be treated, the idea of having regard for the needs and desires of other people—in a word, the idea of unselfishness. The statement that all men recognize the same morality means only that the idea of the obligation to behave thus is found, in some shape or form, in greater degree or less, in every human society; that this is the pith and marrow of whatever morality any particular human society does actually recognize. Does it require learned disquisitions in anthropology, expeditions to the Antipodes, the ostentatious display of "evidence" gathered from the ends of the earth, to prove that this is true? Surely not. For how could it possibly be false? It is impossible to believe that human beings exist, the core of whose essential relations to one another does not consist in at least an elementary consideration for one another's needs, desires, and feelings—that is to say, in some form and degree of altruistic action. For such consideration is the necessary prerequisite of any sort of social intercourse. And social intercourse of some kind is universal in all humanity, because it is as necessary to the human animal as is bread. Human beings simply could not meet, live together, exchange amenities of any kind, without such consideration. It is therefore not conceivable that there should exist social groups who are without the notion of altruism, or among whom the notion is not the foundation of their relations to one another. Morality is nothing but the necessary relations to one another of human beings. It is simply the set of principles which governs those relations. And it is a necessity of human nature that these principles should always be of the nature of altruism, that is, that they should be based upon mutual consideration. And it therefore follows that the essential idea of morality must be the same everywhere. There is no need to penetrate the jungles of Africa, the steppes of Siberia, in search of evidence of this. One must believe it, unless one thinks, with Hobbes, that there are, or may have been, men fundamentally anti-social, living in a war of all against all, even against their own children. And I am not aware that any anthropologist supports Hobbes's abstractions in this respect.

I have, however, already quoted Westermarck's writings as tending to show, by actual empirical evidence—in
the teeth of his own convictions—that the altruistic sentiment is found even in low-grade moralities, and that
progress in morals largely coincides with the growing extension and application of the sentiment to wider and
wider spheres of humanity. And I will here refer to the
same authority again. Westermarck recognizes that an
essential characteristic of what he calls moral emotion is its
real or apparent "impartiality" or "disinterestedness." [1]
Thus it is resentment which, on his view, gives rise to
moral disapproval. Not all resentment, however, but only
that resentment which is, or appears to be, impartial;
which is directed against an act of injury as such, irrespec-
tive of whether the person injured is or is not myself. In
the same way moral approval is based, according to the
same author, upon kindly emotions which are impartial.
Plain resentment or kindly feeling, without this element of
disinterestedness, are not *moral* emotions, and do not give
rise to moral approval and disapproval. They give rise to
quite other things, such as gratitude, anger, revenge.
Impartiality or disinterestedness is the essential mark of
moral, as distinguished from non-moral, emotions. So
says Westermarck. But what is all this save the recognition in all morality of a common element, that of the idea
of impartiality? And is not this impartiality precisely
what I have described in Chapter 7 as justice? According
to view developed in this book the essence of morality—
of morality in all lands and in all ages—can be described
indifferently either as justice or as altruism. This conclusion was reached on general grounds without specific
appeal to the data of anthropology. And now we find that

[1] *Ethical Relativity*, Chapter 4.

precisely these two characters of altruism and justice are found by Westermarck, as a result of his elaborate anthropological investigations, to be essential marks of all moral codes. (Strictly speaking I should say that he finds justice or impartiality to be essential to the existence of morality, and altruistic sentiment to be only associated with its growth. But this makes no difference to my contention.) This agreement between two writers whose methods and beliefs are in general utterly opposed, is curious and striking. And I cannot but suggest that, if the reader cannot be happy without empirical and anthropological evidence for the thesis for which I am contending, I cannot do better than refer him to the writings of Westermarck! This is an odd enough situation. Westermarck is made to appear as a witness against ethical relativity. But the really extraordinary thing is that Westermarck should fail to see that he *is* attributing a common element to all moral systems, and that this is utterly inconsistent with the position of ethical relativity which he purports to derive from his facts.

In Chapter 2 I pointed out that ethical relativity renders meaningless many moral judgments which form an essential part of the beliefs of all cultured persons, and which we are all persuaded, in practice, do have both meaning and truth. Among these were all judgments which compare one moral code with another for the purpose of deciding which is the "higher," which the "lower" —judgments such as that Christian ethics are higher than the ethics of Australian bushmen. Also all judgments which assert that there has been, or ever could be, any "progress" in moral ideas were, we saw, meaningless if ethical relativity is true. For according to that doctrine there can be no common moral standard by which different moral systems can be judged. Hence the ethical relativist can give no better account of such judgments than to say that they express nothing but our egoism and self-conceit. "Higher" can mean nothing except "more like me and my ideas." Thus the ethical relativist made complete nonsense of our moral beliefs.

It is already partly possible to give intelligible meaning to such judgments in the light of the considerations adduced in this chapter. They cannot indeed be finally and fully justified until we have discovered, as we hope to do in the next chapter, the empirical meaning of the word "ought." But already we can go a long way towards understanding them. This is because we have discovered a common standard by reference to which all local and ephemeral standards and ideas can be judged. This common standard is the principle of altruism. A lower morality is one in which the altruistic principle, though it is present, is undeveloped. A higher morality is one in which it is more perfectly developed. The difference is a difference in the degree of unselfishness demanded by the moralities in question. If Christianity contains the highest ethical doctrine yet given to the world, this is because in it the principle of unselfishness shines out pure and clear, and because the principle is extended to all human beings; whereas in lower moralities the idea of altruism is dim, is obscured by other elements, is encrusted with barbarisms and even cruelties, is narrowly and meanly interpreted, and is extended only to a man's immediate friends, family, fellow tribesmen, or fellow nationals. Progress in moral ideas means, in our view, not egregious self-conceit, but the steady development and unfolding of more and more altruistic rules of conduct.

This is surely a more sensible view than that which

denies to the idea of higher and lower moralities any legitimate meaning at all. It is no wonder that plain sensible men are suspicious of philosophy and reject its claims to intellectual leadership when they find that philosophers become so dazzled and bewildered by their own brilliant but empty dialectic that they lose all touch with the actual world, lose touch with man's moral intuitions, cannot keep their feet upon the earth, but drift off into a cloudland of clever falsehoods. For this is what they do when they allow themselves, in the interests of a hair-brained theory, to deny meaning to plain statements of fact of which everyone, except themselves, knows the meaning. Then it is that we see exhibited before our eyes the spectacle of cleverness without wisdom, of learning without sense.

CHAPTER 11

WHY SHOULD I BE MORAL? (I)

After I have barely surmounted the first two waves, you are now bring-
ing down upon me the third breaker, which is the most mountainous and
formidable of the three. . . .
I am now on the point of confronting that very statement which we com-
pared to the huge wave. Nevertheless it shall be spoken, even if it deluge me,
literally like an exploding wave, with laughter and infamy.

Plato's *Republic.*

AT the end of Chapter 2 we set before ourselves
three questions which we were to attempt to
answer in this book. I will quote them in full
as they were there presented.

> What is the universal moral law? What is its actual
> content? What, in short, does it command men to do?
> In what sense is this law universal, and how can its
> universality be shown to be consistent with the actual
> plurality of moral codes in the world?
> What is the basis and foundation of this moral law,
> and of the obligation which it imposes, and how can
> it be shown that the universal "ought" which it
> implies is empirically meaningful?

To the first of these questions the answer—such answer
as I am capable of framing—was given and fully explained
in Chapters 5 to 9. The second question received part of
its answer in Chapter 10, and the rest will have to be
explained here. But the main purpose of the present
chapter is to find the solution of the third of the three
problems. It is this which I compare to Plato's third huge
wave.

250

For in truth it is the one problem of ethics which must fill a man with terror—terror of its vast importance and of its vast difficulty. I approach the attempt to solve it with trembling and hesitation, conscious that what I am about to say may meet with scant sympathy, may even "deluge me with laughter and infamy." And yet before I go any further I would say this. Even if, at the end, the problem remains utterly unsolved, if I fail completely to find the true basis of morals, if I fail to discover any convincing reason why any man should be moral at all, I shall still stick to my belief that there is a universal morality, and that what has been already set forth is at least, so far as it goes, a rough approximation to moral truth. For it cannot be—as the ethical relativist supposes—that morality is nothing but a chaotic, crazy, unintelligible jumble of irrational whims, prejudices, and superstitions. It is my faith that the universe in which we live is not a madhouse. It is my faith that man's moral consciousness is not a kind of universal lunacy. Our moral nature bears witness to some truth. If I fail to surmount the third great breaker—and who is there who is so blindly arrogant as to feel confident here?—then I shall have failed to give a final rational and intelligible account of that truth. But because I have failed, because all men have failed, it is not to be thought of that there *is* no truth. By such vision as we have of it, dim and incomplete though it be, let us abide. Men hope, and will keep on hoping so long as there is intellectual vigour and life in them, that they may find for it a rational justification. But if it is not found, let us not deny such vision as we have, and let us not acquiesce in being stone blind.

At the beginning of the book I pointed out that one among the causes of the decay of belief in a universal morality was the fact that philosophers have been unable to give any clear account of the sources from which a universally binding moral obligation could flow. Supernaturalism, in its time, provided a ready foundation. The moral law was the will of God, and the will of God was naturally binding upon all his creatures. Or the moral law was the outgrowth of the deep-laid metaphysical structure of the universe. Since such views no longer convince the men of our time, there appeared to be left no possible foundation for a universal moral law. And the way was therefore left open for the destructive creed of the ethical relativist.

If therefore we are still to believe in a universal morality, there falls upon us the task of attempting anew to exhibit its rational foundation. I have attempted to show *what* morality is. It is, in brief, the command which is addressed to each individual man "You *ought* to be unselfish." I have tried to prove that all men do, in some sort, either more dimly or more clearly, recognize this obligation. But now we confront at last the final, the supreme, question, Why, after all, ought I, why ought any man, to be moral? And this means for us simply, why ought I to be unselfish? The point of the question, and the difficulty of the question, are at once obvious. There is no difficulty in saying why I should take care of *my own* happiness. That is self-evident. But why should I concern myself with *yours?* Morality says that I ought to. But is this a mere dogmatic command? *Why* ought I to? No reason seems, on the face of it, to be forthcoming. To find the reason, to convert into something intelligible this apparently blind and despotic order which issues from the dark depths of a seemingly irrational world—this is our problem. This is what is conventionally called the problem of the basis of moral obligation. And we shall find as we go on that it involves, or rather is identical with, the problem of finding an empirical meaning for the word "ought."

The Socrates of Plato's *Republic* contended that there is a necessary connection between morality and happiness; that to be moral is to be happy; that morality is the only road to a happy life; that the good man is necessarily happy, the bad man necessarily unhappy.

It was admitted, both by Socrates and by his philosophical opponents in the dialogue, that morality does often as a matter of fact bring substantial rewards— success in life, wealth, power, access to good society; and that immorality does often as a matter of fact bring heavy punishments, failure, poverty, loss of friends. But this was *not* what Socrates meant by the necessary connection between morality and happiness. The special point of his ethical creed, as portrayed in the *Republic*, —and the point which he was especially challenged to prove if he could—was that *apart from* these external rewards the good man is, and must be, happy; and that *apart from* these external punishments the bad man is, and must be, unhappy; that goodness *in itself*, and without regard to its material consequences, brings happiness; that badness *in itself*, without regarding its consequences either, brings misery. In order to make the point doubly and trebly clear Socrates even undertook to prove that the good man, if deprived of all rewards, material advantages, wealth, power, comfort, would still be happy if he retained only his virtue; and that the bad man, even if rewarded, if given all that the heart could desire, would still be unhappy. Perhaps this last position is one which we should think too strong. Man's happiness is not, and cannot be, wholly independent of external goods. And we should at least say with Aristotle that it is absurd to assert that the good man can be happy on the rack. But even if this extreme position could not be finally maintained, it served in Plato's hands the literary purpose of bringing home his real meaning with absolute clarity. A point can often be best made by putting it in its strongest form, even by exaggerating it. And the essential position of the Socrates of the dialogue is that the good man has, in his goodness itself, and apart from its consequences in the way of rewards, a supreme source of happiness. He took seriously the view that virtue is its own reward, and that this reward is sufficient.

Now the essence of what I have to say in this chapter is that the insight of Socrates was a true insight; that the only road by which a man can reach his own happiness is the road of morality. Morality means altruism, that is, it means forgetting or neglecting (to a large extent) my own happiness in order that I may bend all my actions towards making others happy. Therefore the doctrine which I preach is that if a man would be happy himself, what he must do is to forget his own happiness, to cease seeking for it, and to strive for the happiness of others; and that in doing this he will *find* again that happiness of his own which he seemed, by his altruism, to be losing and giving up. Further I say that this is the solution of the problem of the basis of moral obligation. The question is, why should I work for *your* happiness? And the answer is that this is the only way to reach *my own* happiness. This will have at first the appearance of being a species of egoism. We shall see that it is not.

The same doctrine gives us the empirical meaning of

the word "ought." "You ought to be moral" means that
if you wish to be happy yourself, the only means to adopt
is to be moral. And all men are so constituted that this is
true of them. Therefore one and the same moral obligation falls upon all men. All men ought to be unselfish because all men wish to be happy and because for all men
unselfishness is the only way of attaining that end. This,
in briefest outline, is the thesis which I have to present.
And I have before me the heavy task of convincing the
reader that it is true.

To say that the insight of Socrates was a true one is by
no means equivalent to saying that the arguments which
he used to support it were valid. Actually they were partly
valid, and partly not so. It will be worth our while to
examine the substance of his argument in order that we
may see both its weakness and its strength. This will
give us the clue to our own procedure.

When we examine the structure of the human soul, said
Socrates, we find that it is essentially composed of three
parts. These are, firstly, reason or intelligence; secondly,
"spirit," by which he meant what we should perhaps call
spiritedness, that is to say, the aggressive principle in
human nature, the principle which gives rise to bravery,
honour-seeking, ambition, and also to some forms of anger
and indignation; thirdly, the sensuous appetites, such as
hunger, thirst, and sex. A further examination of the
human being shows that each of these three parts of
the soul has its own special function. An examination of
the structure of the body shows that nature intended
the stomach to digest, the lungs to purify the blood, the
brain to coördinate nervous impulses, and so on. Examination of the structure of the soul reveals likewise the essential purpose of its three parts and the work which each is

intended to do. The office of the first part of the soul,
reason, is to govern, to be the ruler, to decide what the
human being as a whole shall do. The office of the sensuous appetites is to provide the motive power of action,
and to be guided and controlled by reason as to the direction in which this motive power is to work. If reason is
the ruler, the appetites are the ruled. The function of
spirit is to be an ally of reason, and to see that the appetites carry out its orders.

Now morality, according to the definition given by
Socrates, is nothing but obedience of the passions and
appetites to their ruler, reason. The moral man is simply
the man whose appetites are kept under strict control.
The immoral man, on the contrary, is the man in whom
passion rebels, takes the upper hand, overrides reason,
and controls the whole man. Hence it follows that the
moral man is he in whom the three parts of the soul function in the *natural* way, in the way in which an examination of their structure shows that nature intended them to
function. He is thus the man whose nature is operating
healthily. The immoral man is he whose parts are out of
order, are operating as they were never intended to operate, unnaturally, unhealthily. He is to be compared
to a man whose stomach usurps the place of his brain.
Quite apart, therefore, from any question of external
rewards and punishments, the good man is certain to be
happy, or at least possesses the first condition of happiness, while the bad man is certain to be unhappy. For
goodness means simply acting in accordance with our
essential human nature, and this must necessarily spell
happiness. Badness means acting against our nature and
necessarily spells unhappiness.

One might make the point of the argument clearer by

using an illustration which has not the authority of Plato himself, but which well accords with the spirit of his contention. Inspection of a tree will show that it is composed of several parts, roots, trunk, branches. Further, it is obvious on such inspection that the roots are intended by nature to be in the ground, the trunk and branches to be in the air. Suppose we were to turn the tree upside down, placing its leaves and branches in the ground, its roots in the air. Could such a tree—if we imagine it to be conscious —be "happy"? It can only be happy if its several parts are in the place in which nature intended them to be, and are doing the work which nature intended them to do. So it is with man. He can only be happy if his reason is on top, controlling the passions which should be underneath. Turn him upside down, as you did the tree, put his passions in control of his reason, and what have you? In the first place you have the bad man, for the rebellion of appetite against reason is, for Socrates, the definition of badness. And in the second place you have the man who is, and must be, radically unhappy. He is unhappy because his whole personality is upside down, because it is operating in a manner contrary to its own essential structure. But the good man is he the parts of whose soul are functioning as they should, naturally and healthily. And he therefore is happy. And this argument will hold independently of any question of external rewards and punishments. Even if the good man finds no such rewards, he will be happy because his soul is healthy. Even if the bad man gains power and wealth and fame, he cannot be happy because his soul is unhealthy.

I do not wish to spend time in pointing out in detail the weaknesses in this argument. I have not quoted it for this purpose but in order to extract from it what is good, and what will be helpful to us in our own enquiry. I will therefore content myself with making very briefly three points of criticism. In the first place, the argument, even if all the facts on which it relies are genuine facts, only proves half of what it is intended to prove. What it shows, the most that it shows, is that goodness (here equated with health of the soul) is *one* necessary condition of happiness. From this it follows that the bad man must be unhappy, since he is without an essential condition of happiness. But the other half of the doctrine, that the good man must be happy, does not follow. For there may be other essential conditions of happiness which he lacks. This is why the argument can never prove, for example, that the good man can be happy on the rack. For although goodness may be one essential condition of happiness, the absence of physical agony is another. Hence the good man in physical agony is not happy. One might add that for most people a certain measure of possession of external goods is also a necessary condition of happiness, and that therefore without these even the good man will not be wholly happy.

This criticism is not, however, really important for us. Perhaps it would not have been important for Plato either. For in order to give a rational basis for moral obligation it is not necessary to establish that goodness is the *sole* condition of happiness. It is enough if we can establish that it is one indispensable condition. If so, we can answer the question, why should I be moral? The answer will be that without morality it is impossible that I should be happy. It is not necessary that we should be able to give an absolute guarantee that if a man is moral, this *alone* will ensure his happiness. This indeed is not our opinion. In addition to morality a man requires for his happiness absence of physical pain, some external goods, some "pleasures," and so on. This is why he cannot be expected to be *absolutely* altruistic, to deny himself everything, but is entitled to be just to himself as well as to others.

A second criticism is that the definition of morality, on the correctness of which the whole argument depends, is quite inadequate. No doubt morality does involve the control of the passions by the intelligence. But it involves much more than that. Positive altruism is necessary to it, and this is not mentioned in the definition. A man might control his appetites, and yet be quite selfish. The Greek conception of morality is simply moderation. It leaves unstressed the note of altruism or self-sacrifice which is the special mark of Christian ethics. Thus Plato's argument only shows that a man cannot be happy if he does not control his appetites. This is reasonable enough. But what ought to be shown is that he cannot be happy if he is not unselfish. And that is quite another matter.

The third criticism is that Plato's psychology is hopelessly out of date. The soul is not divided into the three parts, reason, spirit, and appetite. Nor do its parts operate in the manner which Plato suggested. I do not of course mean that there is no truth at all in what Plato said about all this. There is a great deal of truth. But I mean that his psychology is so primitive and over-simplified and inaccurate that no certain conclusions can be based upon it.

I turn now to consider the strength of Plato's argument. Its strong point is its *method*. It is on this that I would dwell, and it is from this that we can learn. The essence of Plato's method here is based upon the view that *morality grows out of human nature itself*. Plato finds the foundation of morality in the structure of human personality, *in that structure which is common to all human beings*. He was well aware that men differ from one another. He knew that a barbarian was different from a Greek, an Egyptian from an Ionian, one Greek or one Egyptian from another. He was, in principle if not in detail, just as conscious of the different customs, moral codes, tribal regulations which exist in the world, as any modern ethical relativist. But he believed that all human beings have a common fundamental structure of personality. This he found in the tripartite division of reason, spirit, and appetite. And it was on this common structure of human personality as such that he founded morality. It is true that the detailed account of this structure which he gave is quite unacceptable to us at the present day. It is also true that this humanism, even naturalism, of Plato's ethics, seems to be contradicted by other elements in his teaching. Whereas here he finds the basis of morals in human nature, elsewhere he seems to find it in a transcendental world of eternal forms. Whether there is any real inconsistency, or whether a good Platonist could succeed in reconciling these two elements of his doctrine, does not concern us. The first lesson which is taught by the argument which I have quoted is that morality has its foundation in human nature. The second lesson is that its foundation is in the *common* elements of that nature, and not—as the ethical relativists would have it—in the peculiar whims, irrational prejudices, or emotional biases of particular tribes, cliques, or individuals. It is founded, not upon human differences, but upon human samenesses.

The third point in which, in my opinion, Plato is right, is that *morality means the proper and natural functioning of human personality*. This, of course, is the central idea of Plato's whole view. And it is the vitally important point for us to get hold of. I disagree both with Plato's view of what morality in its essence is, and with his particular account of the common structure of human personality on which morality is to be founded. The universal pattern of humanity is not described by a tripartite division of it into reason, spirit, and appetite. But I believe that if we can discover what really is the universal pattern of humanity, its essential structure or nature—what Plato would call its "parts"—we shall find that the moral man is, as he declared, the man whose "parts" function properly and in accordance with their nature. And we should conclude, with Plato, that such a man possesses in himself for that reason the prime requisite of happiness.

What, then, *is* the common structure of human personality? What can we substitute, in Plato's argument, for his tripartite division? Now fortunately for us it is not necessary for our purposes to describe the *whole* of the common pattern on which human beings are made. If it were, I should despair of my task, since nothing less than a complete system of psychology would serve. It is on only a *part* of that common pattern that morality is founded; and it is only this part which we shall have to describe here. This is equivalent to saying that morality takes its rise from certain specific characteristics which are common to all human beings, and not from the whole of human personality. And this after all is just what we should expect. There are, I believe, common elements in the human make-up which are the basis of man's esthetic appreciations. There are other common elements on which his mathematics and his logic are founded. But mathematics, logic, and art, are not parts of morality—though I do not mean to deny that there are connections between them—and neither are those common elements of his personality on which mathematics, logic, and art, are built up identical with those common elements upon which morality is built up. Nor are the latter factors identical with the whole of his being.

What, then, are the special parts of human nature which give birth to morality? They are, in my opinion, two. And it is, of course, essential to our argument that both of them should be common to all men. It is not, however, essential that they should be equally developed in all men. And we find, in fact, that they are very unevenly developed. In some men they, especially the second, are extremely rudimentary. But if they are there at all, even in germ, they are capable of being the seeds out of which morality and moral obligation grow. The first is *the social nature of man*. The second—which is closely connected with the first, but not identical with it—is his *capacity for being made happy in some degree by the bare fact of the happiness of other persons*. I will treat of these in order.

First, man is by nature a social animal. We must be very careful not to import into this expression more meaning than it is intended to convey. A social animal, as I mean the phrase to be understood, is not synonymous with Aristotle's "political animal." The political level is much higher, much more developed, than the social level. Two men on a desert island may satisfy in some measure their social natures by the simple fact of cultivating friendly relations. But they could hardly constitute any sort of a "polis." The social level would not be impossible of attainment by them, but the political level would be. In saying that man is by nature a social animal I am not asserting that it is part of his essential nature to live in cities or states or to have governments. This may or may not be true. Personally I think that much semi-mystical nonsense has been talked about man's personality finding its supreme expression only in the state. I think it is at least conceivable that men could in certain circumstances satisfy their entire natures if they lived in very small social groups with no government at all, or only with the barest minimum of organization. Governments and elaborate political states are adventitious things rendered necessary as a matter of practical convenience by the human habit of congregating in huge masses. But in any case, whether this is true or not, what I am saying here about human nature is something much *less* than that the state is a necessity to it. It is not certain whether it is a necessity of men's nature to live together in political states. But it is unquestionably a necessity of their natures to *live together*. And that is all that I mean by speaking of man as a social animal. I mean only that no man can live by himself, that he must have the society of other human beings—wife, children, relatives, friends. Social intercourse is a necessity of his nature, and without it it is impossible that he should be happy.

Perhaps someone will say that what I am describing should rather be called mere gregariousness. But this would be to mistake my meaning. Men, of course, are gregarious. But so are many animals. Animals, however, are incapable of genuine social intercourse, implying as it does not only affection, but exchange of ideas, friendship, and the like. Just as the social level is in itself a lower stage of development than the political level, so is the gregarious lower than what I am here calling the social.

It will repay us to specify a little more in detail that content of man's social nature which distinguishes it from mere gregariousness. Sociality is distinctively human, whereas gregariousness is shared by men and animals. Social intercourse achieves for men a number of different, though closely related, ends: a few of which may be mentioned. In the first place men require from their fellows the warmth of human affection. And conversely they need the opportunity to exercise towards their fellows their own affectionate natures. Both to receive and to give affection are amongst the greatest sources of human happiness. Perhaps in the end they are the greatest of all. For of all other satisfactions, not excluding even those of art and religion, the final fruit is not seldom weariness and disillusion. But human affection remains as solace and comfort when all else is gone. So that men, when they come to die, and when all desire for everything else has ceased within them, ask that those who care for them and for whom they care should gather round them. Now this end, the giving and receiving of affection, is attained mainly in the social intercourse of the family—the love of husband and wife, of parents and children, of brothers and sisters—but also in the intercourse of intimate friends.

But social intercourse may extend beyond these limits, and have other ends. In normal conditions men have, outside the inner circles of family and intimate friends, a variety of fellow beings with whom they like to associate. These are their less intimate friends and also what are sometimes called "acquaintances." We look to less intimate friends and to acquaintances, not for the deep love and affection which is largely the support of our inner lives, but for lesser goods which are, however, profoundly important to us. These include occasions for the pleasant interchange of ideas, for laughter, for sympathy and encouragement, for exchange of esteem and respect, and for mutual appreciation of one another's activities. There are indeed lonely spirits who flourish best with but little society. But no man can live completely lonely. And the vast majority need the society of both friends and acquaintances as an opportunity for self-expression. They need the stimulus of human fellowship to stir into activity their otherwise dull and immobile functions. Given this, they blossom forth. They unfreeze. Their whole personality expands as flowers open to the sunlight. Or we may change the metaphor. In those who live more or less solitary lives the wheels of personality move harshly, creaking and grating like rusty machinery. Immersed in congenial society they move swiftly, smoothly, and soundlessly, like wheels well oiled. Now the stirring of our activities, their lively and pleasant functioning, is one of the major conditions of our happiness. That happiness is not found in static ends, but in activities, in moving towards ends, was one of the major insights of Aristotle. And because social intercourse quickens up the whole tempo of all the activities of the soul, the happiness of men depends in no small measure upon it. In pleasant society we feel a warm glow of the mind not unlike that warm glow of the limbs which accrues from healthy bodily exercise.

In the same way men of great intellectual power, philosophers, scientists, artists, often depend in great measure upon intercourse with men of their own type. Without this stimulation their powers remain sluggish, inert. Intellectual or artistic conversation excites them and may be the inspiration of their best work. This is the truth which lies at the basis of Mr. Flexner's educational efforts. It is true that there are some men of intellectual tastes who do their best work in loneliness, isolated from their own kind. But this is the exception, not the rule. And even such men, it will be found, need human intercourse of some kind. They depend deeply upon the love of family and the affection of friends. And very often such men find, in the company of simple and unintellectual people—plain half educated men, or even peasants and workmen—a real and lasting source of satisfaction. These are men whose minds are naturally so intensely active in themselves that they require, not so much stimulation, as relief and contrast in quiet and unexciting society.

Thus for all men, in one way if not in another, social intercourse is an absolute necessity of happiness—not only a source of happiness, but an indispensable condition of it. And for our purposes it is essential to note that this is as true of the savage as it is of ourselves. Sociality is a *common* element of human nature, and an *essential* part of it. So that a man without it would be as much a freak or monster as a man born without a face. No doubt the sociality of the savage is extremely crude, and expresses itself in the most outlandish ways. But it is there. Even he cannot live alone. He must have his family and his companions. For all men great loneliness is great unhappiness. And a really complete solitude is torture, a fact well known to those who organize penal institutions.

This social nature of man is one of the two sources of moral obligation. It is the most primitive source and perhaps the most important. It is this which in the first instance *forces* morality upon us. For without society men cannot be happy, and they cannot have society except upon the basis of a greater or lesser degree of altruism. The only condition upon which men can live together is that they shall have regard to the needs, desires, and feelings of each other. Thus it is impossible for me to be happy unless I am prepared to act for the happiness of other men. And to say this is to say that morality, at least the rudiments of it, is a necessity for happiness. Why, then, should I be moral? Because I myself can only be happy if I am moral, that is, if I consult the happiness of my fellows.

No doubt this gives only the germ of morality, not morality highly developed or fully fledged. Men may doubtless live together in social groups with some sort of success—may rub along together somehow—with a very grudging recognition of the obligations of altruism, with a bare minimum of morality. This is what we find in very primitive peoples. Nevertheless the moral idea has already, in this bare minimum, been born. And thereafter it will grow. It comes to be found that the bare minimum of morality is not enough to secure the *full* blessings of social life. The happiness thus engendered is real, but rudimentary. It is incomplete, broken up by the intermixture of misery produced by that vast selfishness which overlays and almost crowds out the little altruism there is in such a society. It comes to be realized that a higher degree of altruism will generate a higher degree of happiness. In this way more exalted moral ideals are born. In this way higher and higher ethical codes are developed.

Let no one say that this is to give a merely genetic account of morality—that it may tell us how it arose, but does not tell us what it is. This would be completely false. The point is that, quite independently of history, morality in its own nature *is* the proper and full functioning of the inherent element of sociality in human personality. I *must* be moral—this is where obligation enters —because to be so is a necessary condition of the natural functioning of my personality, and therefore of my happiness.

But this is to found morality upon mere feeling and even upon "emotion." For sociality is concerned with our feelings and emotions towards our fellow beings. Emotions, however, are variable, and cannot be the basis of a universal morality. So it will be said.

It is one of the perennial delusions of philosophers—largely fastened upon them by Kant—that only reason is universal, and that feelings and emotions are not so. This dogma is now uncritically accepted as the truth even in quarters otherwise thoroughly unKantian. So that Westermarck actually gives it as a proof of ethical relativity. There cannot, he says, be a universal morality because morality is founded upon emotions, and because emotions, as Kant saw, are variable elements of human nature.[1]

But it is a patent fact that emotions are just as universal as is reason. For instance, fear, love, and anger, are a part of the structure of all human personalities whatever. It is true that the emotional ingredients of personality are differently mixed in different individuals. Some men are more fearless than others, some more affectionate, some more jealous, and so on. But then the same is true of reason. Some men are more rational than others. In some men reasoning power is highly developed, in others little. It is possible, though I doubt it, that some men are born without any fear at all. If so, they are freaks. But in any case men are also born without reason. They too are freaks and are shut up in suitable institutions. It is also true that fundamental human emotions are directed by different people upon different objects. Some people fear spiders. Others reserve their fearfulness for more formidable enemies. But again the same thing is true of reason.

[1] *Ethical Relativity*, page 60.

Some people direct their reason upon philosophy, others upon household accounts.

Here again Plato was right as against Kant. He founded a *universal* morality upon the supposed three elements in human nature, reason, spirit, and appetite. Morality, for him, is the harmony of these three parts of the soul. And it is therefore essential to his argument that spirit and appetite should be parts of every human soul. He saw no impossibility in this notwithstanding that "spirit" is largely emotional, and that appetite is variable in the same sense as emotions are variable. He thought that spirit and appetite are *universal* elements in human nature. I do not say, of course, that Kant was wholly wrong. There is a certain sense in which reason may be said to possess a kind of universality which is lacking to feeling. The word universal is ambiguous. Reason is universal in the sense that it is coercive, so that if a piece of reasoning is valid for one man it must be valid for all rational beings. Emotion does not possess *this* kind of universality, since the concept of validity has no application to the emotions. Kant was therefore right in asserting that in this sense reason is universal while emotion is not. But there is another meaning to the word universal. Whatever character is possessed by all the members of a group is a universal character of that group. Thus fear is a universal ingredient of human nature. So are love, jealousy, desire, appetite. It is this kind of universality which is possessed by emotions. And my point is that the first kind of universality, which reason possesses and which the other elements of human nature do not possess, is not relevant to morals. Feelings—or at any rate those feelings which constitute sociality, with which alone we are concerned—possess the only kind of universality which is required to render them a suitable basis for morality, namely, the second kind. This kind of universality consists in the simple fact that sociality is a part of the essential psychological structure of all human beings. Sociality is not, as a matter of fact, wholly emotional. It is shot through with intellect. This is why it is distinctively human, and is not owned by animals. But we need not trouble about its analysis in this respect. The prime fact is that the love of wife and children, the desire for friends, the necessity of having social relationships with one's fellows, the horror of loneliness—these are human facts at least as universal—in the only relevant sense—as "reason." They assert their demands as insistently among the lowest savages as among the most highly developed races. They can therefore suitably form the basis of a universal moral standard.

I now pass to the second source of morality. This is the fact that men are so constituted—i.e., this too is a part of the fundamental structure of human personality— that each one of them finds happiness, in greater or less degree, in the bare fact of the happiness of others; and finds unhappiness in the unhappiness of others. I expect, on the part of the reader, a greater degree of scepticism towards this than towards the social nature of men. But I will proceed, hoping to overcome this scepticism slowly.

Why there should be such a fact in human nature I do not know. How it has come about, what are its biological causes, we need not enquire. For we are not—let the reader mark—giving a genetic account of morality. And I am only concerned to assert that, whatever its causes, this fact *is* a fact.

Let us first of all try to see what this alleged fact really is. It is not merely that *indirectly* other people's happiness affects mine through the increase or decrease of the satisfactions with which they normally supply me. It is that *directly* their happiness or unhappiness tends to communicate itself to me. It is, of course, true that if my wife is ill or miserable, she will not manage my house so well. She may forget to order my dinner. If my friend is unhappy, he may treat me with indifference or even unkindness. If the grocer is in jail, he cannot send me the butter. If society at large is wretched and oppressed, I cannot obtain from it the usual supplies and satisfactions. These are the kind of crude reflections in which ethical egoists indulge, and on which apparently they would base morality. It is only for reasons of this kind, they think, that I need to concern myself with the happiness of my fellows. But I have in mind a fact of human nature quite other than this. It is that, quite apart from these selfish considerations, unhappiness in one man tends to make others unhappy; and happiness in him to make them happy. Doubtless I am inconvenienced if my wife's unhappiness prevents her from properly managing my house. But entirely independently of this her unhappiness *in itself* makes me unhappy. And I am really sorry that the grocer is in jail, quite apart from the fact that he cannot send me the butter.

Conversely a man tends to be happier for seeing those around him happy. He takes pleasure in their happiness quite apart from the selfish consideration that they will serve him better. A good employer wishes his workers to be happy and contented because this is good business and their work will then bring him more profits. This is quite as it should be, nor has the employer the slightest reason to be ashamed of such a motive. But there must be at least some employers who *also* wish to see their work people happy independently of these mercenary considerations; who themselves obtain satisfaction directly from witnessing the happiness of those who work for them. I am not suggesting that even the best employer in the world is an angel. I am not taking a sentimentally rosy view of human nature. But neither am I taking a cynical one. Sentimentality and cynicism are both alike unscientific. They are opposite deviations from the truth. I am dispassionately pointing to plain facts of human nature. It may be true that mercenary motives enormously outweigh in all ordinary human beings the disinterested desire to see others happy. But even if there is to be found a single almost microscopic grain of disinterestedness amid the immense masses of human selfishness, my point is sufficiently gained. That grain is a *fact* of human nature.

This disinterested desire to see other people happy varies very greatly in its incidence and mode of operation—just as sociality does. In general we care greatly about the happiness of those who are near to us, such as our family and our friends, and are relatively indifferent to the welfare of those who are remote from us. The mild illness of my son makes me distraught. But the devastations of a flood in China, and the fact that it drowns thousands, leaves me comparatively cold. But individuals vary very greatly. There are people who are made miserable by cruelty to a dog, but seem far less moved by cruelty to a child. Some men, the best, are highly sensitive to the weal or woe of their fellows. Others are comparatively callous. There may even be men who sometimes take pleasure in the sufferings of their fellows. And indeed we nearly all do this on occasion, if the sufferings are not too shocking. For cruelty too is a part of human nature.

But in spite of variations, sensitiveness to the happiness and unhappiness of others is a universal part of human nature. It is part of the structure of human personality as such, and is not confined to any age or race. It is possessed by savages. Indeed it seems to be possessed by many animals. Nor does the occasional occurrence of genuinely cruel men at all disprove these facts. For as a rule the cruel man is perverted. He too must have had in him the roots of human sympathy. But evil associations, bad training, cruel treatment administered to himself, or some other psychological cause, have smothered them. It is even possible that men may be born really and literally destitute of that part of normal personality to which I am pointing. No doubt this poses a problem, and I shall return to that problem later. For the moment I will content myself with a single remark. The theologian who asserts that Jesus Christ died for *all* men doubtless lays himself open to the question of Anatole France regarding the monstrous progeny of a man and a beast "Did Jesus Christ die for this?" And we who say that moral obligation falls upon *all* men may likewise be asked whether it falls upon all the moral and psychological freaks and monsters ever born into the world in human shape. And for the present we will only say that the fact of there being such monsters no more disproves that the disinterested desire to see others happy is a part of the common pattern of the human mind that the existence of men without arms, legs, or face disproves that arms, legs, and face are parts of man's common bodily pattern.

Thus this second universal fact of human nature is also one of the foundations of moral obligation. For it is an essential basis of altruism. It means that men cannot be happy unless they work for the happiness of others. Why should I be moral? This means, Why should I be unselfish? One reason has already been found in the fact of sociality.

The other reason is now before us. That I am, willy nilly, made directly happy by the happiness of others, and unhappy by their unhappiness, means that I can only attain complete happiness for myself through unselfishness, through seeing others happy and making them happy. Work for the happiness of others is the most valuable source of *my own* happiness.

Here too, however, as with sociality, there is development in the human race. In primitive societies the principle involved obtains a recognition so bare and grudging that it may easily be overlooked altogether. Savages may seem almost totally insensitive to the weal or woe of others. As civilization advances there is a growing realization of the value of this source of happiness. But in the majority in any civilization men still in practice believe that other sources of satisfaction—wealth, power, fame, or what not —will bring them more happiness than will the sacrifice of these things combined with work for others. It is only the saint who knows, who truly believes not only with his intellect but also with his whole personality, that his own true source of happiness lies in sacrifice for the sake of others. And the reason why this is true is because, in the scale of values of higher and lower satisfactions, disinterested unselfishness is highest, that is, it yields the greatest happiness. And the proof of this is the fact—empirically verifiable in history—that supreme happiness does as a matter of fact come to the saint.

With this, it will be observed, the problem of the empirical meaning of the word "ought" is solved. The radical empiricist truly tells us that there can be no such thing as an unconditional ought, and that such an ought has no meaning. But he recognizes that a proposition of the form "if you want X, then you should do Y" has meaning.

For it is translatable into the form "Y leads to X." And this is empirically verifiable. An "ought" sentence has been translated into an "is" sentence.

Our hypothesis fulfils the conditions demanded by the radical empiricist. For the sentence "You ought to be moral" means simply "You ought to be moral, if you wish to be happy." It asserts the alleged experiential *facts* that the best or the only road to happiness is through morality, that good men tend to be happy, bad men unhappy. This is a proposition which may be true or may be false. But it is at any rate a proposition which has meaning. And of course it is my contention that it is not only meaningful, but also true. Finally it is true of all human beings because it depends upon their common psychological structure. And therefore the same moral obligation falls upon all men. All men wish to be happy. And for all men there is but one road, the road of morality. And let it not be said by some clever person that there are men who do *not* wish to be happy. All men wish for something (else they could not continue to live). And *what* they wish for—however strange it may be, however it might make most of us miserable—is that which *they* conceive will make them happy.

In this same teaching there is found the proof of the second part of the doctrine of the universality of morals. That doctrine meant, we saw, two things: first, that as a matter of fact all men do in some sort recognize the duty of altruism; and this was shown in the previous chapter. Secondly it meant that, whether they do recognize it or not, they *ought* to. And what this means has been shown in the present chapter. It means that for all men the real road to happiness is the road of altruism, and that this is true, *whether men recognize the fact or not.*

CHAPTER 12

WHY SHOULD I BE MORAL? (II)

LET us attempt to get our perspectives right and to see what place morality occupies in life generally. It is not asserted that *no* happiness can come to men from any source except morality. However important morality is, it is not the whole of life. The sources of human happiness are many. They include the satisfactions of art, of religion, of intellectual exercise, of bodily function. And they also include the two specific sources of satisfaction, sociality and disinterested altruistic feeling, on which morality is founded. Therefore we must not exaggerate by saying that without morality no happiness at all is possible. We cannot say either that the bad man can have no happiness; or that the good man can be completely happy if all the fountains of happiness, except his virtue, are cut off. Exaggerations of this kind are what breed scepticism of moral truth. Men will disbelieve our whole case if we thus overstate it. But what we can say is this. In the first place, sociality and disinterested altruistic feeling are two among the many sources of happiness. *Some* happiness is possible without them because there are other sources from which it may be derived. But the highest degree of happiness is not only impossible without morality, but is impossible without the highest degree of it. Very great happiness is attained only very rarely in the world, and only by those men whom we call moral geniuses, or saints.

But we put the matter much too low if we say merely

that morality taps two out of many sources of happiness.
If that were all, we could hardly see any obligation to it,
since there would be alternatives. We have forgotten the
conception of "higher" and "lower" satisfactions. A
higher satisfaction, as we have seen, means one which
contributes more to happiness. The next point to be made,
therefore, is that the two sources of morality are exceedingly high in the scale of values. They are so high that
between them they are probably capable of yielding more
happiness than all the rest of our satisfactions put together. So that he who neglects them, though a dribble of
happiness may pass into his life, is yet a maimed creature
with the possibility of but little happiness.

It would be foolish to attempt to arrange human satisfactions in a precise order of value. They are far too complex. And their value is not capable of precise measure-
ment. Nevertheless there are considerations which are
relevant here. Let us consider the two satisfactions of
morality separately. Sociality, I should say, including as
it does the satisfactions of friendship, family love, ordinary
social intercourse with the expansion of personality and
the stirring of all our activities which it produces, stands
very near the top of the scale. It is incalculably higher
than the brute pleasures of the body. For it yields incalculably more happiness than these. And disinterested
altruistic feeling is probably, I think, higher still. Either
it stands supreme at the head of the scale or (perhaps) it
shares that position with the exalted religious satisfaction
of the mystic. (In actual life, of course, these two are often,
perhaps usually, conjoined. They are not rivals.) One can
only rely here on the evidence of those rare souls in whom
disinterested altruistic feeling is very highly developed.
For the high development of it is far rarer than the high

development of sociality. And those few who have sufficient magnificence of spirit to set aside all petty and selfish
aims and to live whole-heartedly for humanity, forgetting
all but the service of others, these as it seems to me—
though one can observe them only from afar off—attain
a pinnacle of happiness undreamed of by us others.

Art is rightly reputed a high and noble satisfaction.
Yet I cannot think that it contributes to life anything like
the happiness which is found either in human affection
(sociality) or in the disinterested service of others.

Why should I be moral? Well, in the first place, *some*
degree of morality, though doubtless a comparatively low
one, is absolutely forced upon us by our social nature. I
cannot live with my fellows at all without at least a measure of regard for their wishes, desires, happiness. Even
criminals, in a criminal society, must exercise towards one
another such consideration in some degree. Even savages
must do so.

But this is clearly not enough. Why, you will go on to
ask now, should I observe any higher degree of morality
than that bare minimum which is sufficient to enable me
to get along with my fellows? And I answer that with this
minimum you can indeed "get along" somehow. But you
cannot be a truly happy man. Your life and your happiness will be utterly incomplete. You will live, that is, keep
barely alive. But yours will not be a full life. On the other
hand, the higher the morality which you observe, the
greater—other things being equal—will be your happiness.
And you can only achieve supreme happiness by reaching
up to, and practically carrying out, the highest imaginable
moral ideals. Most of us, with our low level of morals,
may *say* that we are happy enough, that we do not want
any more. And therefore we may ask why we should be

more moral? But all this is a lie—a lie that we tell to ourselves in order that we may conceal from ourselves the inner emptiness of our lives. It is the nature of man to want happiness, and to want more and more of it, to want the highest happiness that he can conceive. Even the savage wants the highest happiness that he is capable of understanding, and would want a higher still as soon as it could be brought within his ken. All men, then, desire the greatest happiness of which our kind is capable. The road to this happiness lies through morality. That is the meaning of obligation, and that is why it is universal to all men. You ought to be moral because without morality you cannot attain that fulness of life more abounding, that high happiness, which you yourself desire. We saw that it was self-evident why a man should care for his own happiness. We could not see why he should care for that of other men. Now we see. It is because this is, in the end, the only way of caring for his own.

But now I shall be told that this reduces morality, after all, to egoism. After elaborately repudiating and refuting the doctrine of ethical egoism in Chapter 9 I have now in these final chapters shamefully capitulated to it. I am to be moral only because I can thereby find my own happiness. So my motive is selfish after all.

But to argue thus is merely to resurrect the wretched fallacy which I endeavoured to expose on pages 221–223. All human actions whatever, from the greatest to the most trivial, aim at the satisfaction of some impulse of the actor. Whatever a man does aims in one way or another at *his own* satisfaction, and this is equivalent to saying that he aims at his own happiness. But this is merely to say that no man acts without motives, and that his motives are always his own and not someone else's. Therefore the distinction between selfish and unselfish motives falls *within* the sphere of motives which aim at a man's own satisfaction. And the difference is found in the *kind of end* which yields him satisfaction. The unselfish man is he who finds satisfaction in the happiness of other people, and sorrow in their sorrow. The selfish man is he who does not make the happiness of others his end at all, because he receives no satisfaction from it. He may still make the happiness of others a means to other ends which do satisfy him, and so act altruistically. But his motive is selfish none the less. And his is the only kind of altruism the existence of which is admitted by the egoist. We, on the contrary, assert that it is possible, and indeed frequently happens, that a man may seek the happiness of others as an end which gives him satisfaction *in itself*, and not merely as a means to some ulterior end. But it would be absurd to ask that he should not himself obtain any satisfaction from the end which he seeks, namely, the happiness of others. In that case, of course, he would not act at all, having no motive to do so.

In the light of this, consider the two sources of morality. One is the disinterested desire to see others happy. The fact that a man who has this desire, and who acts upon it, himself receives happiness from the happiness which he gives, does not make his action egoistic. It is true that if I relieve a fellow being of his pain, if I increase his opportunities of positive happiness, and if I do this without any hope of receiving from him, or from my act, directly or indirectly, any sort of reward, I may still be said to act as I do because to do so gives *me* happiness. But this is disinterested altruism, not egoism. The egoist holds that I never can or do act in this way. According to him, if I give a man bread or heal his wounds, this must be because

I hope that either he, or someone else, will some day give me bread, heal my wounds, or do me some other service. Morality, according to him, is founded solely upon such crudely commercial and selfish motives. But my view is quite different from this. It finds the source, or rather one of the sources, of morality, in *disinterested* altruism.

Moreover it must be remembered that although the ultimate reason and justification of the good man's altruistic action is found in the increase which it brings to his own happiness, yet the good man, in acting, has not this end normally in view. It is conceivable that a man might consciously seek to lead a moral life for the deliberate purpose of making himself happy. But human nature is so constructed that this is not usually the case. Normally the good man acts morally without asking himself the question "why should I be moral?" This question is one which the philosopher puts as he watches the good man act. It is not one which the good man himself, as such, asks at all. He acts without thinking of his own happiness, without even being aware that he is adding to it. He is *thinking* of the happiness of others, not of his own. And from this there flows into his soul a happiness for which he has not asked, has not sought—a happiness at which he has not consciously aimed. "Seek ye first the kingdom of God, and all these things shall be added unto you" was the advice given to the apostles. And it is in this spirit that the good man acts. What he seeks is not his own happiness, but the happiness of others. And his own happiness is thereupon "added unto him." It comes to him unseen and unsought. And it is the more blessed for that. But of these things the egoist knows nothing. He continues to gather up the offal and the dung with his muckrake, not seeing the light above his head.

Consider the other source of morality, man's social nature. Some of the reasons for which men desire the society of their fellows have been mentioned above. They include the cultivation of affectionate feelings, both those given and those received, the exchange of ideas, laughter, mutual esteem, intellectual stimulation, the stirring of activities, the unfreezing of personality. Now these ends are not entirely disinterested. There is in them an element of exchange, which can be brought under the categories of egoism. I like to make my acquaintances laugh. But if they cannot make me laugh in return I consider them dull fellows and I avoid them. If I give pleasure to others who associate with me, I expect to get pleasure from their company too. Yet this is not the whole of the story. If sociality is not wholly disinterested, it is not wholly interested either. There is something in companionship which the crude categories of commercial exchange allow to escape through their net. The fact is that real sociality is impossible unless, in addition to the exchange which it involves, there is an element of disinterested pleasure taken by each in the pleasure of the others. It is true that I enjoy your society because you make me laugh and loosen the free flow of my ideas. But I also enjoy it because it gives me pleasure to see *you* laughing and happy and exercising the free play of *your* activities. And this part of my pleasure is disinterested. Without both these elements genuine companionship is impossible. One soon detects the man who seeks one's society *only* because it amuses *him*, and who ceases to tolerate one immediately it ceases to do so. That man is not a genuine friend.

The egoist can understand the business man who is hospitable to his fellows and invites them to his table for the sake of increasing the circle of his customers. This is for him the type of all hospitality, of all friendship, of all morality. The simple desire to enjoy the society of other men for its own sake, to find one's pleasure in giving them pleasure, without any ulterior motive, this is to him apparently incomprehensible.

One may ask the question why did men ever come together in societies at all? Why did they not live solitary? Hobbes apparently thought that the "natural man" would be perfectly happy provided that he had all the food, clothing, houses, lands, wealth, that he wanted, without any human society at all. He supposed that men only enter into societies in order to get more food, clothing, etc., and to preserve what they already have from depredation. But this is nonsense. No doubt developed social relations are largely governed by such commercial considerations. But the prime reason for the existence of any social relations at all is simply the desire for human intercourse for its own sake. Men did not come together in order to exchange bread, tools, clothes, furniture. They came together—or rather they always were together—simply because they like being together, because they enjoy each other's society, because they need human companionship and affection. Companionship involves, as I showed, elements both interested and disinterested. And I think that it must always have done so. And this means that at least the germ of disinterested pleasure in the pleasure of others must have been present in all societies from the very beginning. Society is ultimately founded, not on economic, but on friendly considerations. That it can also be used to serve the conveniences of economic exchange was a subsequent discovery. To place this at the foundation is absurd.

If I have surmounted the criticism that my doctrine is

nothing but a disguised egoism, another objection is sure
to confront me. "It is not in fact true" the critic will say
"that unselfishness is the best road to happiness. Morality
may be obligatory, but it cannot be for this particular
reason. For if this were true, all men would know it and
would be moral. Every man seeks his own happiness. And
if in spite of this the majority of men are immoral and
selfish, it must be because experience has taught them that
to be selfish and immoral—making, at any rate, only the
minimum possible concession to altruism—is in reality the
best way of attaining each his own happiness. In practice
this is the opinion of all men. And this opinion is based
upon thousands of years of human experience. Why, if
to be unselfish is the best way of attaining one's own
happiness, are men still almost universally selfish?"

Alas, why indeed? If one must give reasons they will be
somewhat as follows. Men are bad because they do not,
with all their cunning, know their own best interests.
They tear themselves to pieces, cut their own throats.
Yet it is not true that the majority of men do not know
that the best way to be happy is to be unselfish. The truth
is less simple than that. The truth is that they both know
it quite well—and yet are ignorant of it. On the surfaces
of their minds they are without this knowledge. But deep
down in the obscure depths of personality, they *divine* its
truth.

My critic quotes against me the apparent opinion of the
masses of humanity. But I have on my side the few, the
wise men, the sages, the saints, the prophets, of all ages,
of all countries, of all races. I have on my side the authority of Plato, of Buddha, of Christ. But it is not my purpose
to rely upon authority. My purpose is to ask a question.
Men in general in their actions, as well as in much of their

talk, ignore the witness of these seers. They act as if they believed, and indeed they really do believe, that they can best attain their own happiness by selfishness mixed with the smallest leaven of altruism. Why, then, if they really think the sages wrong, do they still honour them as sages? Why do they still pay them even the lip-service that they do pay? Why are these names which I have quoted held immortal even among the many who disbelieve their doctrines? Why are they not remembered, if at all, only for their consummate folly in teaching something which everyone knows to be false? Is it not because, in some obscure way, in some dark corner of their minds, men *know* that the sages are right and that it is they themselves who are wrong. Thus they both know the truth and do not know it. They both know it and yet disbelieve it.

I cannot pretend to explain the reasons for this. To do so would be to write the mental and moral history of the world. Yet one reason, I think, is plain. In explaining it I am going, for the moment, to use the word "pleasure" to mean those satisfactions which are other than the two satisfactions which are the sources of morality; and in particular to mean the "lower" satisfactions. This is quite in accordance with ordinary usage. And speaking in this way, I shall say that men in general *mistake pleasure for happiness*. Expressed in more philosophical language this means that they wrongly suppose that the lower satisfactions will yield them more happiness than will the higher ones. And they make this mistake because the lower satisfactions are as a rule more intense, and they mistake intensity of satisfaction for greatness of happiness. To mistake pleasure for happiness—this is indeed the great illusion. This is the veil of Maya. All men are deceived by it sometimes, and some men always. Men see the phan-

toms of pleasure glimmering and shining in their eyes.
They grasp at the vision, taking it for happiness. But the
vision is hollow. The happiness which they sought eludes
their grasp. It is chiefly for this reason that happiness has
been figured as a blue bird which turns black when it is
caught. The parable is not wholly true. For happiness
is within men's grasp if they go the right way to find it.
Pleasure, when mistaken for happiness, is what turns
black.

Now the pursuit of pleasure is selfish. It must be, since
we have defined pleasure as excluding the genuinely altruistic satisfactions. Therefore if men think that pleasure
is happiness, they will also think that the way to reach
happiness is the selfish way. This accounts for the fact
that with one part of their minds they disbelieve the deep
truth that morality is the road to happiness. And yet
because they have a dim sense of real values, of what is
truly "higher" and "lower," they know also that this
is untrue. They are deceived by the illusion. And yet
they know that it *is* illusion.

But, it will be said, if happiness is a natural consequence of morality, one would expect that the more
moral races would be the happier. Can it be claimed that
this is a fact? Are the European races, with their higher
Christian ethical standards, happier than the races which
follow lower moralities? Do we not in fact often wonder
whether the contrary is not the case, whether the less
advanced, more simple and child-like races of the world,
are not actually happier than those with more advanced
and complicated civilizations?

Whether we are, as suggested, actually less happy than
people with lower moral standards I do not know. I do
not believe that anyone knows. One cannot take a census

of the happiness in one community, and then in another, and compare the results. But let us suppose, for the sake of argument, that the people of Tibet, or Ethiopia, are on the average happier than we are. What does this prove? Certainly not that a higher morality does not lead to a greater happiness. For it is quite possible that these simple people are *more* moral than we are, not less. We may place before ourselves a higher moral standard than they do. But this is merely our theory, not our practice. That we subscribe in theory to a higher code of morals than they do by no means indicates that we are actually in practice more moral. And there is some reason for thinking that the contrary is the case. Among many races which would not be considered "advanced" property may be left unguarded in the public view with impunity, property which among ourselves would be stolen at once. This is but one small example, and the reader can doubtless supply others for himself. It is also well known that contact with European civilization has corrupted and demoralized many innocent "lower" races. The progress of what we call civilization is by no means synonymous with the progress of morality. Rather the reverse. As life becomes more complicated, and especially as wealth and luxury increase, morals have a tendency to deteriorate. And it is certainly doubtful whether a race which pours deadly fumes, mustard gas, and other poisons, upon harmless, if rather uncivilized, shepherds, killing them by the thousand, can claim to be more moral than their victims.

The unhappiness of the modern European man (if it is a fact) is certainly not caused by his exalted morality. It is at least arguable that it is in large measure caused by his inferior morals. But it is also in part due to factors which have no direct bearing one way or the other upon the argument. These include the growing complexity of life, the fatigue and weariness which this involves, economic conditions, and a thousand other factors.

Objection may also be made that our account of the basis of moral obligation will not extend that obligation over the whole human race. Even if we admit that sociality involves moral relations between members of the same society, it does not follow that they are thereby necessitated as between members of different societies. To live happily with my friends I must behave morally towards them. And this idea may perhaps be applied to a whole social group. Since, in some sense or other, all the members of a single social group live together and have social relations with one another, each, it may be supposed, has moral obligations to all the others. But sociality cannot give rise to any obligation outside the particular social group to which we belong. I can see on this basis why I should behave unselfishly to another member of my own nation or society. But why should I behave unselfishly to a Chinaman or an Australian bushman?

In part the answer is that all humanity is implicitly one social group. In days when a society in the western hemisphere was utterly cut off from a society in the eastern hemisphere it might be argued that a westerner had no moral obligations to an easterner. But the statement would be purely academic. For since there was no communication between them at all, no question of moral relations between them could ever arise. Immediately communication is established, as soon as the westerner does begin to have relations of any kind with the easterner, they have *ipso facto* become members of one society. It may be so far rudimentary, but it is real. We must not mix up the idea of a society with the idea of a politically organized group having a government. It is the fact of having social relations, of living together in any sense, which is the basis of morality. Sociality, as we saw, is a different thing from politicality, and may exist without it. As soon, therefore, as men begin to have relations at all, the obligation imposed by sociality begins to operate. The idea of morality has been born, and once born its logical implications will carry with them the whole of morality. The closer the relations between different communities become, the more that improved communications cause them to be interlocked, the more plainly will the moral obligation—which was, however, there all the time, implicit and unrealized—emerge into view.

It is because morality is founded upon sociality, and not upon politicality, that there is such a thing as international moral obligation, however little it is practically recognized or acted upon. I am not a member of the German political state, but I am a member of the same society to which Germans belong. Civilization brings me into contact of various kinds with them, and these contacts imply social relations between us. And those persons who are bound together by social relations are members of a single society. It is a false doctrine that moral obligation holds between individuals, but not between states. Moral obligation holds between all the members of one state and all the members of the other. And therefore it holds between the states.

But we have not given the whole answer to the question why moral obligation exists between members of different social groups. What has been said was from the point of view of the basis of morals in sociality. But this is not its only basis. And the other source, that disinterested happiness which we derive from the happiness of other persons, is not only implicitly, but explicitly and from the first, intercommunal. It overleaps all sectional boundaries. A man may derive happiness from the happiness of another whether that other belongs to his own social group or not. Upon this can be founded at once, therefore, an obligation which is universal and is not confined within the boundaries of any particular society.

It is on this basis too that our obligation to treat animals with kindness must rest. It can hardly be founded upon sociality. But it is a part of human nature to feel pain even at the pain of an animal. And although this may hardly be apparent among lower races, or even among the more coarse and uneducated members of our own race, I think the germ of it at least must be present in them as it is present in all normal men.

There is a final objection which must be met before I bring the subject to a close. It is useless, the critic will urge, to attempt to found moral obligation upon feelings of sociality and benevolence. Such feelings can doubtless explain why some men, who happen to have these feelings, do as a matter of fact act altruistically. But you cannot explain *obligation* in this way. For if a man does not possess the feelings referred to, or if he possesses them in so low a degree that they do not impel him to be moral, on what basis can you say that he *ought* to have them or that he *ought* to be moral? If a man is by nature social and benevolent then no doubt the cultivation of these elements of his nature—which is morality—will yield him happiness. And therefore you can say to him that *if* he wishes to be happy, he ought to be moral. For him, in fact, the suggested solution holds. Morality will be for him a road to happiness. So far, so good. But if a man simply does not possess the feelings on which morality is based, moral obligation will, according to the account here given, have no application to him. You cannot say to him "You ought to have the feelings which you do not have," for on what basis could any such obligation rest? Moreover, apart from the case of men who are literally and absolutely destitute of these feelings, it must be admitted that in many men, savages and criminals for example, they are utterly rudimentary. These rudimentary feelings will be fully satisfied by the barest minimum of morality. Why then should such a man cultivate a morality any higher than the minimum which satisfies his nature? Are you going to say that he ought to develop *more* of the feelings than he now possesses? But this is in principle the same as saying that a man ought to have feelings which he does not possess at all. And as we have seen, there can be no possible basis for such an obligation.

There exist men of almost inhuman callousness. You may say that even they have the rudiments of the moral feelings. They may feel in some slight measure altruistically towards their own children, even towards a few close friends. To the majority of humanity they are utterly indifferent. It gives them no pain to see others brutally treated, to treat men brutally themselves. It gives them no happiness to see others happy, nor to make them so. How can you say to such a man "You ought to behave with unselfishness to all men, because this will yield to yourself a greater happiness"? This will be simply untrue of him since as a matter of fact he will derive no happiness at all from the happiness of those whom you say he ought to benefit. Hence on your own showing there is no reason why he should behave morally; there is for him no moral obligation.

What answer can be made to these charges? I will take

separately the two cases imagined, namely, that of the man who is literally destitute of social and altruistic feelings, and that of the man in whom they are very rudimentary. And I will take the latter case first.

The position here is this. The feelings which are the basis of morality are part of the universal psychological pattern of humanity in the same sense as fear and anger are parts of it. They may be stronger or weaker. But they are always present, except perhaps in pathological cases. The more they are developed and exercised in a man, the more satisfaction and therefore happiness they yield to him. Therefore if a man has them in low degree, he would, if by exercise he developed them and made them stronger, be capable of a happiness much greater than any which can come to him now when these feelings are undeveloped. And as all men desire a greater happiness than they now possess, he ought to do this. To develop more fully these feelings *is* a road to better happiness even to the man in whom they are very rudimentary. And feelings can be developed by exercise in just the same way as muscles can. Hence there *is* a basis for the obligation to feel these feelings more strongly than he does now. And that basis lies in the rudimentary feelings which he already possesses. It is perfectly meaningful to say to him "*if* you want to be happier, you ought to cultivate the feelings on which morality is founded, water them, make them grow; you ought to be more moral; in the end, if you wish for the highest happiness, you ought to reach out to the highest imaginable moral ideals." It is perfectly meaningful, and furthermore it is true, if this is said to the coarsest and most brutal man in the world. Upon such a man therefore there lies the obligation, not only to a bare minimum of morality, but to the highest morality. The *same* moral obligation, that is to say the highest, is universal to all men.

The case is entirely parallel to that of the man whose bodily physique is undeveloped. It is perfectly sensible to say to him "If you would develop your muscles and bodily frame, there would be possible for you a health and happiness which are now out of your reach by reason of your stunted growth. And since you certainly desire such health and happiness, you ought to do this."

And now finally I will consider the case of the man absolutely destitute of social and altruistic feelings. I do not know whether any such person really exists or could exist. But since human beings are born without faces, arms, legs, I suppose it is possible that they may be born without any natural feelings. If there are such men, what can be said of them? How can it be said that any moral obligation falls upon them? *They* would not be made any happier by being moral, since they are without the natural feelings through the satisfaction of which morality yields happiness. Therefore it is impossible to say to them "*If* you want to be happy, you ought to be moral." In their case this proposition would be simply untrue.

Such men, if they exist, are as much freaks and monsters as men born without faces, arms, or legs. They are, like lunatics, defective of essential parts of human personality. Now will anyone assert that moral obligation falls upon raving lunatics, or that an ethical theory is unsatisfactory if it cannot show that it does? I have urged that moral obligation falls universally upon all *human* beings. But those who are literally destitute of even the germ of natural feeling are simply *not* human—however the biologist may classify them. On any moral theory, does it really matter that it may be impossible to show that obligation falls upon lunatics, imbeciles, and other defectives? If morality is founded upon "reason," as Kant supposed, then it cannot apply to the irrational. If it is founded upon "intelligent selfishness," then it does not apply to those who are born without intelligence. If it is founded upon social and altruistic feelings, then it does not apply to those who are destitute of these feelings. And what of it? When we say that its application is universal, we mean that it applies universally to all *normal* men. And if that can be shown, surely that is enough. Society does not expect those poor creatures who are born with half of their humanity missing to be moral. It encloses them mercifully in places where their lives can be made as tolerable as possible, and where they can do no harm to their fellow men.

Morality legislates for men such as we are, men with our human nature. The one morality is universal for them and for them alone. It is not to be pretended that it extends beyond those limits either in the direction just indicated or in any other. Thus, for example, if there should arise on this planet a race of supermen, a race of beings utterly different from ourselves in psychological structure, who shall say that our morality would apply to them? Enough if it applies to man as we know him in all countries and in all the ages of the history of the world.

EPILOGUE

IT was very late when I finished reading my manuscript. I could see through the windows the first streaks of the summer dawn. Jim yawned audibly. Peter had been dozing during the reading of the last two chapters, but woke up with a start assuring me that he had heard every word. As a matter of fact they had both been attentive and interested on the whole, I thought. They sat in silence for a while. Jim lit his pipe and let the long wreaths of blue smoke trail across the room. After a while he began to question me. Do you believe, he said, that there is in the universe any sort of purpose or plan? Do you suppose that it is driving at anything in particular? Do you think that the universe is interested in our values, in goodness and beauty and truth and all that sort of thing?

Why do you ask? I enquired.

Because, he said, nothing of that sort appears in your book, although if the universe had any reason or plan in it one might suppose that morality had something to do with the plan. Picture a universe without a God, a soulless piece of mechanism, perfectly indifferent to any sort of value. Suppose that there were human beings in that universe. They might very well evolve for themselves the sort of morality you describe in your book. They might try to be kind to one another, and to alleviate each other's sufferings. They might invent the ideal of altruism. And they might give for being moral just the reasons you give in your book.

You describe the position perfectly, said I.

But is there in morality nothing more than that? he

asked. Do you not yourself believe that it embodies in some way some sort of a cosmic purpose?

I don't know. What do you think?

It is difficult to say anything definite, he admitted. But I will express myself by saying that even if there is no Mind which consciously supervises the affairs of the world, I think there must at least be some principle in things which drives the world on towards a better state of affairs. Would you not admit that?

The question is beyond me, I replied. One has, of course, vague feelings of that sort. But if one tries to formulate them in intelligible conceptions, one fails. All the attempts which have ever been made to formulate such conceptions either in religious creeds or in metaphysical systems seem to me ridiculous. But suppose for the sake of argument I admit what you say. What then?

Only this, he said, that in that case you will have to admit that the account of morality which you have given in your book is wretchedly incomplete and even shallow. It leaves out all the profounder issues.

I believe, I answered, that what my book says is true so far as it goes. Of course it is incomplete. As to whether it is shallow or profound I have no idea. I express in my writing what there is in me to be expressed. I cannot get out of myself more than is there.

Jim meditated, blowing smoke rings in the air. After a while he said: Then the difference between us is this. You believe in a purely naturalistic morality which does not in any way spring from the essential nature of the world. Our values, you think, are irrelevant to the universe which neither knows nor cares anything about them. I, on the contrary, believe that morality involves something deeper. The feeling of moral obligation is really an instinctive sense of the necessity we are under of coöperating with the cosmic purpose. It appears in our consciousness as a blind driving force which we do not understand. We rationalize it, as you have tried to do in your book. I admit that when we talk about purpose in the world we are probably using hopelessly metaphorical language. Hence the difficulties and contradictions into which we fall when we attempt to systemize the idea. But there is something in the universe which we can only vaguely express by calling it a striving towards a goal. Our anthropomorphism is no doubt very crude. But we cannot express ourselves in any other way.

I do not think, I replied, that there exists between us the sharp difference which you have described.

How so?

I do not deny any of the things which you assert.

Then if you agree with me, why not say so in your book?

You go too fast. I did not say that I agreed with you. What I say is that I do not know whether your ideas are in any sense true or not. They may be the expression of some sort of vague groping towards a truth. We seem to have dim perceptions and intuitions of this kind. Or rather, I do not know whether they are dim perceptions of truth or mere dreams of our own. That is the trouble. Hence I neither assert nor deny what you say.

That is a spineless sort of attitude! said Jim. Why don't you make up your mind? I would rather you went over to the enemy altogether and flatly denied that there is any rhyme or reason or meaning or sense in the world at all.

All this while Peter had remained silent, contemptuous, I thought, of the whole discussion. But now he suddenly burst out saying that he agreed entirely with Jim. This surprised me very much, seeing that Peter prides himself on being tough-minded, scientific, and positivistic; and I could not imagine him agreeing with Jim's semi-religious ideas. I began to twit him gently with his inconsistency.

Stop! he exclaimed. Of course I don't mean that I agree with Jim's beliefs. I mean that I agree with him about you and your intellectual ineptitude. As to the rest of what Jim has said I think it is sheer sentimentalism. It is mere primitive thinking. Purpose can be attributed to human beings and perhaps to animals. But to attribute it to the universe is absolutely meaningless. This is all a sort of hang-over from religion. The world is a world of brute facts and nothing more. Science can tell us what happens. And science alone gives any information about the world. Science alone *says* anything. Religion and metaphysics are both meaningless. There is no reason *why* anything is what it is. There is no sense in asking why things are as they are. I thought I detected, while you were reading your manuscript, numerous signs of primitive thinking and of edifying sentimentality. The fact is that with all your alleged empiricism—for I do not admit that it is true empiricism—you belong to a past generation. You have a pre-war mentality.

I am sorry, Peter, I said, that I appear so feeble. But may I explain why I cannot see eye to eye either with you or with Jim?

Fire away! said he, but you will not convince me.

I shall not try to convince you, I said. But I will try to say what I think. I cannot adopt Jim's position simply because I do not really understand it. I do not pretend to know whether the universe has any purpose—whatever that word may mean when applied to the universe—or not. That is all an impenetrable darkness to me. But for

that very same reason I cannot throw in my lot with Peter.
I do not know what the darkness may hold. And I will not,
with him, declare that it holds nothing. He is too dogmatic and cock-sure. What he cannot understand he
labels "nonsense." And it seems to me that there is quite
a lot that he does not understand—even of things that
other men see quite clearly. And I will add something
more. When I hear music, or when I see the beauty of
sunsets, I feel—as Jim does too, I think—the sense of a
presence which seems to be trying to get in touch with us,
to break through barriers, something—so it seems—which
lies behind and beyond the veils of the world of sense.
And when men talk about the purpose in the world,
though I admit that what they say cannot in any literal
sense be defended, I think they are vaguely groping for
that something. Hence although I am sure that the philosophies which try to express this in intelligible concepts fall
at once into contradictions and absurdities, yet I cannot
be so contemptuous of them as Peter is. There may be
that in the universe which our intelligences cannot grasp.
In my philosophy I prefer to leave a margin for the unknown. All roads, it seems to me, lead in the end to a
question mark and to ultimate mystery.

You are an intellectual jellyfish, said Peter. You wob-
ble about in all directions. Sometimes you are on one side
of the fence and sometimes on the other. As to what you
say about a mystic presence beyond the veils of sense, I
can prove to you conclusively by the modern theory of
meaning that all such statements are meaningless verbiage.
We have developed a technique. I shall begin by demon-
strating—

In the name of heaven, I interrupted hastily, spare us
the demonstration. I know beforehand all the arguments

you are about to use. I have read all the books you got them from. You are going to regale us with tags from Wittgenstein and Carnap and the rest, aren't you?

At this Peter began to sulk. Have it your own way, he said. If you will not even listen to my arguments I may as well drop out of the discussion.

Don't do that, Peter. What you say is always amusing.

Well, he admitted, I suppose it is true that you are acquainted with the arguments of the positivists. So I need not repeat them. But I will ask you what you have to say in reply to them.

Not much, I said. They have done admirable work in checking our tendency to fly off into high-sounding and meaningless phrases. There has certainly been too much of that. I agree with you and your school that all meaning must be definable in terms of some possible experience, and that concepts which do not refer to such experience are meaningless and are not concepts at all. That, I take it, is the much needed lesson which you and your friends have enforced. But this must not be made a ground for narrow-mindedly limiting the universe to what falls within the petty range of our human faculties, and declaring to be non-existent or meaningless whatever *we* cannot grasp. Meaning must be relative to experience—that is your point. But it does not follow that it is relative to *our* experience. There may be other kinds of experience at present beyond our reach. Who does not know, indeed, that there are insects and animals whose members are sensitive to vibrations which do not reach us? They apprehend these vibrations, of course, through senses which are still physical. But it is mere dogmatism to confine the term experience to sense-experience as you do. There may be non-physical senses of which we have no knowledge. Mystics claim that direct non-physical experiences sometimes come to them. Possibly they may be deluded by mere subjective visions of their own. But this is not certain. And I know of no ground but prejudice for refusing to listen to their claims. Will you say that their experiences are "private" and cannot be checked? But in the country of the blind the experiences of the one-eyed man would be private and could not be checked. It is possible that if all men had the faculties of the mystic, what the mystic sees could be as easily checked and verified as what we now see with our physical eyes. However that may be, my point is that for a genuine empiricism the term experience ought to mean any direct objective impinging of the world upon any conceivable mind. To say that non-physical experiences are not objective is merely to beg the question. And to a genuine empirical theory of meaning, meaning must be relative to any such possible experience. Our senses are the only channels through which come to us—or to most of us at any rate—news of the outside world. Do you really suppose that what little gets through to us is all there is to know? It is possible that there may be millions of channels through which the world might flow in on minds more developed than ours or on beings differently constituted—channels which in us are not opened at all. There may be millions of possible kinds of direct experience of which we have no knowledge. The dim intuitions of something beyond our ken, of a presence behind the scenes, may be faint indications and premonitions of direct experiences of the world which may flood in upon our remote and more highly evolved descendants, the supermen of the future, as clearly as the sunlight now floods our eyes. Suppose that there existed men who had lived all their lives within a hollow sphere, whose walls were composed of almost, but not quite, sound-proof material. Such faint sounds as filtered through from the outside world would be heard by a few who might be possessed of exceptionally acute ears. Those of duller hearing would suppose these latter to be involved in some illusory experience of their own. They would say that this experience was "private" and "not empirically verifiable." But if a hole were suddenly knocked in the wall of the sphere, then the noise of the outside world might break in like thunder upon them all. You and your friends are very logical, but you have no imagination. You parcel out the universe with your concepts into neat little piles. But there remains the sense that you have unaccountably left out something, something too subtle to be caught in the crude meshes of your blundering conceptual machine. And if I cannot say *what* that something is, that simply means that my concepts too are too crude to catch that faint elusive experience. It escapes as soon as we try to grasp it.

I glanced at Peter to see the effect of my eloquence. He was fast asleep.

Peter! I shouted, Peter! You were asleep, and I was uttering some of my most interesting thoughts.

I heard most of what you said, he replied. You were uttering the wildest and most fantastic nonsense. You accuse me of lack of imagination. You certainly have it yourself.

I give you up, Peter. Go to sleep again. But I still have a word for Jim. I want to come to an agreement with him.

What sort of an agreement? asked Jim.

Well, I said, it is quite possible for you to accept everything I say in my book and retain all your own beliefs as well. Let us suppose, for the sake of argument, that we accept a purely conventional theistic creed. There is a personal God, a being like ourselves, only bigger and more powerful. He has a plan for the world. Moral action on our part is action which furthers that plan. Immoral action is action which tends to thwart it.

Well?

You can believe all that if you want to. There is nothing in my book which contradicts it.

But according to you, said Jim, the reason for being moral is that morality is a means to happiness. On the theistic view the reason for being moral is that to be so fits in with the divine plan.

Both reasons, I answered, might be true at the same time. That morality should both forward the divine plan and advance our happiness would be part of the infinite cunning of God. And morality might have just the nature which I attribute to it in my book. And if what I have written is perfectly compatible with a crude theism, it is still more obvious that it is compatible with your vague religiosity.

What you say is true, admitted Jim. Still your account of morality is utterly inadequate. You have left out all that is truly profound in it, I mean its cosmic importance.

I quite agree, I said. I have probably said very little that is of importance. That is because I know so little. I would say more profound things if I knew them. I do not deny that the full truth about morality may be much *more* than I have written. What I am concerned to teach is that at any rate it is not *less*. And I do think this is of some importance. For nowadays philosophers are found who deny that morality has any meaning at all. They make utter nonsense of it. According to them it is mere irrational emotion. It is an unintelligible chaotic jumble of baseless and mutually contradictory ideas. I have at least tried to show that this is false, that morality is rational, and that it is in some sense really binding upon men. And if I can accomplish that, I am willing to let the rest go. There are doubtless men of greater vision than mine. Let them utter their vision. Let me give, with the tiny lamp of my intellect, what light I can. What do any of us know of the universe? Each of us is like a man wandering in an infinite impenetrable darkness carrying in his hand a ridiculous little candle. The candle lights up faintly about a foot or two around us, and beyond there are billions and billions of miles of black darkness. And if what I can see with my candle is very little, do not for that reason despise it.

Very well, replied Jim. But you will please nobody with your book. The idealists will have none of you because of your empiricism and naturalism and your complete neglect of what they will consider the only issues worth considering. As to your radical empiricist friends, they will refuse to admit that you are one of themselves. You do not follow the crowd. You do not repeat their usual catchwords. You do not wave their banners. And they will look askance at anyone who calls himself a radical empiricist and yet admits into the foundations of his philosophy anything other than sense-experience—introspective experience, for instance, and the moral experience of humanity. That, they will say, is not empiricism.

So be it, I replied, I shall please nobody. But in the end one writes a book to work out one's own intellectual salvation and to please nobody but oneself.

That, said Jim, is merely your variety of conceited affectation. Since nobody takes any notice of what you say, you pretend that you have been talking to yourself and that you didn't want anyone else to listen.

Goodnight, I said hastily, goodnight. You know too much.

INDEX

305

PB-6481-8
516-17

PB-64812-8
516-17